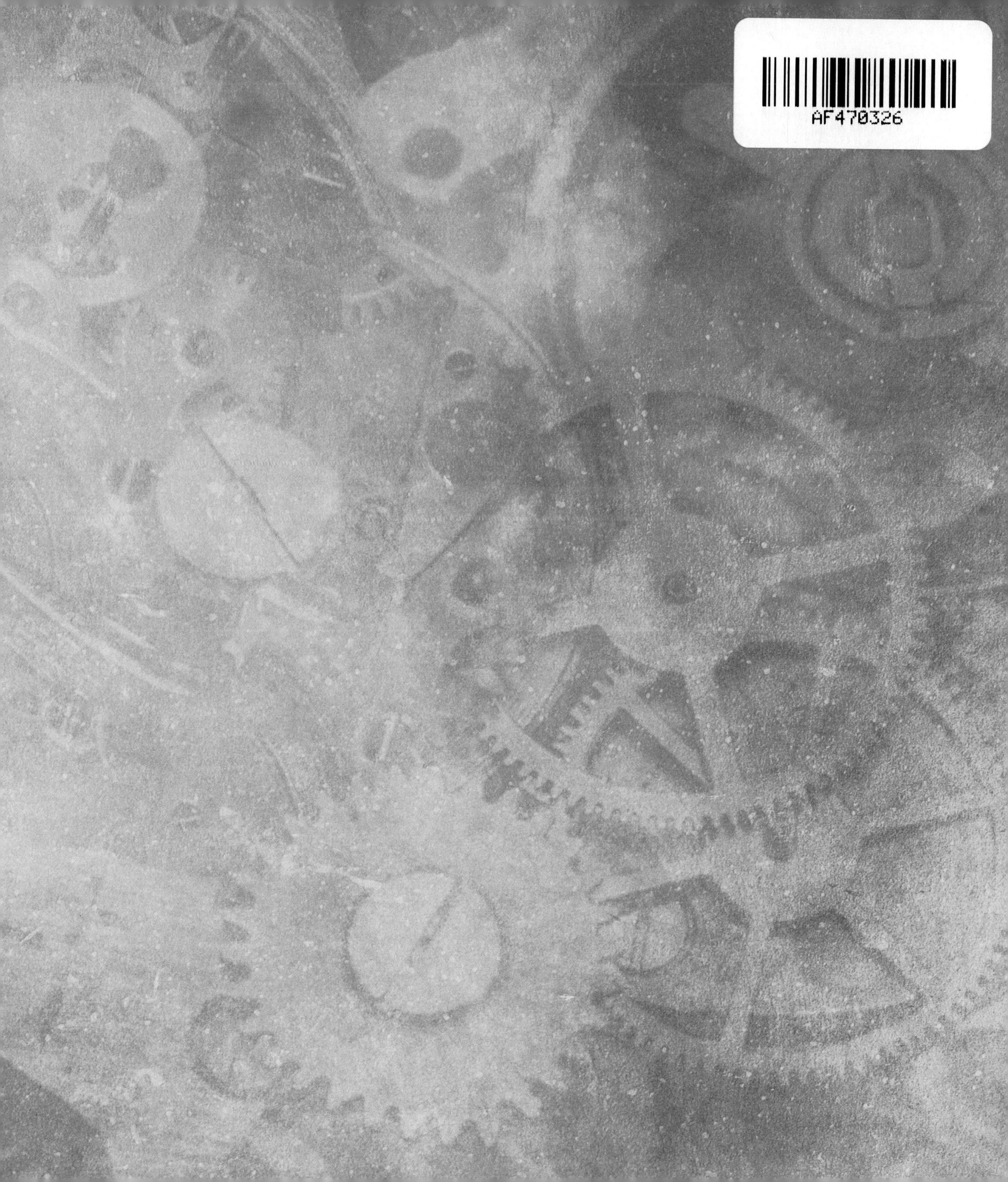

Gothic Dreams

Steampunk

Fantasy Art, Fiction, Fashion and the Movies

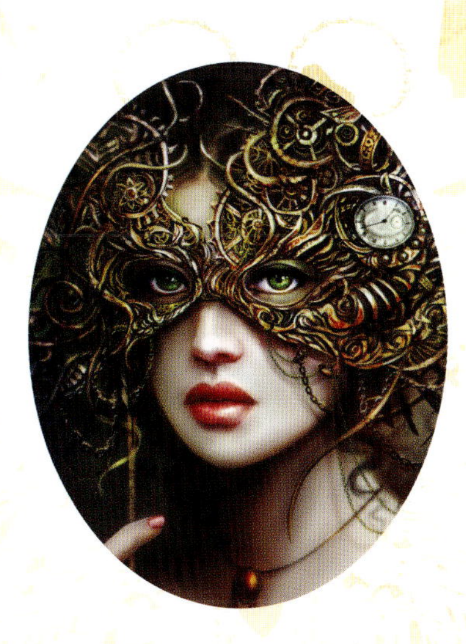

Publisher and Creative Director: Nick Wells
Project Editor and Picture Research: Laura Bulbeck
Art Director: Mike Spender
Digital Production: Chris Herbert

Special thanks to: Frances Bodiam, Catherine Taylor, and the artists who allowed us to reproduce their fantastic work

FLAME TREE PUBLISHING
6 Melbray Mews
Fulham, London SW6 3NS
United Kingdom

www.flametreepublishing.com
www.flametree451.com

First published 2014

16 18 17
3 5 7 9 10 8 6 4

A CIP record for this book is available from the British Library upon request.

ISBN: 978-1-78361-122-5

Printed in China

Gothic Dreams

Steampunk

Fantasy Art, Fiction, Fashion and the Movies

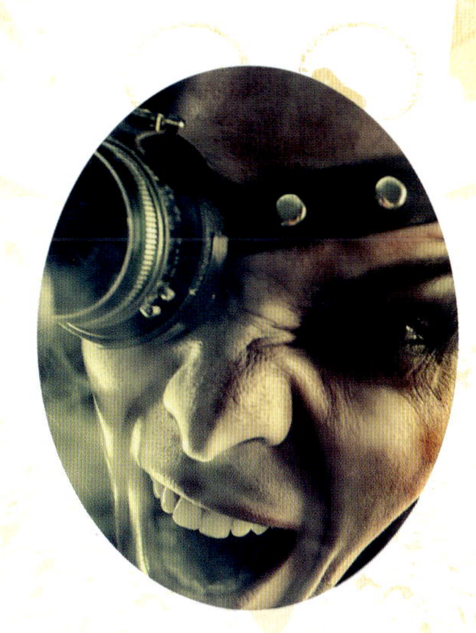

HENRY WINCHESTER

Foreword by G.D. FALKSEN

FLAME TREE PUBLISHING

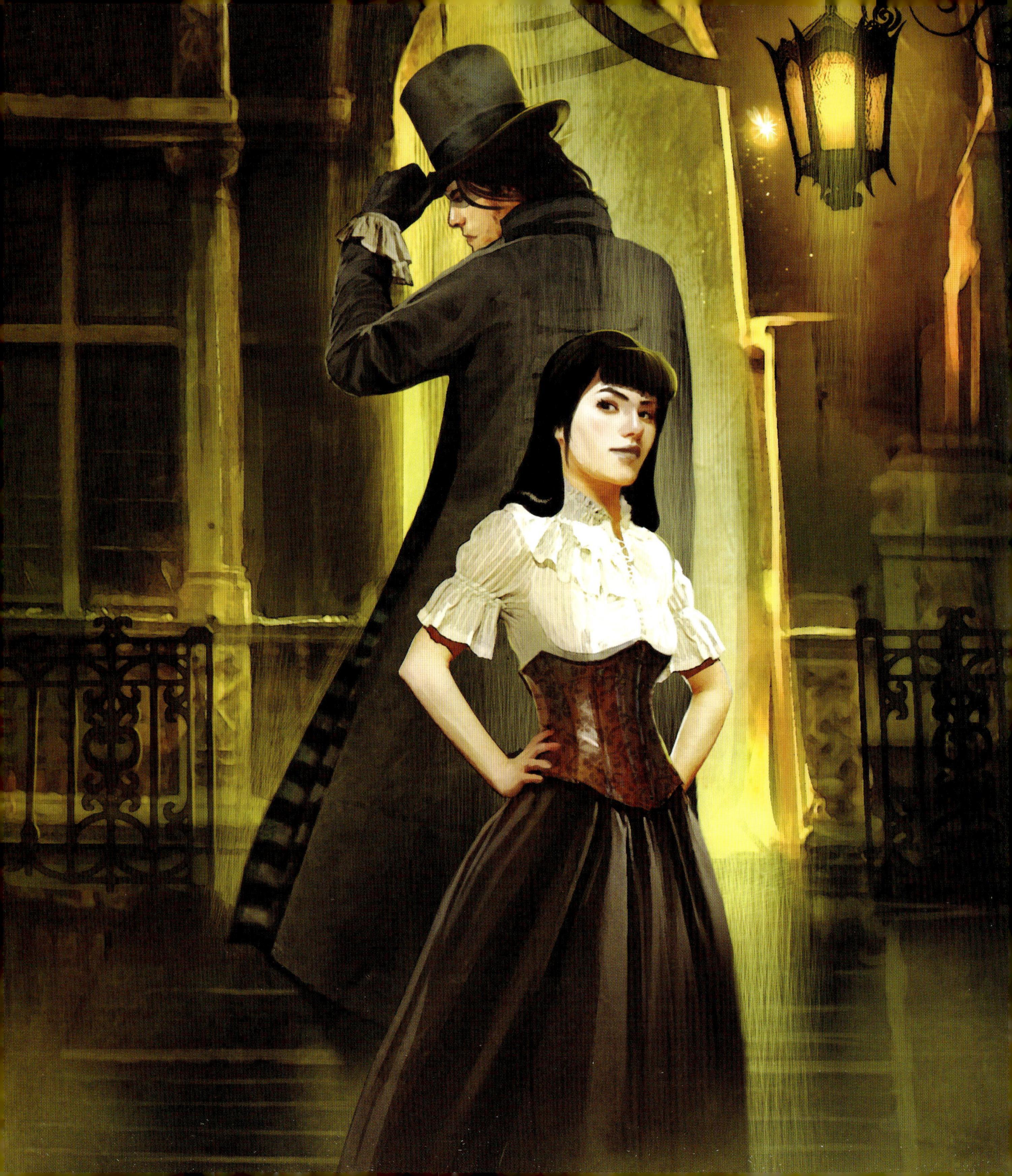

Contents

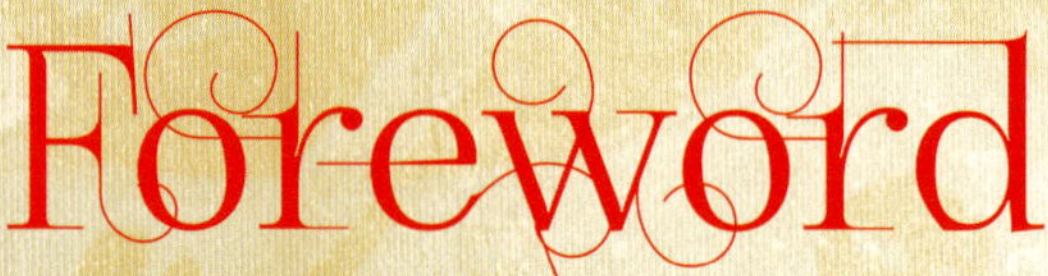

Foreword

'Steampunk is Victorian science fiction.'

It's been several years since I first coined that phrase to help explain steampunk to the general public. Now, with steampunk far more visible in pop culture and entertainment, the statement seems so very obvious; but at the time, with steampunk still relatively obscure and only just beginning its growth from a literary genre into an aesthetic and a subculture, it was the obvious observation that needed to be said. Since then, it has been repeated, expounded upon, rephrased, and presented in a myriad of different ways, but all leading back to the same basic meaning: Steampunk is the science fiction of the industrialized 19th Century. It is Victorian science fiction.

It has been a pleasure watching the steampunk community grow from a small collection of enthusiasts spread all around the world into a vibrant and growing subculture. Steampunk fans are wonderful, intelligent, and highly creative people, and I am honoured to have played a roll in bringing them together. It has always been my wish to foster fun, community, and imagination, and to open people's eyes to the great complexity and wonder inherent in the steampunk genre. That has been the purpose of my various articles and lectures on steampunk, and if my writing has inspired people to dive into steampunk and explore just what it is they truly love about it, unfettered by a fear of having to do it like everyone else, then I have succeeded.

And that really is the core of steampunk. It's why I love it. Steampunk is about creativity and imagination, history and beauty, community and at the same time deep individuality and diversity. Steampunk is a vast and majestic world waiting to be explored, and I invite everyone to join in the search.

Steampunk is Victorian science fiction. And it is marvelous.

G.D. Falksen

www.gdfalksen.com

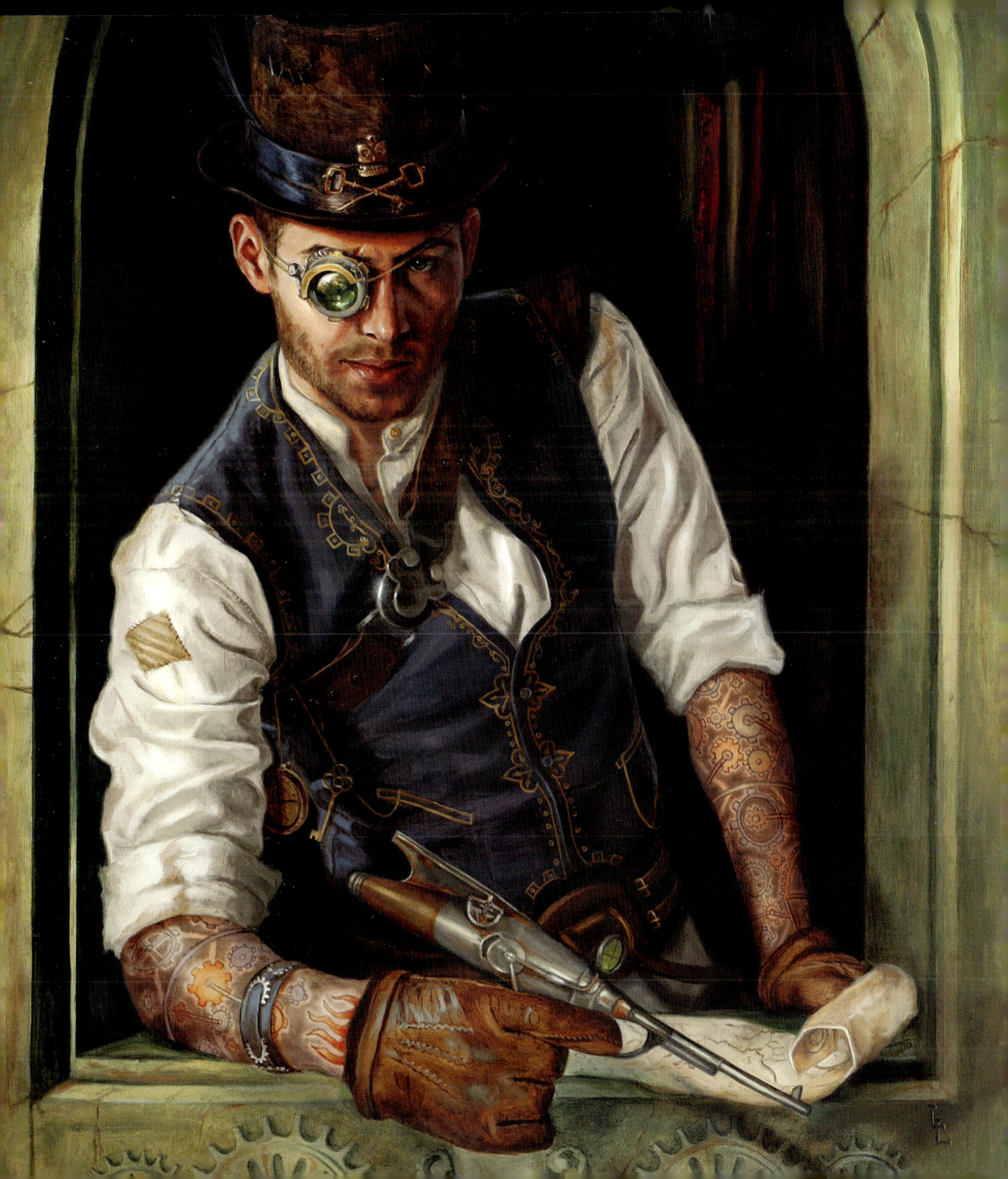

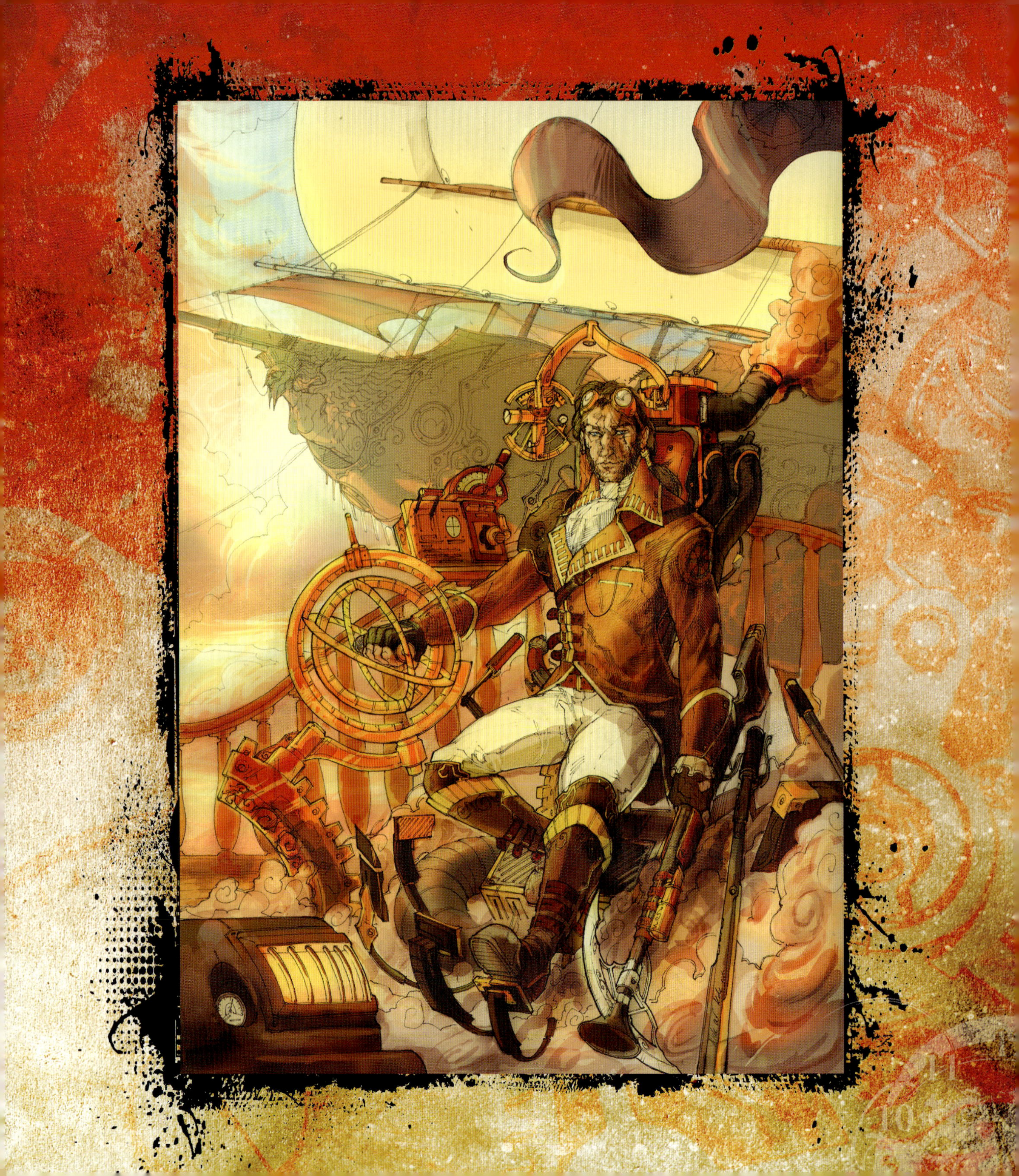

A Steampunk Revolution

Welcome, weary traveller. You've come a long way. Let me take your leathery suitcases while you slip off your tweed jacket and relax in our chaise longue. You're about to enter our airship and embark on one of the most marvellous of journeys; one which will take you simultaneously back to the past and thrust you into the future.

On the way you'll meet all sorts of characters. You'll sit shoulder-to-shoulder with eminent Victorian authors such as H.G. Wells and Jules Verne. You'll witness the heroic escapades of Captain Nemo and James West. And you'll come across the fierce adversaries Frankenstein and Jack the Ripper. Of course, you'll also have all the ancient but modern equipment you'll need for your perilous journey.

Cityscapes

Our journey begins a long time ago, in a place familiar yet different: London in the Victorian age. It was a time of great change, of tectonic shifts that changed the face of the earth. But this isn't London as you or anyone remembers it. This is a London that's been mutated by the obsessions of the modern age. It's a London in which empires never fell, in which vampires came to occupy the throne, in which steam powers just about everything.

So strap on your brass goggles, take one last glance at your pocket watch and prepare to join us on a voyage into the heart of steampunk....

'Steampunk is an eclectic world of cogs .... It is romance. It is adventure!'

Aether Emporium

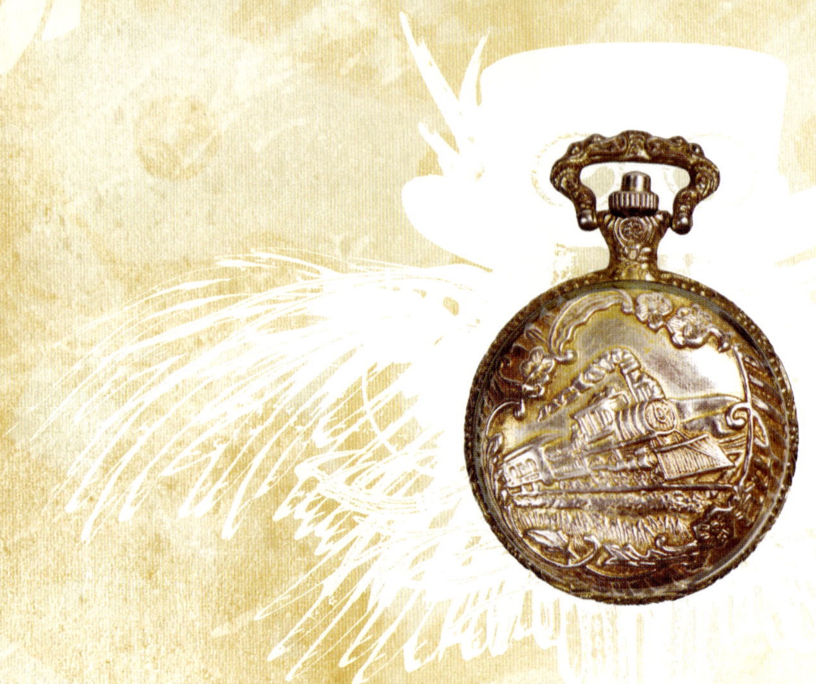

Picking Up Steam

Steampunk is such a wide and varied term that it's quite difficult to nail down, but in a nutshell it's a way of looking at the future based on the collective imagination of the past. The past in question is generally defined as the period of Queen Victoria's rule in Britain, from 1837 until 1901. During this time the Industrial Revolution caused huge social and economic change, and steam-powered factories and vehicles completely changed the face of the Western world. However, steampunk doesn't just take ideas from this period – it also raids other parts of history, such as Wild West conflicts and 1930s Art Deco.

From Whence Did it Come?

As we look back through time, it's easy to see things that we could now consider 'steampunk' – the design of the submarine in Disney's movie ***20,000 Leagues Under the Sea*** (1954), or the premise of Ronald W. Clark's novel ***Queen Victoria's Bomb*** (1967), in which a nuclear weapon is created during the Victorian Era. But steampunk as we know it today began primarily as a form of literature in the early 1980s. Its analogue, mechanical nature was intended as a riposte to cyberpunk's tales of the digital and the binary, and a big part of steampunk's attraction

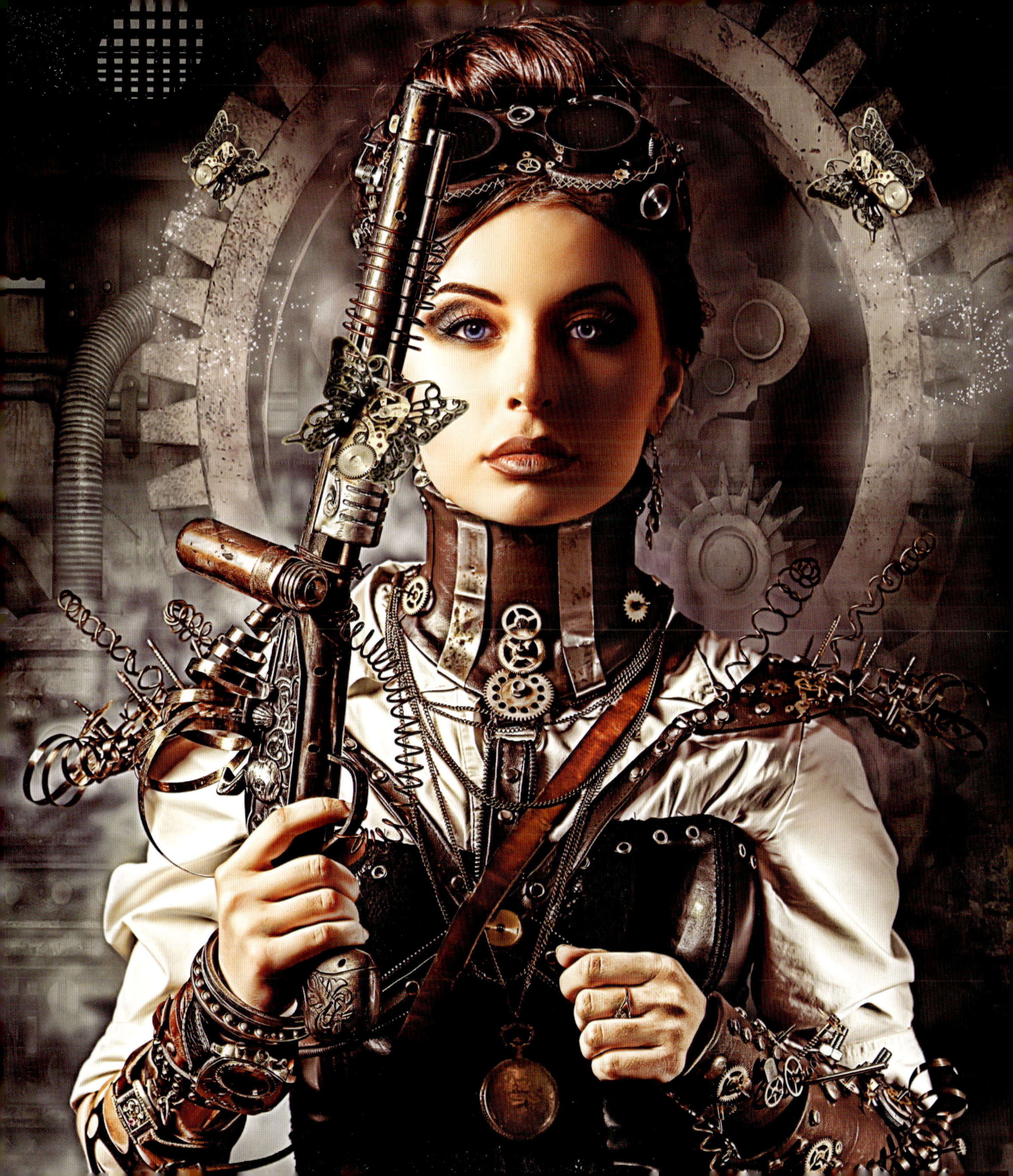

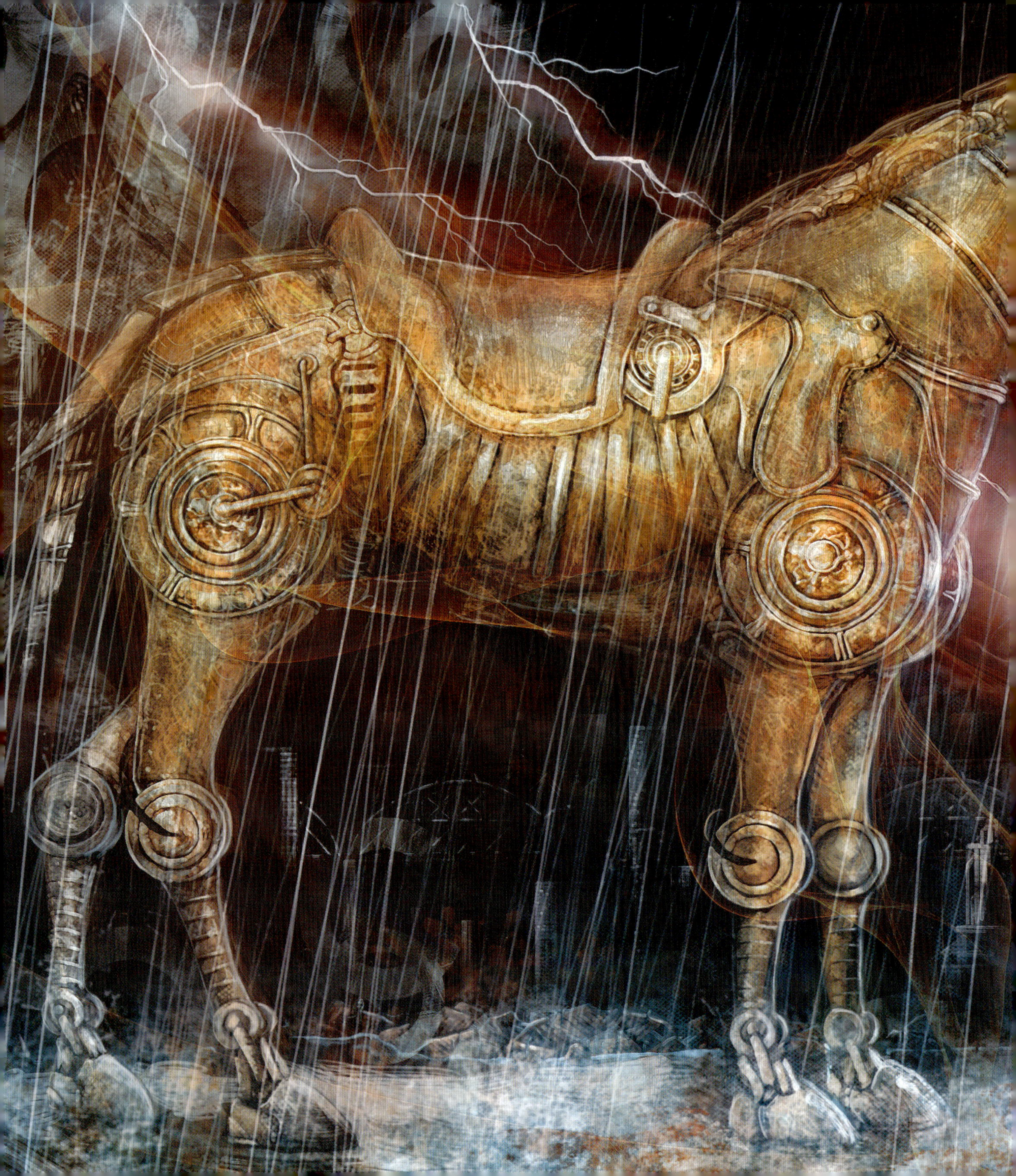

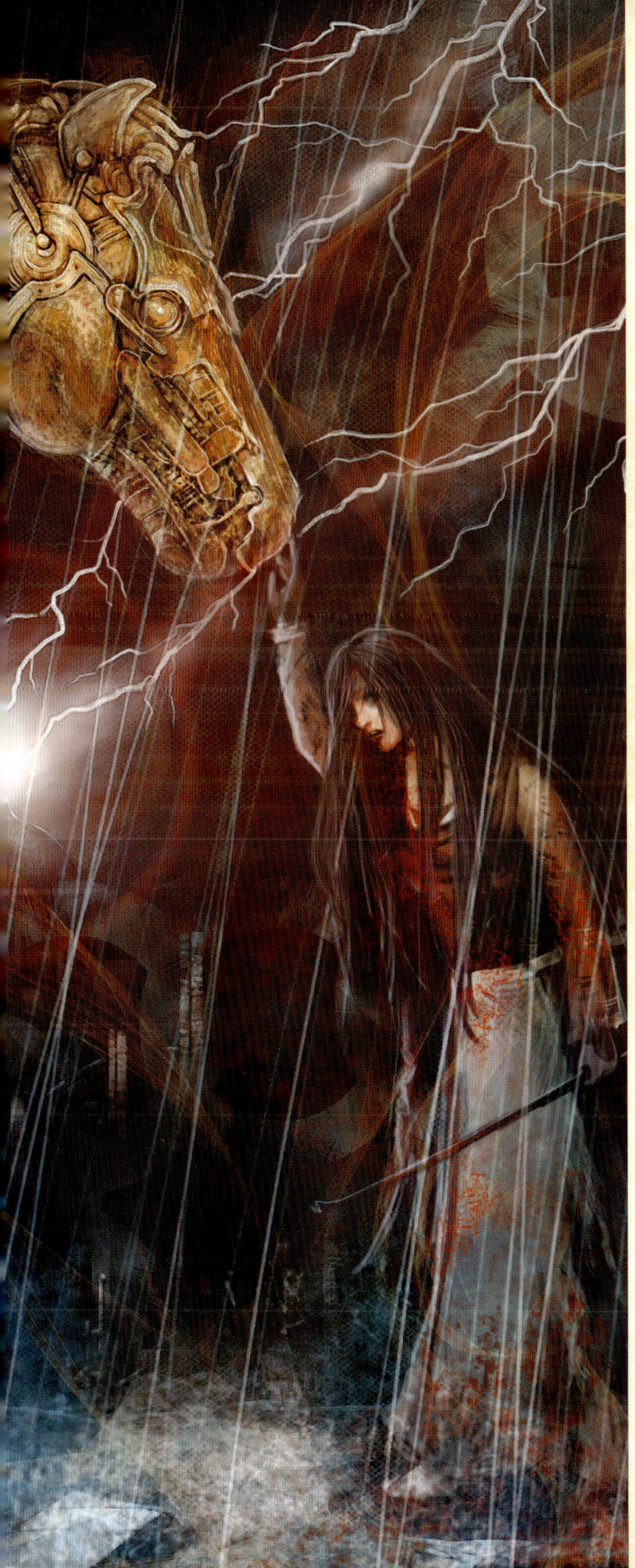

remains the way in which it rejects sleek modern technology in favour of something more primitive.

Mass Media

Despite its origins as a literary movement, steampunk has taken on many forms. In cinema, films such as ***Wild Wild West*** (1999) and ***The League of Extraordinary Gentlemen*** (2003) rendered steampunk in larger-than-life scale, and populated their worlds with real and imagined characters from the Victorian era. On the small screen, series such as 'Warehouse 13' and episodes of 'Doctor Who' and 'Castle' have embraced steampunk. The movement has even found its way into music and video games, which is testament to how fluid and pliable it is.

Full Steam Ahead

Steampunk is far more than just a certain look and ideology for media – it's an entire subculture. Conventions and events have sprung up around the world, in which fans of the sub-genre create magnificent costumes and intricate accessories and weapons. Physical and virtual stores cater to steampunk collectors and enthusiasts, and there's a whole movement dedicated to modifying and customizing items, such as jewellery or electronic accessories, to steampunk them up. Steampunk also inspires science fiction and fantasy artists of all disciplines to create marvellously rich visions of the future-past.

'Push past the artificial boundary of time to ask the real questions: What does it mean to be human? What are we going to do with all this technology? How can we create the future we want and need?'

James H. Carrott

Just Glue Some Gears On It

There remains a great divide in the steampunk world between those who simply embrace its unique aesthetic, and those who delve into its rich literary trappings. It's best summed-up by Reginald Pikedevant's humorous song 'Just Glue Some Gears On It (and Call it Steampunk)', in which he states that: 'Calling things "steampunk" to try to sound cool makes you look like a bloody fool!' It's an incisive view into what steampunk has become to some people, transferred from a well-informed and meaningful discourse into the mere act of applying a layer of fake brass to an everyday object and, indeed, gluing some gears on it.

A Steamy Affair

At the same time, it's important to remember that steampunk is at heart frivolous and whimsical. Even the nature of something being steam-powered is a fallacy; steam is the result of water being heated, and the pressure that this process creates is what drives steam engines. Steam isn't a magical force – although some adherents of the steampunk movement seem to believe it is – and it still requires fuel. Perhaps 'coalpunk' or 'woodpunk' would be a more apt description, but this doesn't quite have the same ring to it.

From the Past to the Future

A quick Google Trends search suggests that steampunk is still very much on the rise, with 'steampunk clothing' at the top spot for most-searched phrase. Hollywood, however, appears to be moving away from the steampunk aesthetic and towards harder, more conventional sci-fi movies such as ***Star Trek*** (2009) and ***Elysium*** (2013). Steampunk has thoroughly planted itself in the popular imagination, though, and a new wave of steampunk novels will undoubtedly result in a new wave of steampunk films as well.

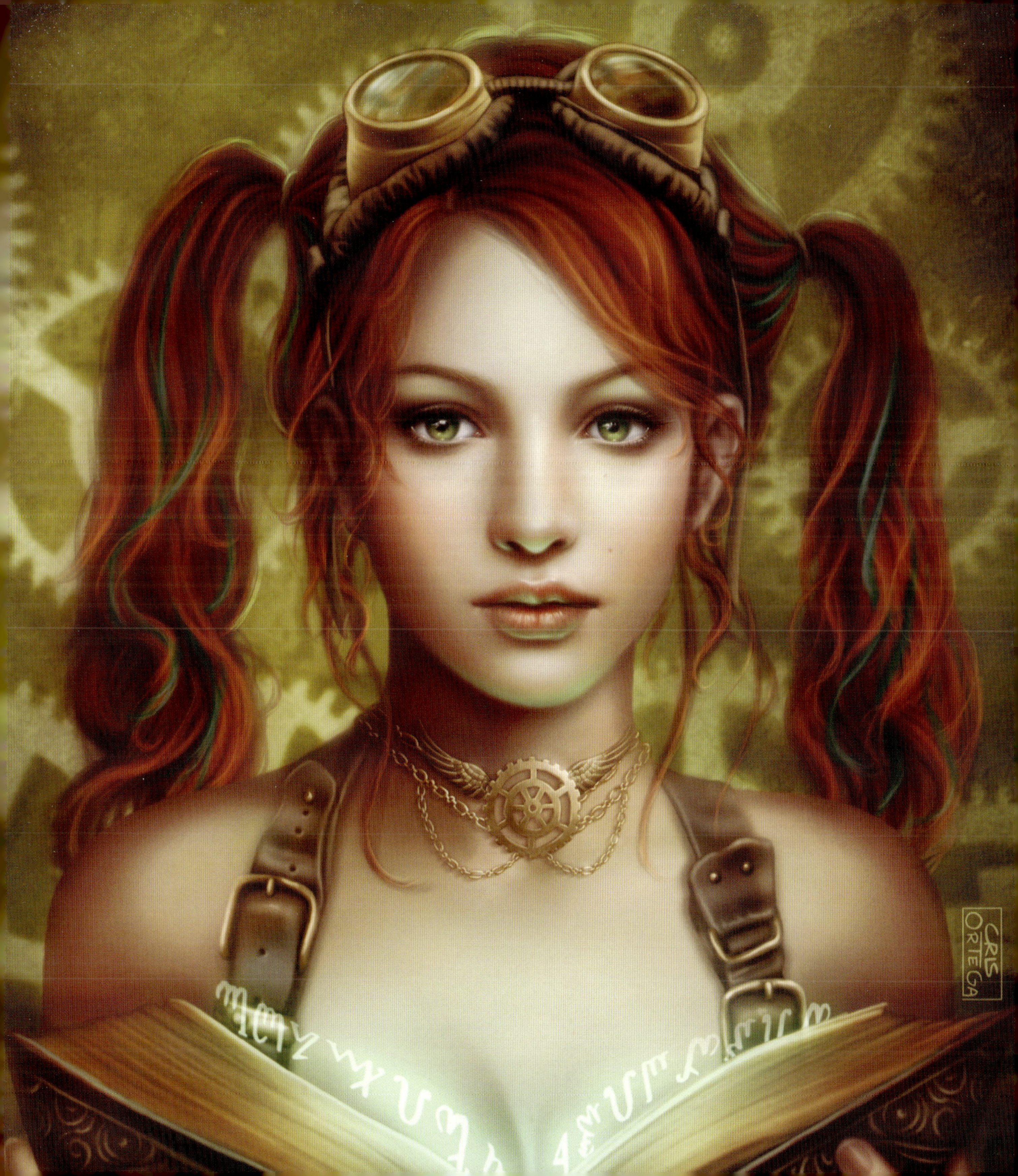
CRIS ORTEGA

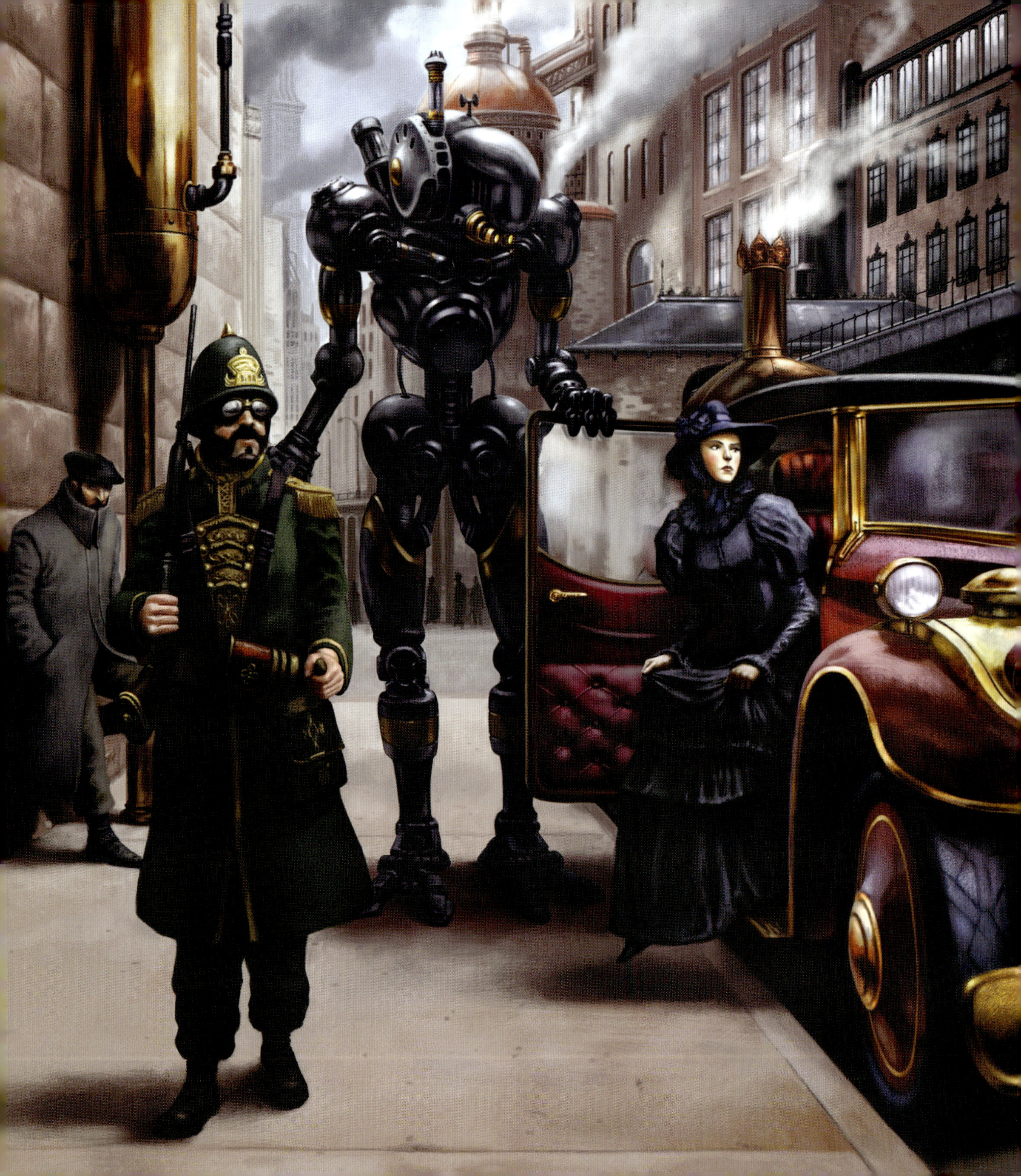

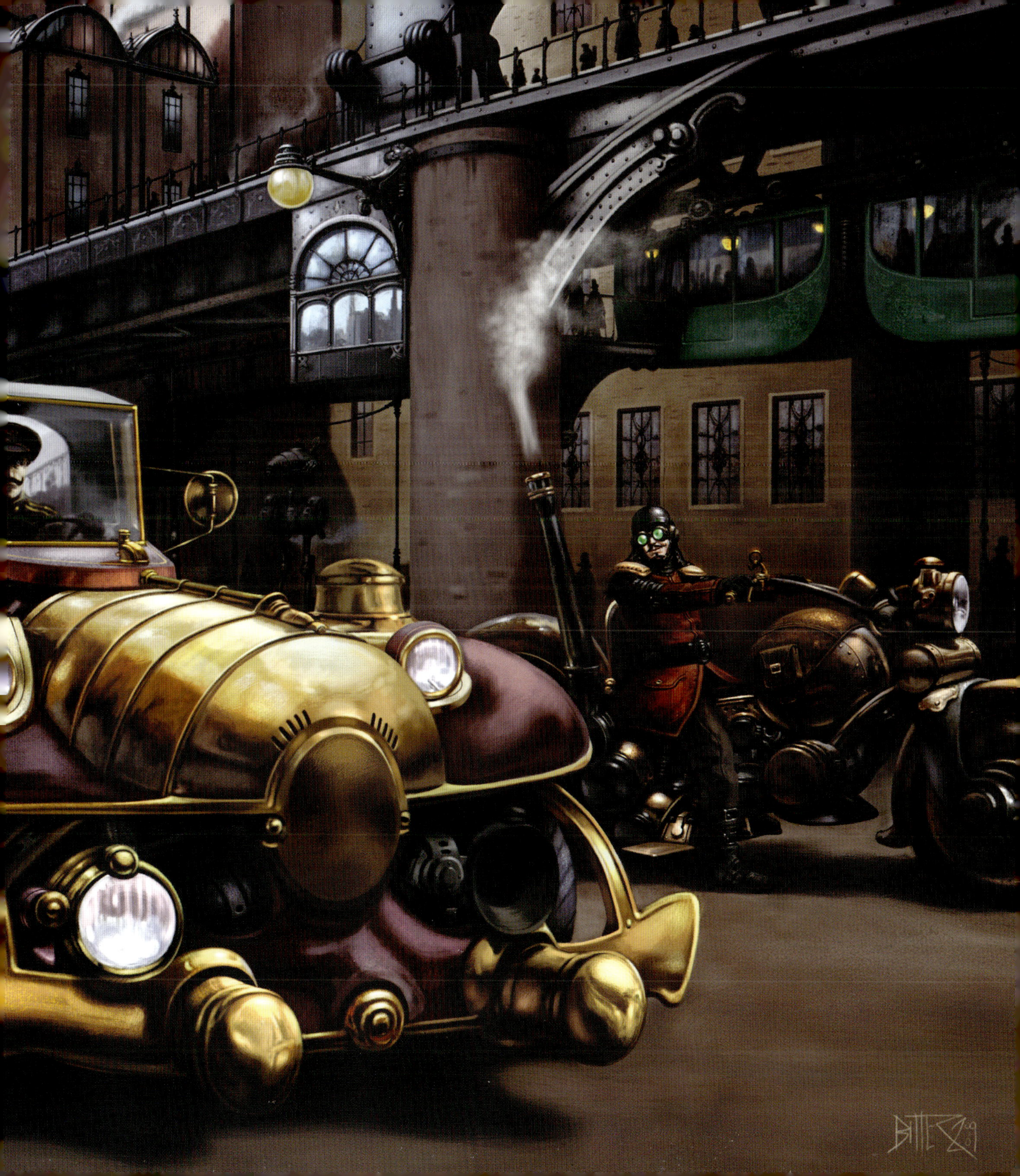

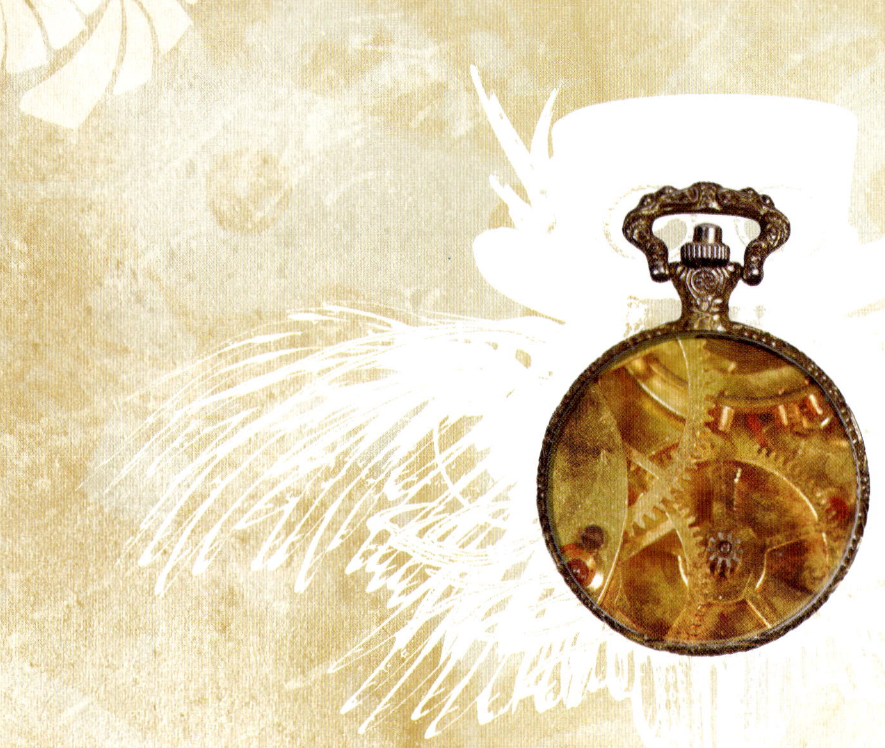

A Fashionable Affair

Steampunk fashion is almost immediately recognizable: think smartly dressed people in brass goggles and top hats and you're there. But, as with other steampunk forms, it's defined by taking certain elements from the past and fusing them into a strangely cohesive whole. There are inevitable anachronisms – we don't think many Victorians would have used smartphones, no matter how many gears and pipes were glued to them – but this is all part of the joy of dressing as a character. This rose-tinted vision of history means that there is a lot of leeway in costumes, too, and you don't have to subscribe to a particular look.

Kitted Up

The best steampunk costumes and characters embrace these dualities between the past and the present, and the normal and the weird. You could, for example, completely go to town with a steampunk costume and festoon every inch of it with cogs, brass plating and pipes, but it's far better to simply go to town on a single element, such as an artificial arm or a bizarre helmet, and wear pseudo-Victorian dress for the rest. This throws people off kilter, and instantly gives them something specific to examine and concentrate on.

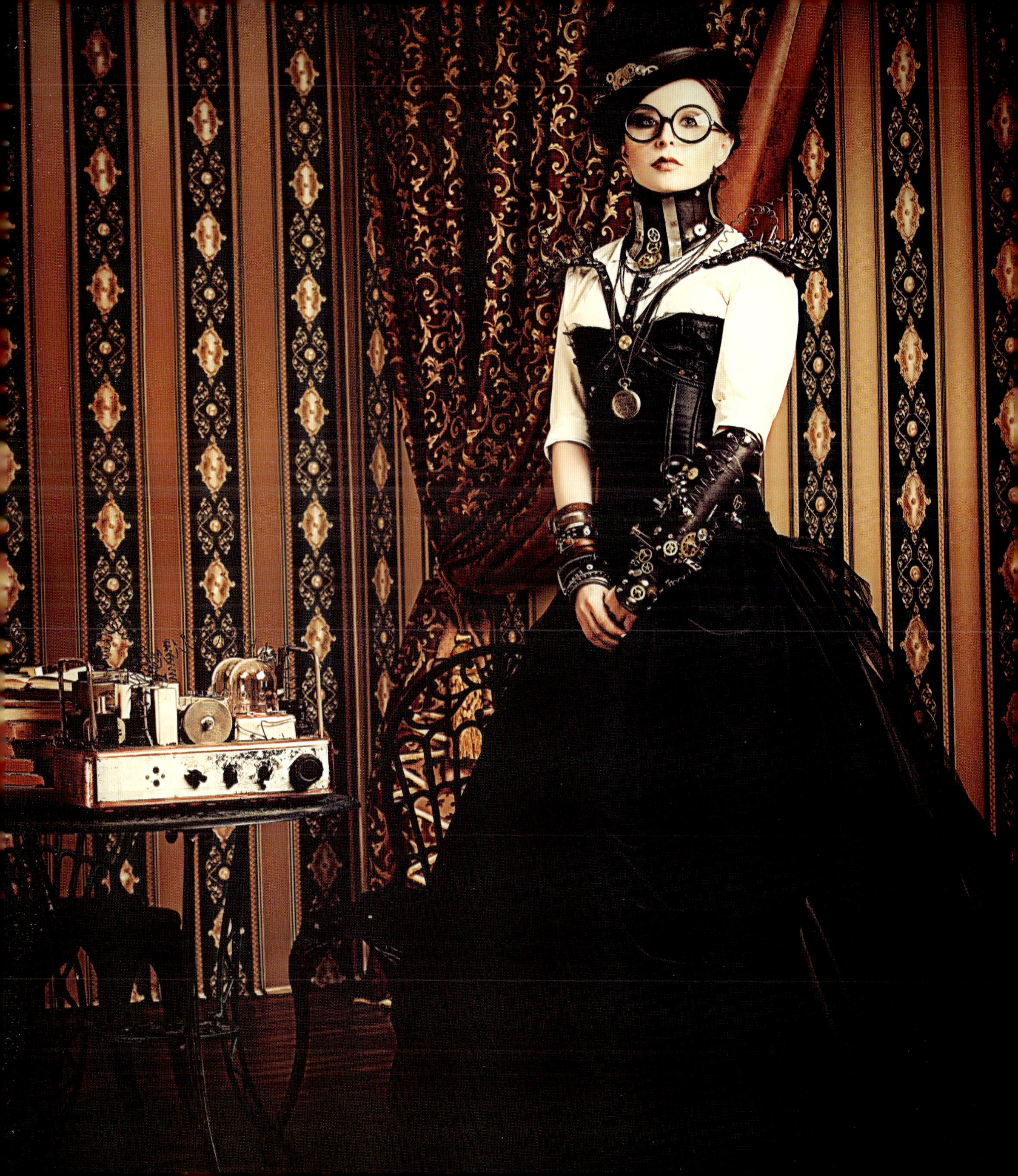

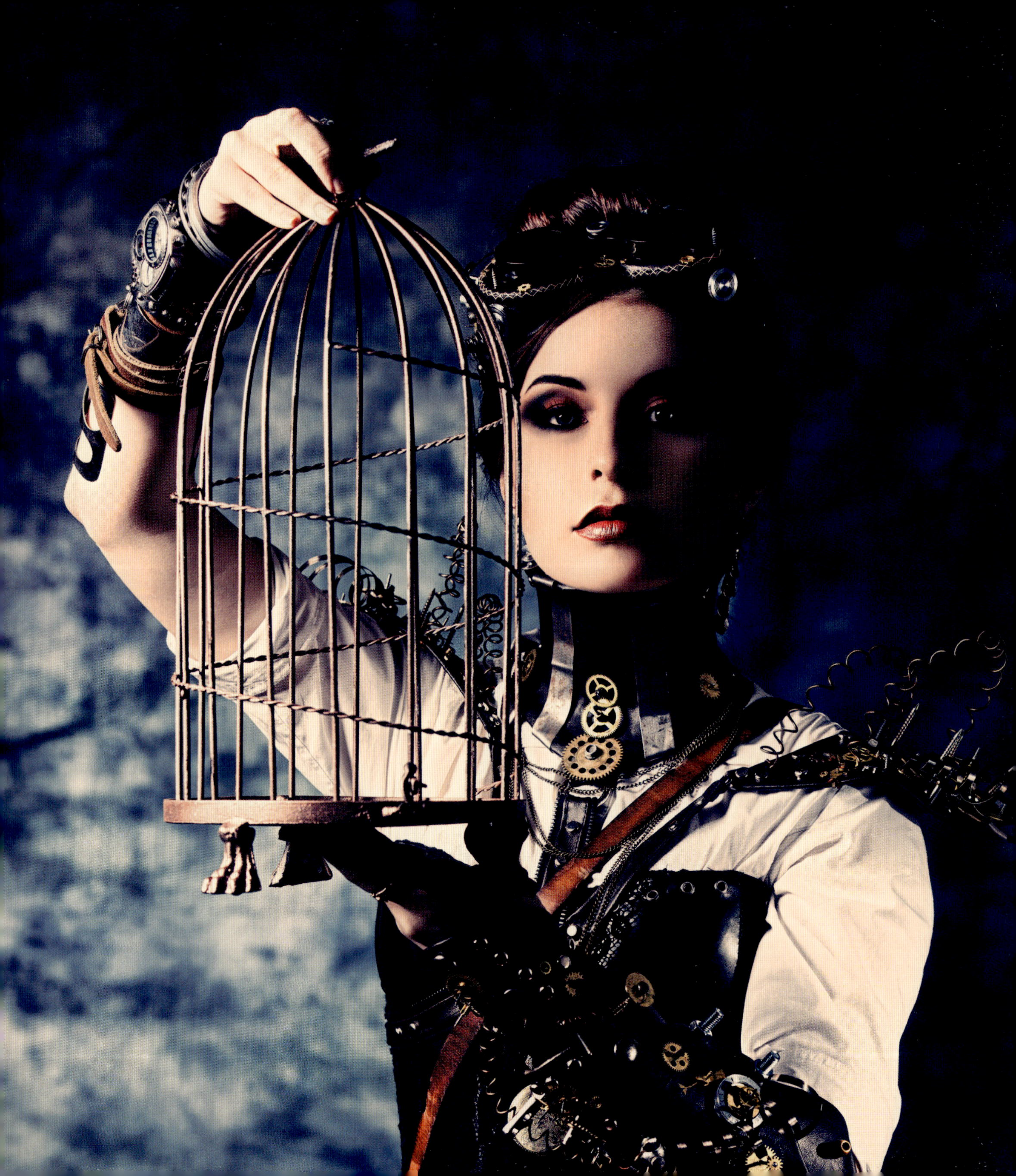

Victorian Fashion

The Industrial Revolution changed everything in the Victorian era – including fashion. The sewing machine was arguably as important an invention as the car or the steam engine, and huge factories could pump out hundreds of items of clothing a day. It became critically important for the ruling classes to be well dressed. However, this revolution was contrasted with a prudish attitude towards what women could wear: at points, even a bare ankle was seen as risqué, and rumour has it that some Victorian gents covered the legs of their pianos.

The Well-Dressed Ma'am

The Victorian era saw the beginnings of a shift in gender politics towards women. Between the 1830s and 1860s upper-class ladies' skirts were huge and flamboyant but by the turn of the century they became smaller and more practical as sports such as cycling and horse riding flourished. Corsets, which drew in the waist and accentuated the hips and bust, were made more forgiving as the century progressed and new manufacturing techniques were introduced. The working-class lady, however, would have to have made do with second-hand clothes, and given the complicated designs of garment, they would often have spent a long time tailoring them to fit.

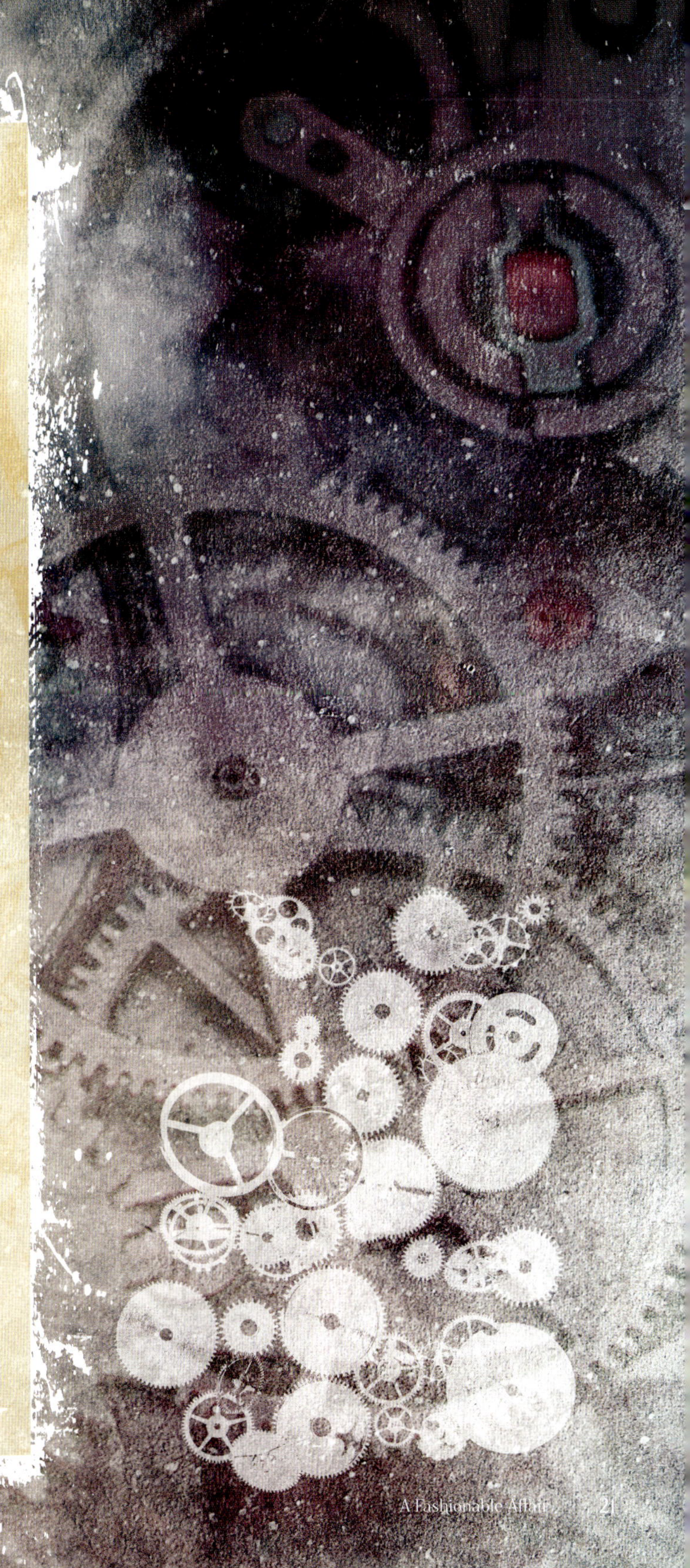

'Steampunk currently applies to t-shirts and shoes as much as literature. It's also important to remember that spiritualism was considered a form of science … ectoplasm, mesmerism, bilocation.'

Tim Powers

'Steampunk is … the love child of Hot Topic and a BBC costume drama.'

Gail Carriger

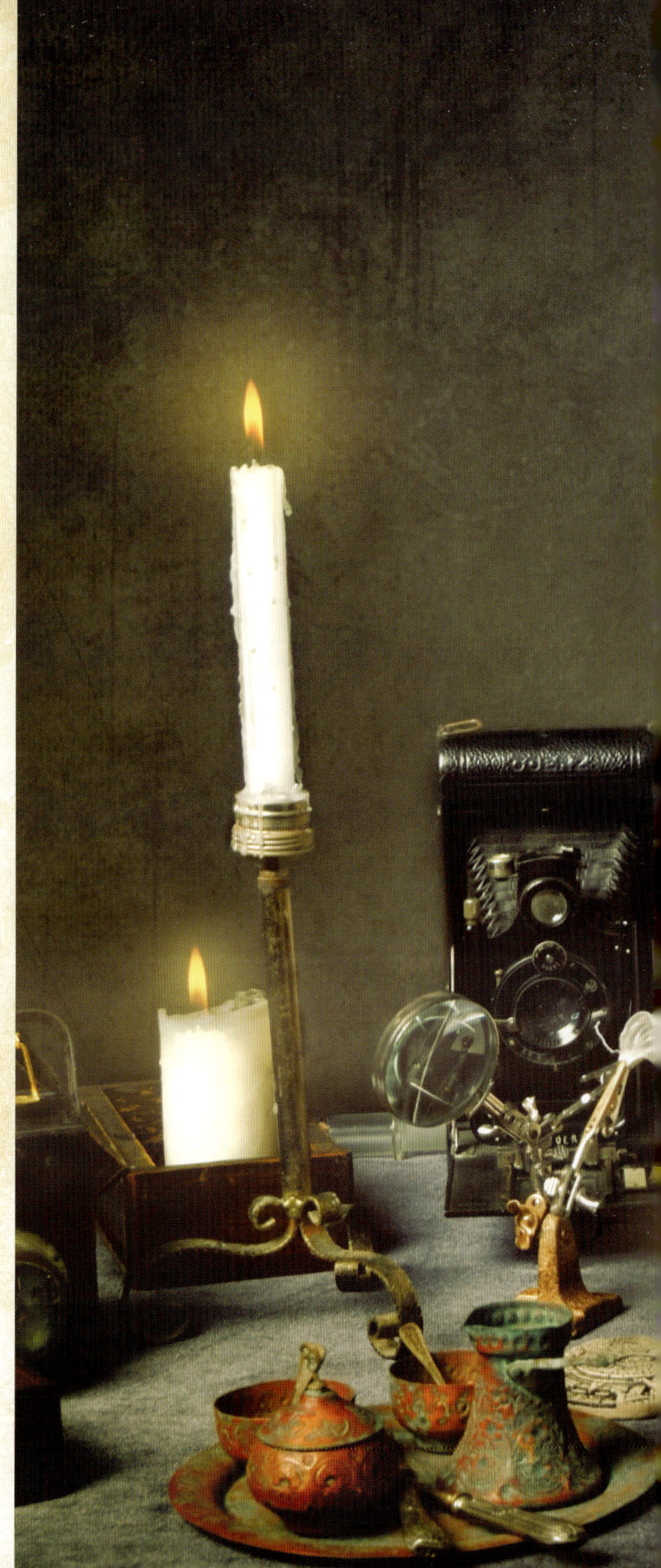

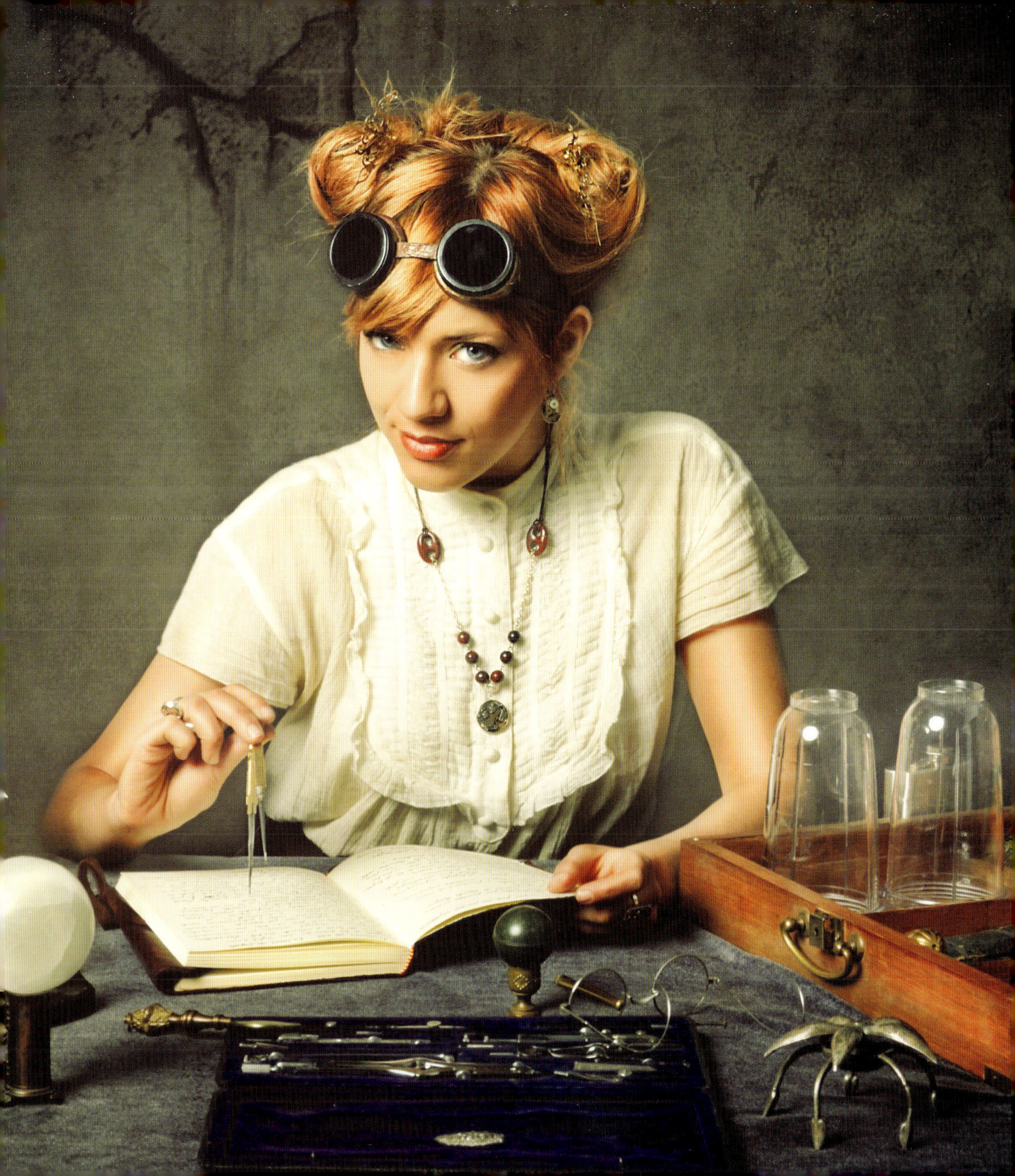

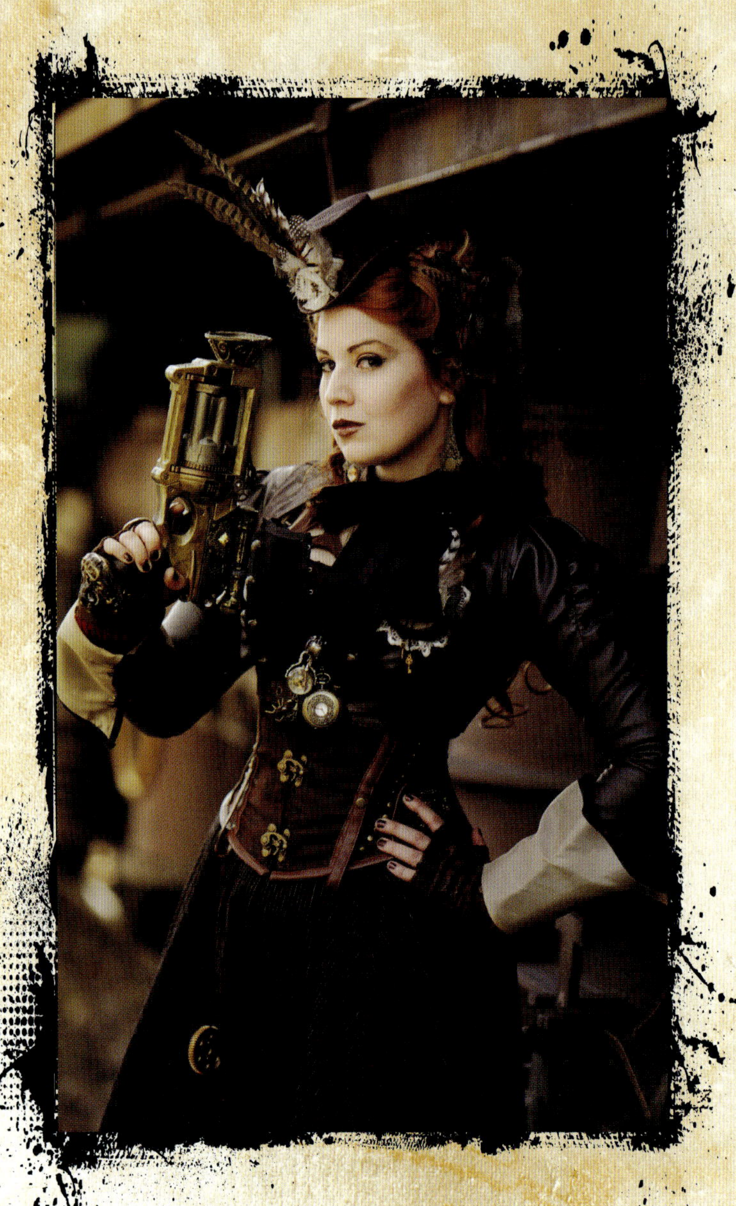

The Dapper Gent

Men had it a little easier in the Victorian period. Upper-class gentlemen were expected to wear a waistcoat in public, with silk as opposed to wool waistcoats being an indication of wealth. Frock coats, which descended to just above the knee, were worn on top, and trousers were usually flat-fronted rather than pleated. The look was topped-off with a hat – bowlers for the working class, and top hats for the more privileged. Colours were usually dour and understated tones of grey and black, in contrast to the dyes which coloured ladies' garments.

Other Influences

Of course, if you dress in a purely Victorian style you'll be mistaken for someone from the nineteenth century. The word 'punk' was added to steampunk for a reason, and the late-1970s movement pioneered both music and fashion. Key to the latter was the idea of recycling items found in charity shops, and customizing second-hand clothes with rips and badges. It parallels the steampunk movement nicely as both are based on ideas of taking something from the past and retrofitting it to create something modern and eye-catching.

Technical Clothing

The 'punk' element in steampunk relies upon layers and modifications on top of standard Victorian dress. The items can be repurposed from just about anywhere in history, from a pair of First World War-era flying goggles to a Wild West-style six shooter or a Victorian pocket watch. Being steam-powered is a bonus, of course, but intricate clockwork devices work just as well, without the inherent danger of being scalded. Some steampunkers even go so far as to craft prosthetic limbs and exoskeletons from brass pipes and cogs.

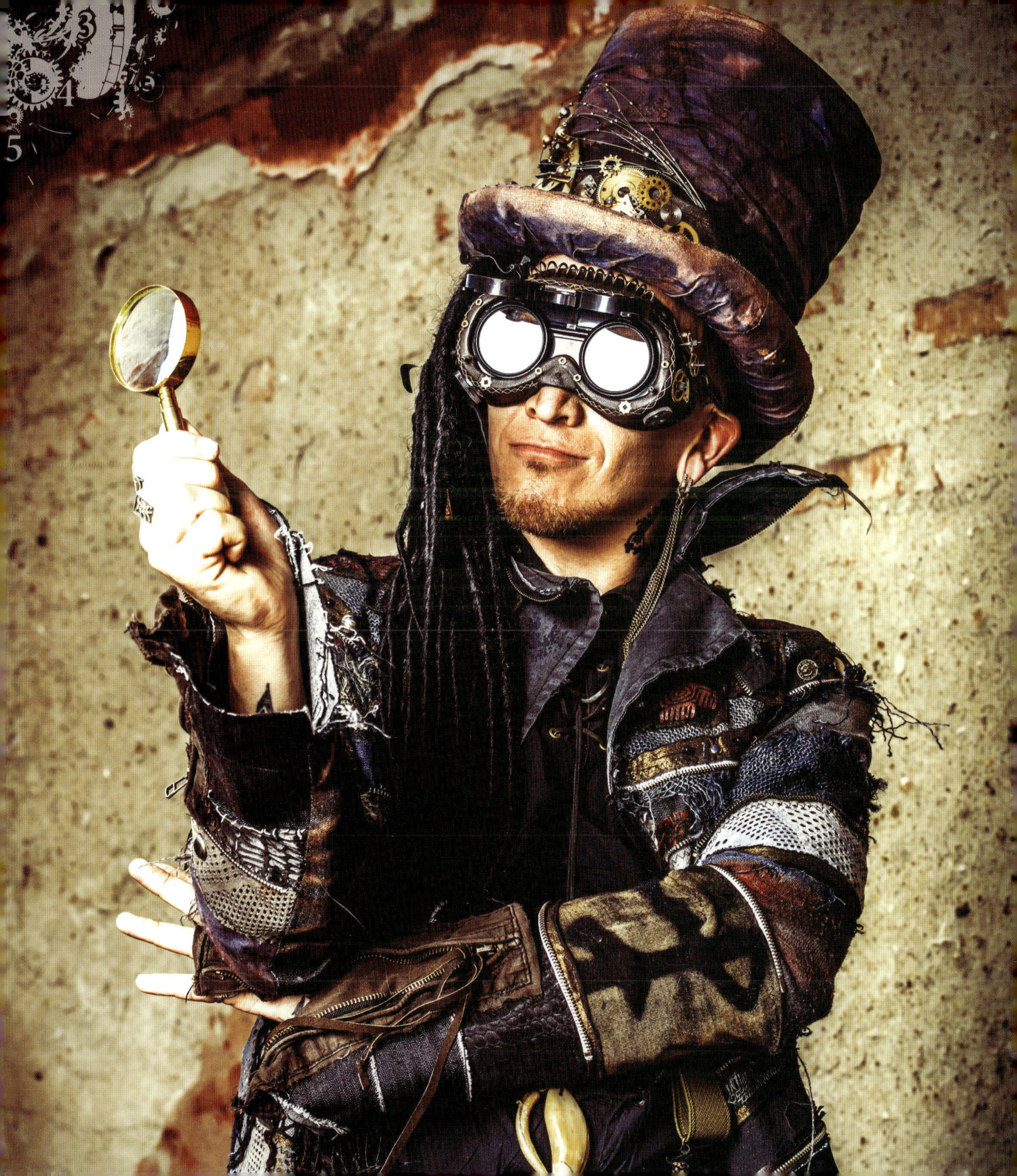

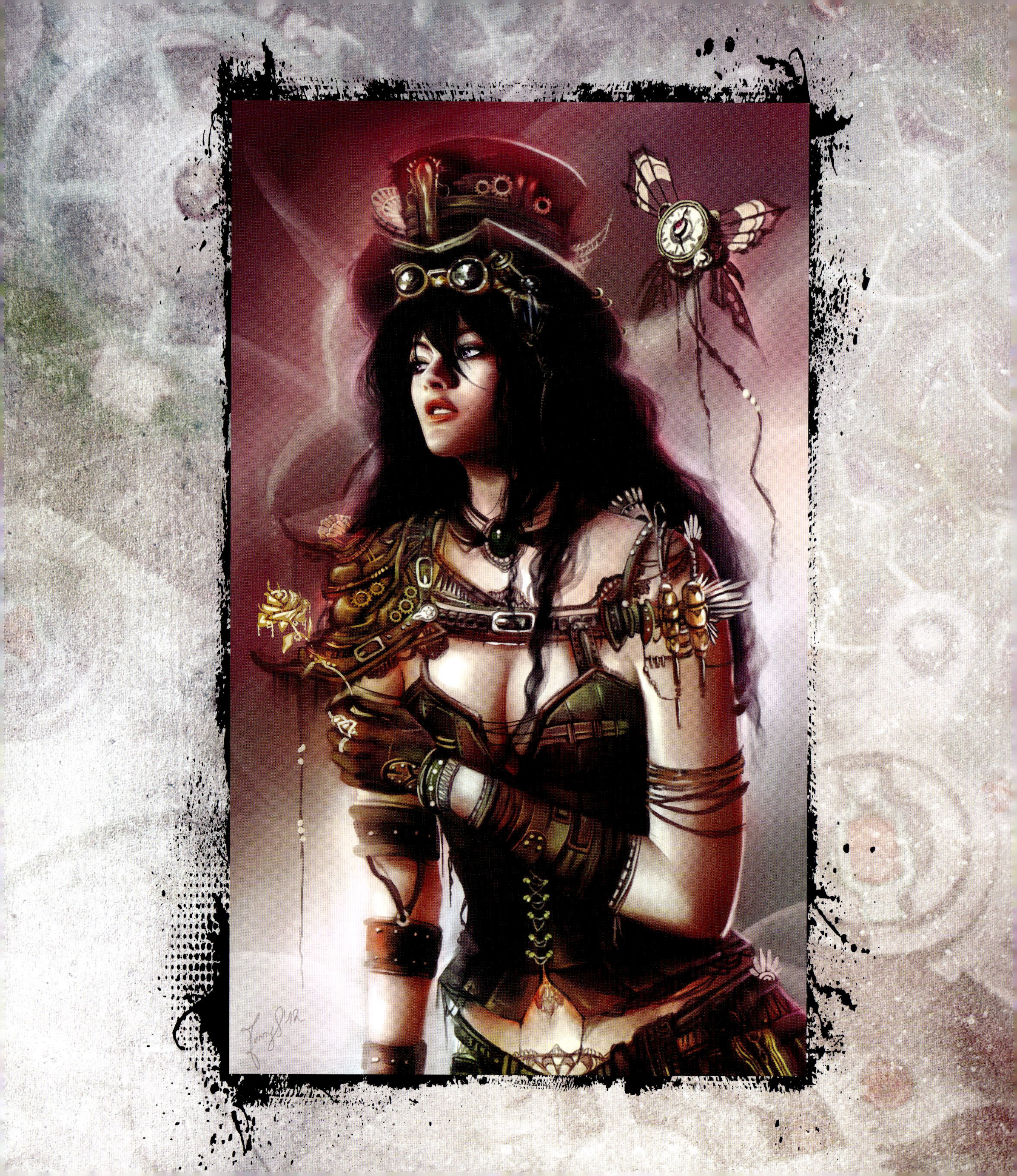

Who Are You?

Dressing up as a steampunk character can be very enjoyable, and it's a unique way to express your character and interests. Before you start, it's a good idea to try and imagine your character and their place in a steampunk world: were they a dashing adventurer, or a quiet inventor, or a war hero? Having an image in your head will make it a lot easier as you piece together your costume. You can also put a steampunk twist on a character from popular culture: what would a Victorian Darth Vader or Professor Dumbledore have looked like?

Becoming a Character

Big clothing labels such as Prada and Dior have embraced the steampunk phenomenon – but you'll have to pay a lot of money to get this designer wear, and it's cheaper and more satisfying to do it yourself. Charity and vintage clothing shops are a great place to start, but if you don't fancy traipsing around the high street in search of a fitted corset, eBay and etsy are good places to look online. It's also worth having a poke through your wardrobe for old clothing – that black t-shirt you haven't worn for years could be jazzed up with stencils or patches.

Accessorize Yourself

Accessories can be found and repurposed in a similar manner – plug 'steampunk' into eBay and you'll find people selling huge piles of cogs and springs from old watches, as well as cheap round sunglasses and goggles. If you're a

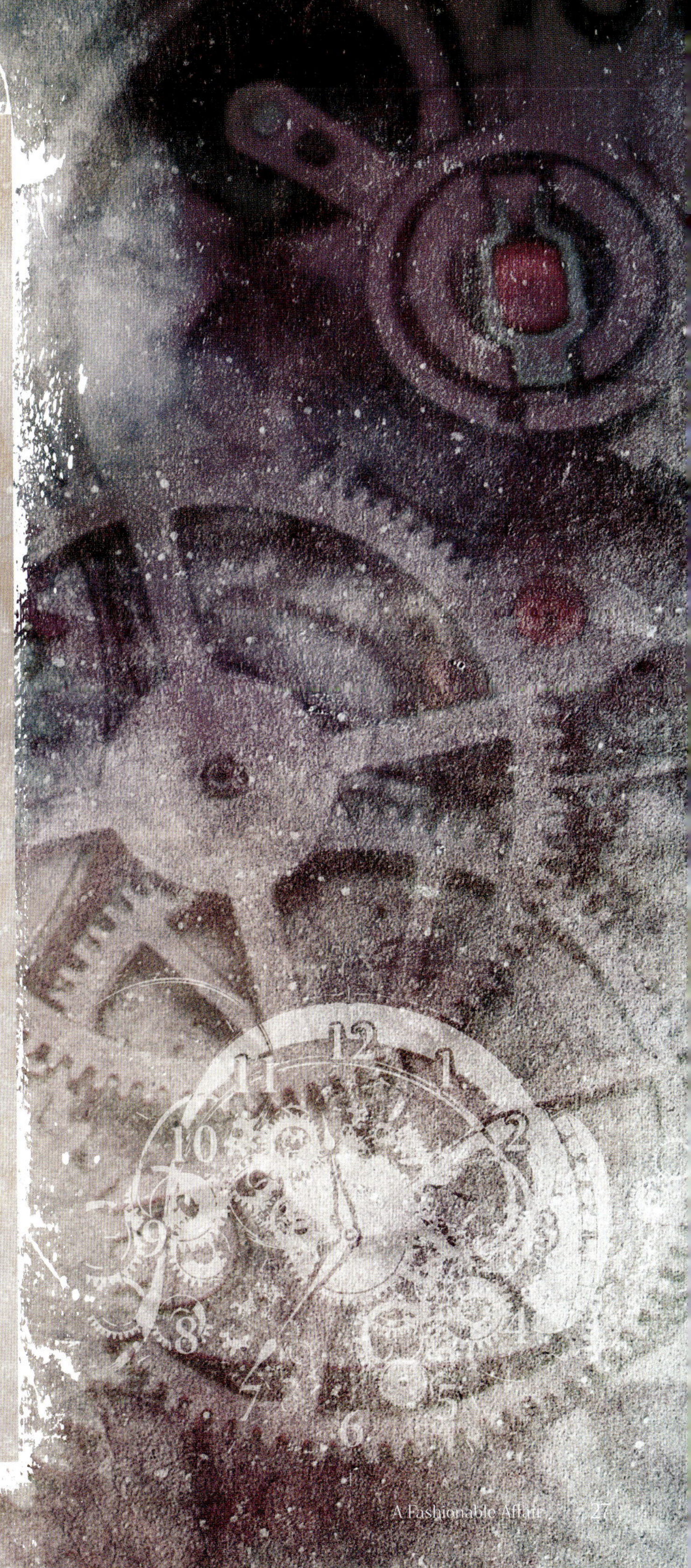

'I'm so sick of baggy pants hanging off your bottom. This is more refined. It goes back to a time when people had some dignity.'

Giovanni James, musician and magician

dab hand with a sewing machine or a soldering iron you can create your own steampunk belts and brooches, and a can of metallic brass Plasti-Kote can make mundane household objects such as lunchboxes and straws look like fantastical machine parts. The blog at www.steampunkcostume.com is – as its address suggests – a wonderful source for inspiration and ideas.

Cosplay Nicely

'Cosplay' refers to dressing up as a specific character from a movie, book, TV show or videogame and replicating their personality and traits. Steampunk is a great source for cosplay ideas – there are thousands of characters to choose from, and they look distinctive and often turn heads. It's also a little more challenging than merely dressing in a steampunk fashion, as you have to approximate a character's looks without the aid of a Hollywood costumer or a talented illustrator. Once you've completed your outfit you can take part in cosplay events where like-minded individuals do the same, and it's kind of liberating to lose yourself in someone else's creation.

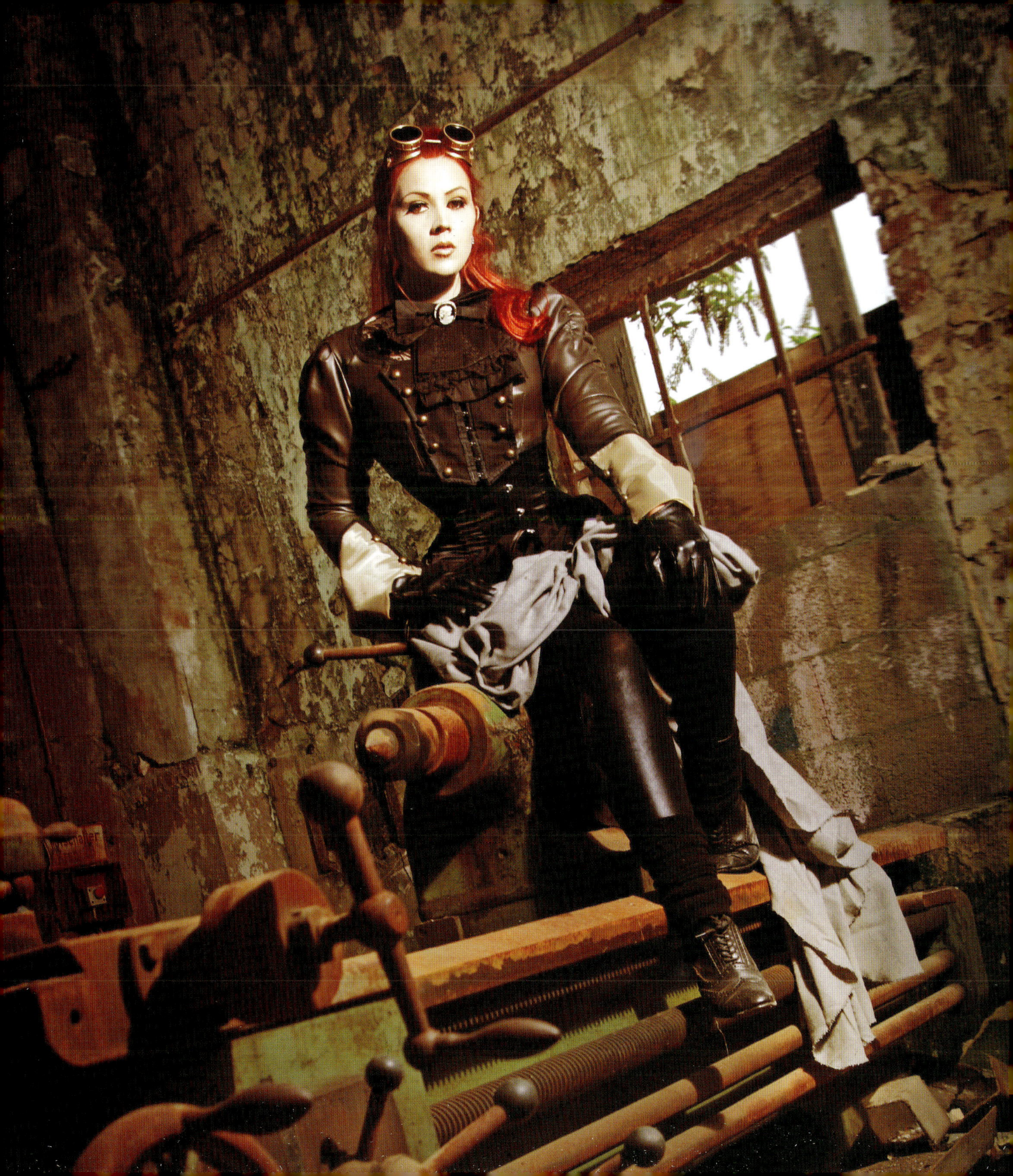

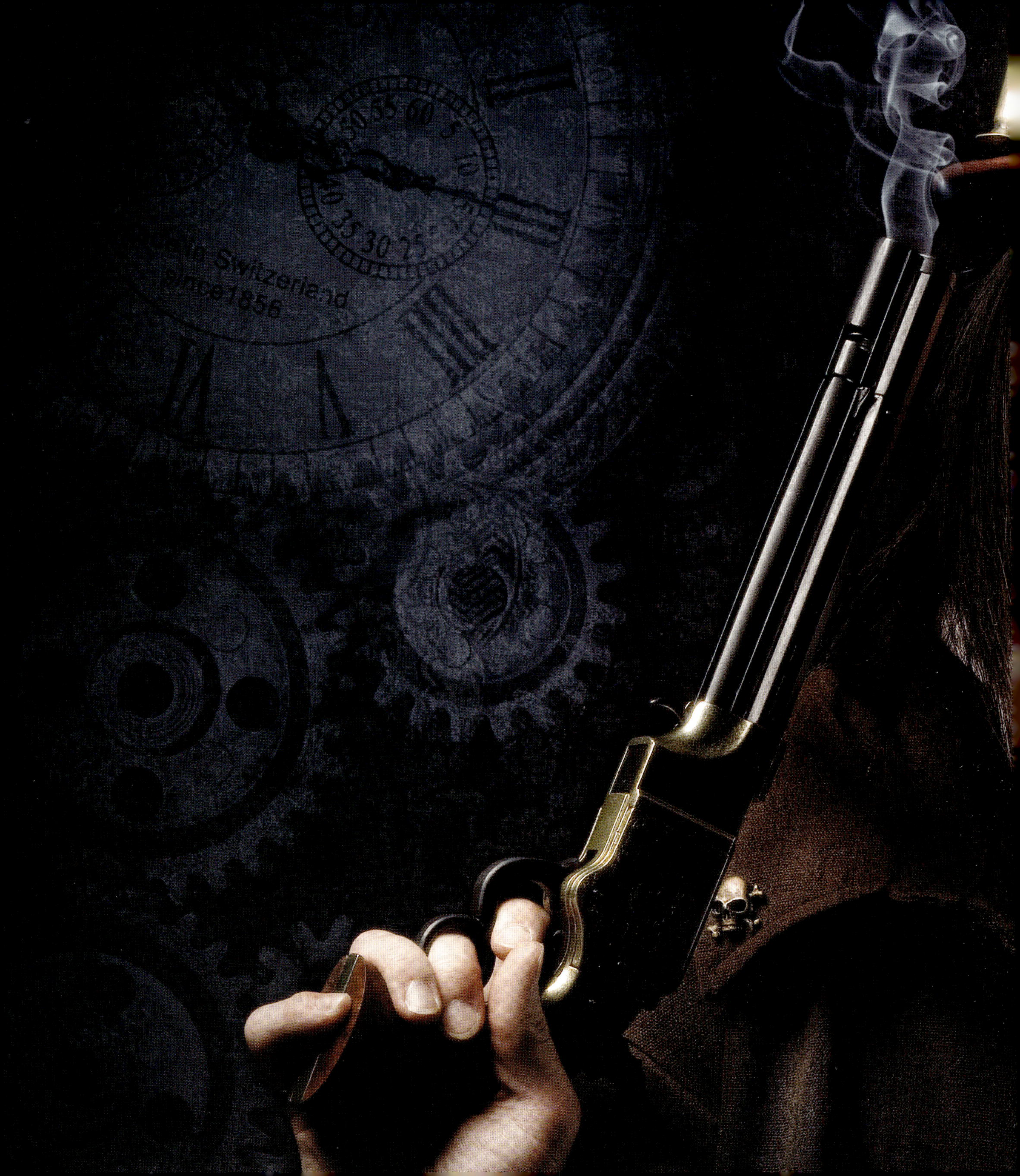
Switzerland

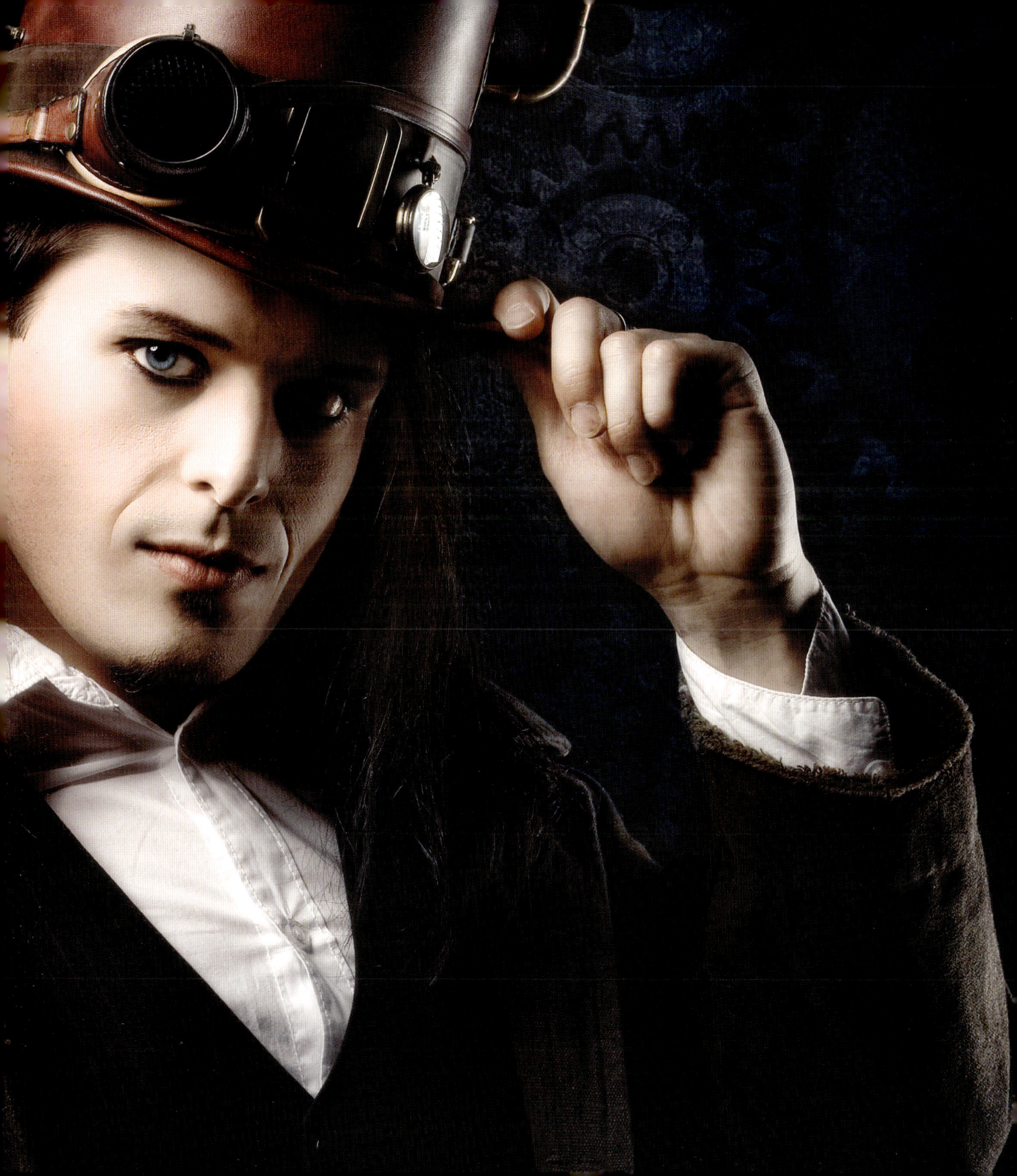

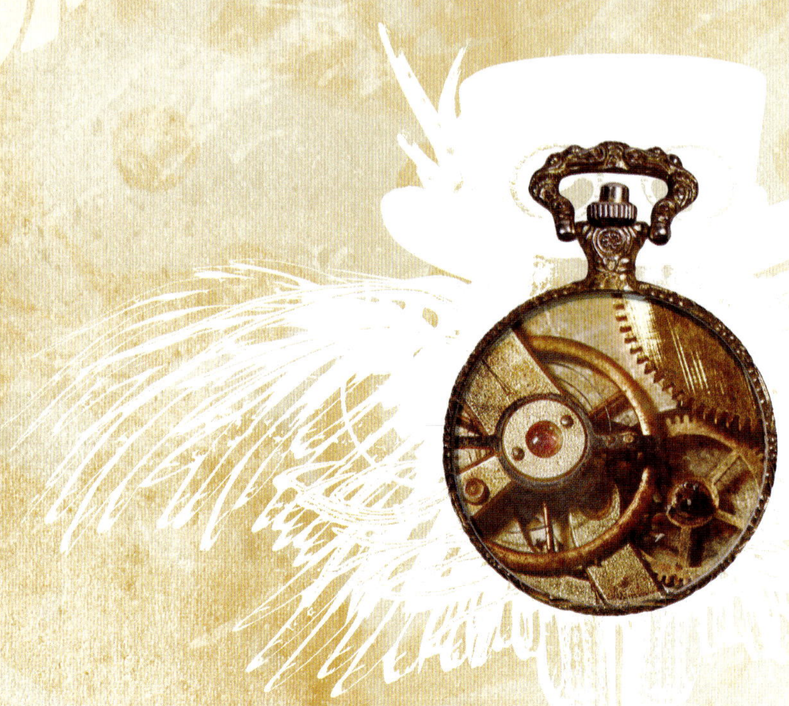

Fantastic Fiction

Despite being such an aesthetically-based movement, steampunk's roots lie primarily in literature. It plucks elements of classic novels by Dickens, Shelley and Wells and stirs in modern facets, or says what could have only been whispered in Victorian times. Steampunk is, in a way, a set template onto which authors can apply their own ideas and build upon those of others. One author may write about the role of women in Victorian society by creating a superpowered heroin, whereas another may comment on the class system by envisaging a race of clockwork robots who do humans' dirty work.

Genre Bending

Victorian London is the setting for the vast majority of steampunk, but it's not the only one – some stories take place in a far-flung, post-apocalyptic future, whereas others take place in an alternative version of the present day. As a genre it fits broadly into science fiction, which predicts tomorrow based on today's technology, but the twist is that it's predicting tomorrow based on yesterday's technology. Steampunk also pulls in many other genres, such as the romance, mystery, adventure and horror novels, all of which are blended to create interesting and exciting tales.

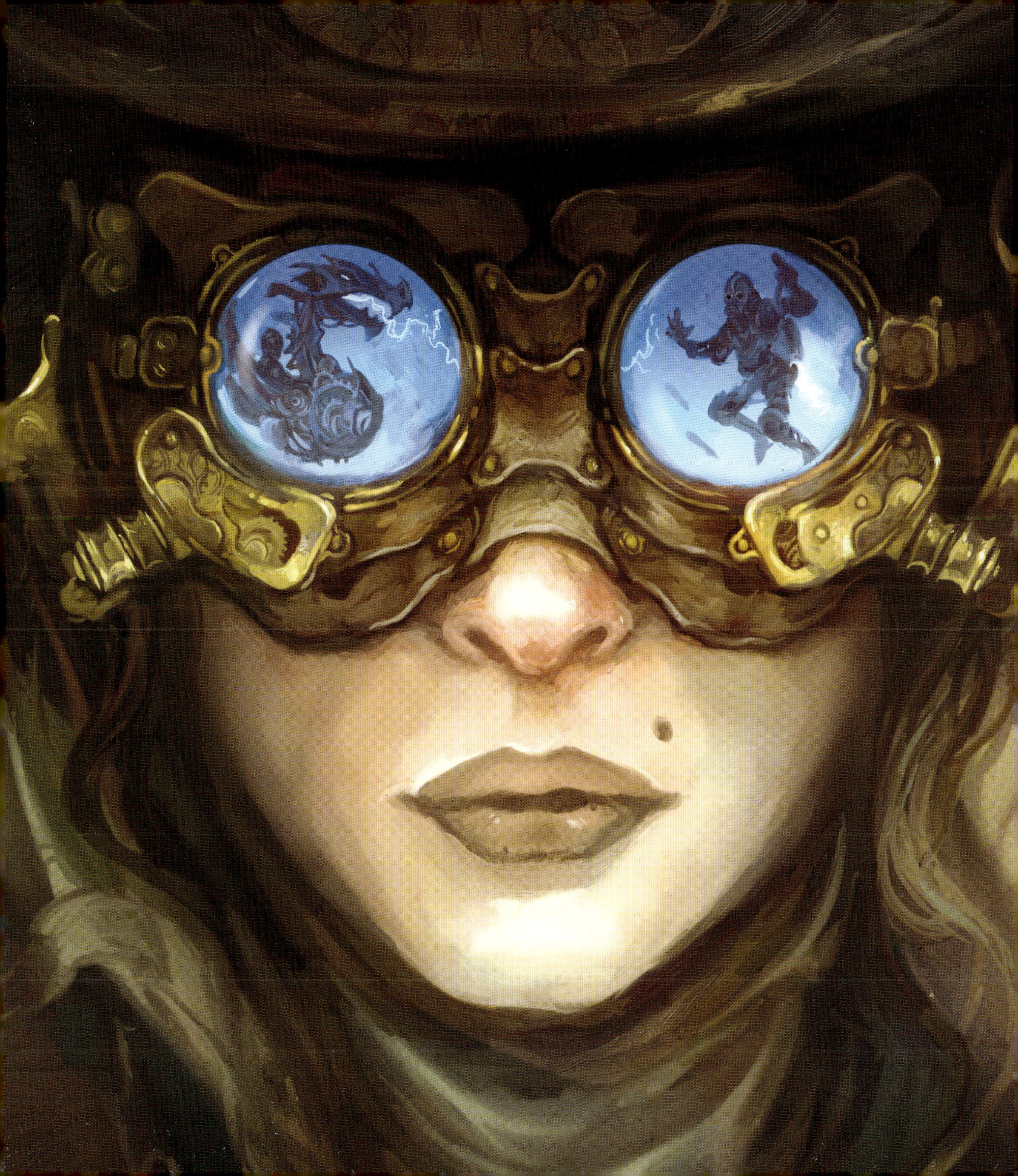

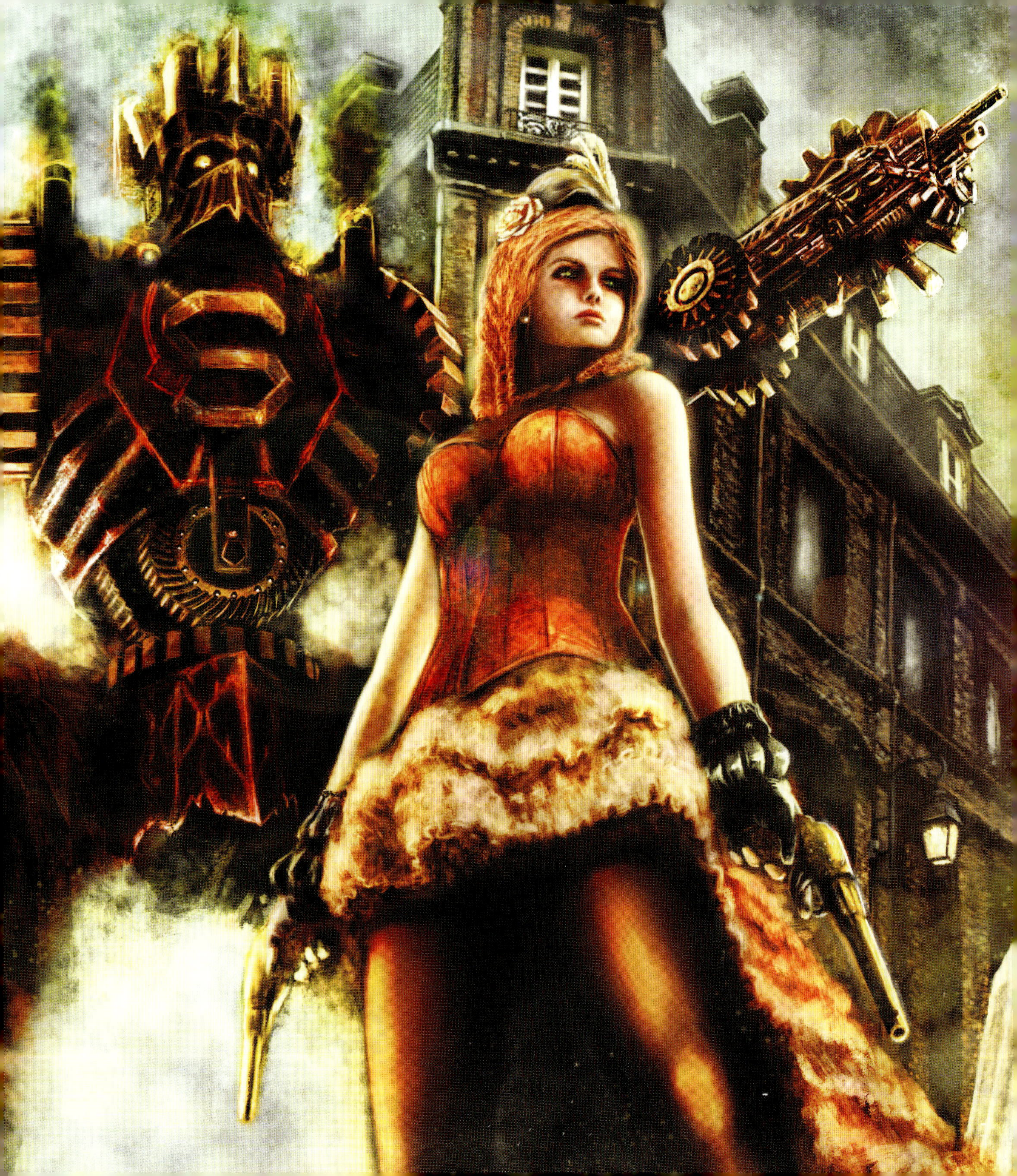

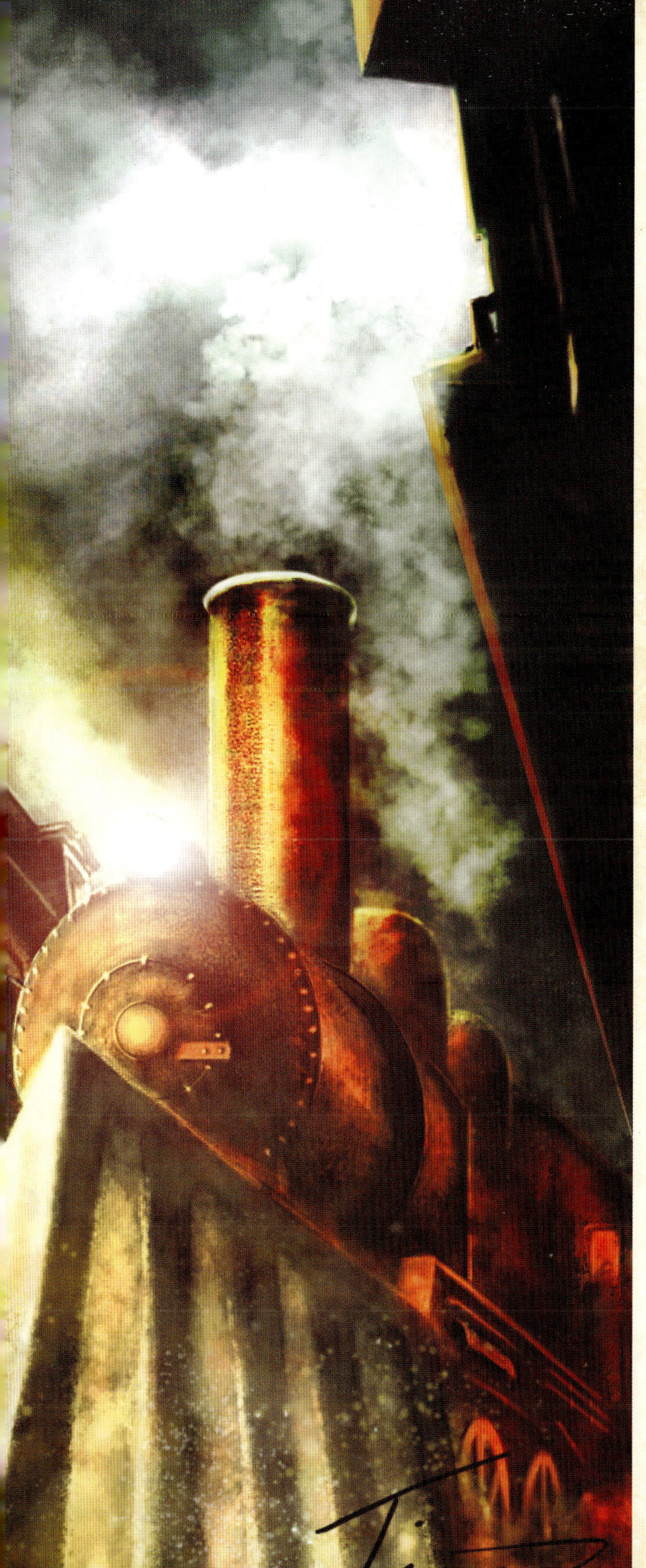

A Modern Prometheus

Arguably the first science fiction novel, Mary Shelley's 1818 story ***Frankenstein*** used the then-mysterious force of electricity to reanimate stitched-together body parts and create Frankenstein's monster. A key theme of the book is that technology allows Dr Frankenstein to play god, and this interaction between science and the occult has become a key facet of the steampunk ideology. It is also a book about identity: the monster doesn't quite know its place in the world, and this theme dominates tales of cyborgs and automatons.

Anglo-French Relations

Following Shelley's lead, a number of authors created science fiction works which are considered steampunk's forefathers. French author Jules Verne explored the worlds above and below us in ***From Earth to the Moon*** (1865), ***20,000 Leagues Under the Sea*** (1870) and ***Journey to the Centre of the Earth*** (1864). But his most steampunky novel was ***The Steam House*** (1880), in which British colonists travel around India in cabins pulled by a mechanical steam-powered elephant. On the other side of the English Channel H.G. Wells was extrapolating visions of the future in ***The Time Machine*** (1895), ***The War of the Worlds*** (1898) and ***The First Men in the Moon*** (1901).

Leaving the Nineteenth Century

The 1800s were nicely capped off with Bram Stoker's ***Dracula*** (1897), in which the immortal and ancient vampire travels to the then-new world of Victorian England with

'I like stories about supervillains. They teach children that you can accomplish great things even when the whole world is against you.'
G.D. Falksen

phonographs and typewriters among the technology on display. Arthur Conan Doyle played a role in the science fiction of the time: his detective creation Sherlock Holmes used a combination of wit and scientific knowledge to defeat his foes, and later cinematic adaptations would take on a very steampunk aesthetic. H.P. Lovecraft introduced new fears to a Georgian audience with his 1928 short story ***The Call of Cthulhu***, the metaphysical villain of which would become a steampunk icon.

Mike's Mechanics

Alternative historical novels began to rise to power in the 1960s and 70s. Ronald W. Clark's ***Queen Victoria's Bomb*** (1967) replants the invention of the nuclear bomb in Victorian times, while Harry Harrison's ***A Transatlantic Tunnel, Hurrah!*** (1973) imagines an alternative coal-fuelled British Empire digging a tunnel to America. But it was a trilogy of books by Michael Moorcock that paved the way for steampunk. ***The Warlord of the Air*** (1971), ***The Land Leviathan*** (1974) and ***The Steel Tsar*** (1981) depict various futures-gone-wrong through the eyes of Oswald Bastable, a British Army Captain.

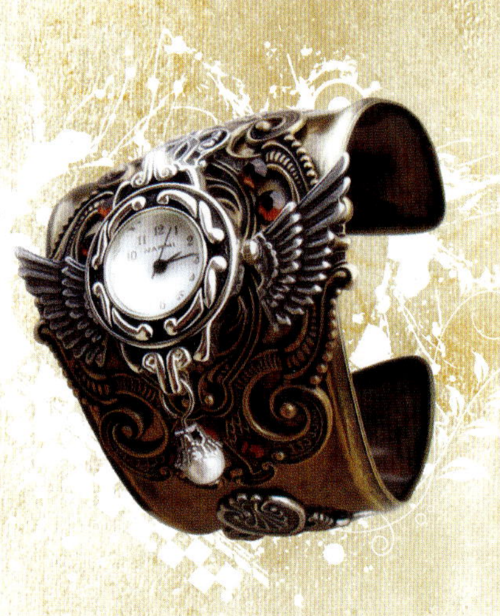

Triple Trouble

While Moorcock's work certainly helped steampunk on its way, it was a trio of writers working around the same time who truly put the 'punk' in the phrase. K.W. Jeter, James P. Blaylock and Tim Powers were a group of friends living in California, united by their love of writing. They would spend time with legendary cyberpunk progenitor Philip K. Dick, discussing stories and

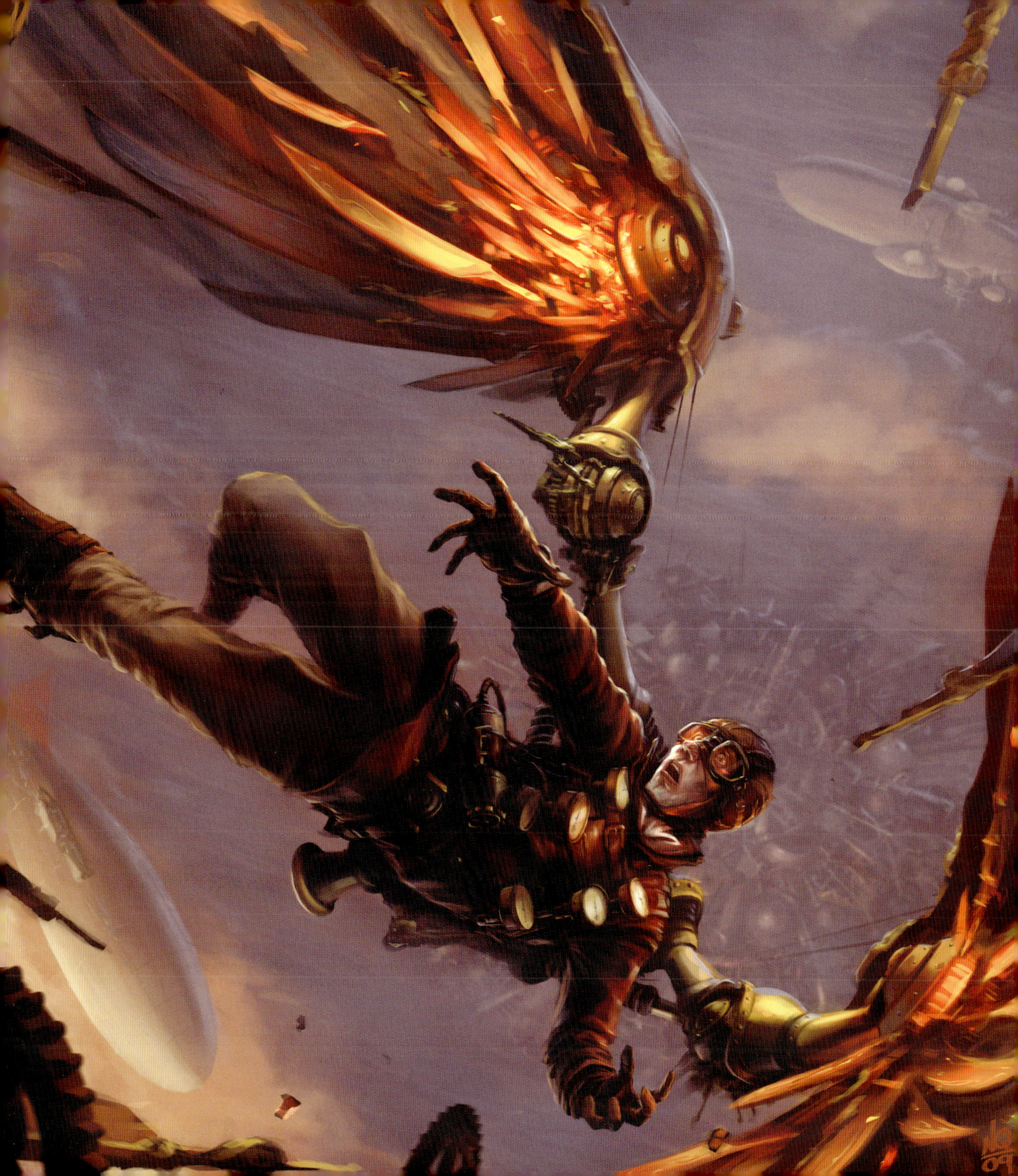

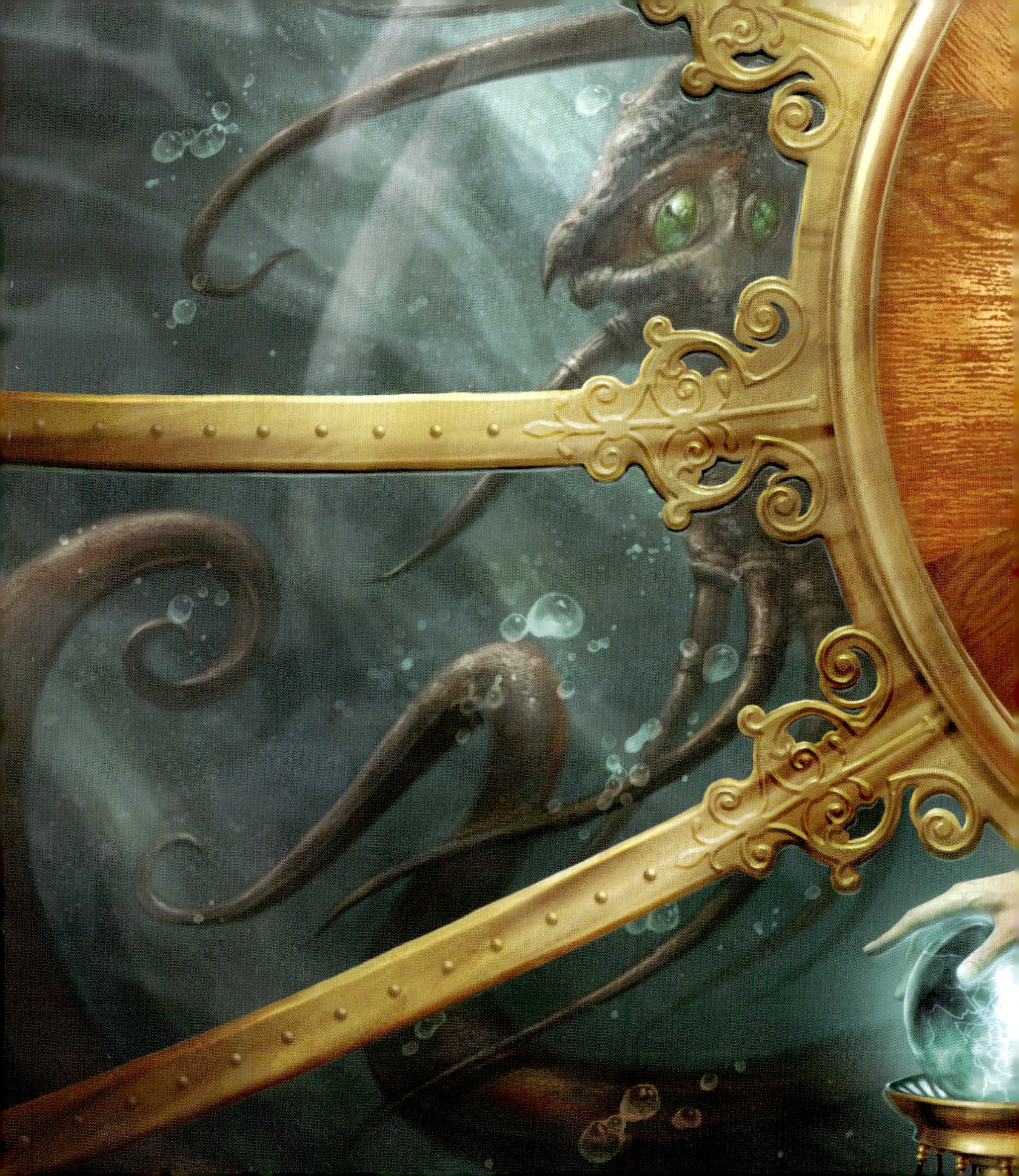

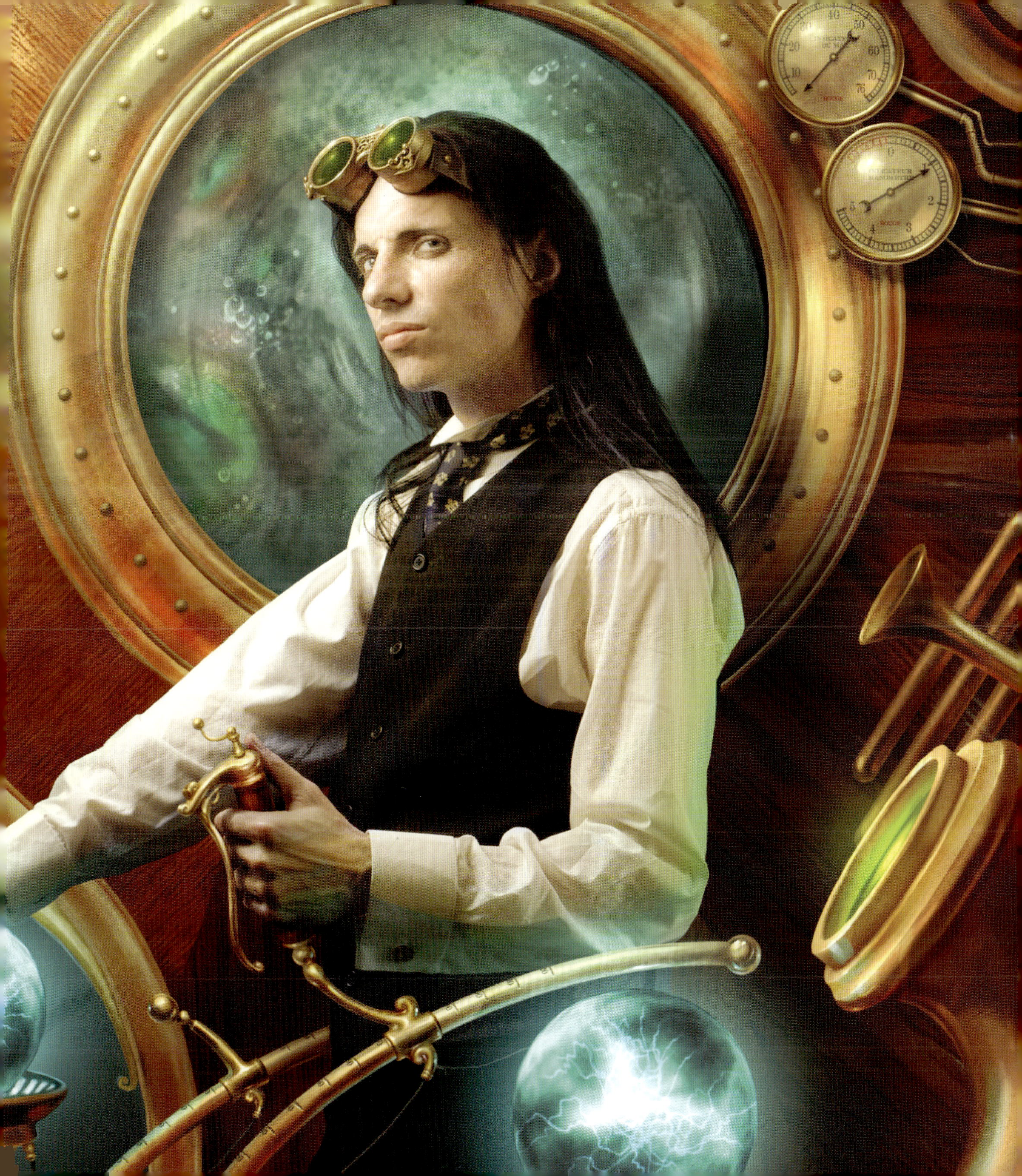

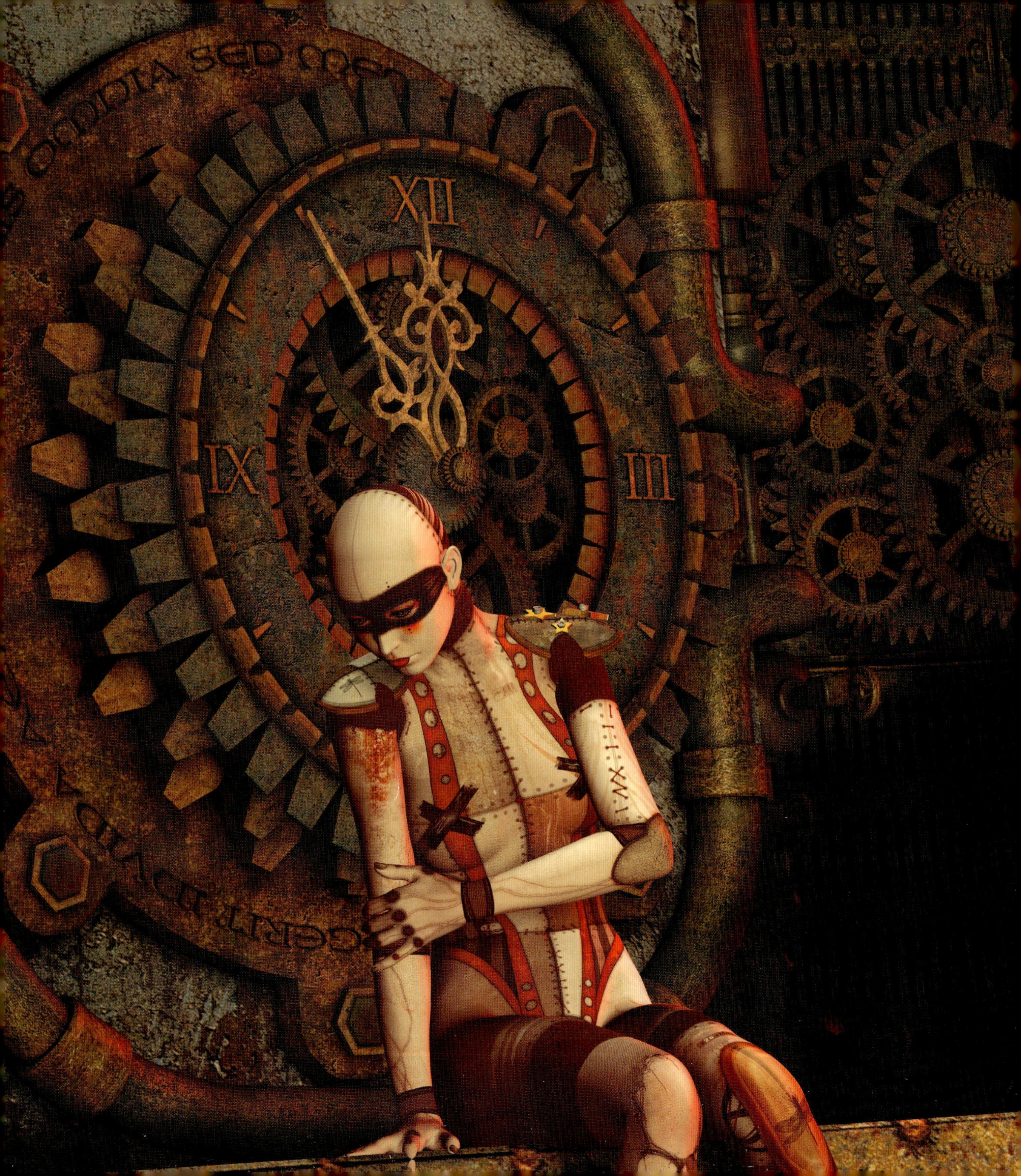
XII
IX
III

giving feedback on each other's work. While they started writing pulpy science fiction and fantasy stories, they were united by a love of Victorian fiction and conspired to create a whole new genre – which still didn't have a name.

The Time Machine 2

A huge H.G. Wells fan, K.W. Jeter reappropriated ***The Time Machine*** in ***Morlock Night*** (1979). In Wells' original novel, the nameless Time Traveller encounters the subterranean and caveman-like Morlocks in the year 802,701; but in Jeter's continuation of the story the brutish creatures figure out how to use the time machine and arrive in Victorian England. Chaos, naturally, ensues, and the saviours of Victoriana from the Morlocks turn out to be none other than Merlin and King Arthur. While it reads like a piece of fan fiction towards Wells, it was certainly the start of the steampunk we know and love today.

The Powers That Be

Meanwhile, Tim Powers' ***The Anubis Gates*** (1983) takes a different tact. Brendan Doyle leads an expedition through a network of time gates left by the Egyptians after a fictional plot to bring down the British Empire in 1802. Doyle becomes trapped in the nineteenth century and finds himself embroiled in a battle between magical factions. Again, Wells is a prime influence on ***The Anubis Gates***, and while it favours magic over bizarre contraptions, its reimagining of the past and the future it creates is key to steampunk as a genre.

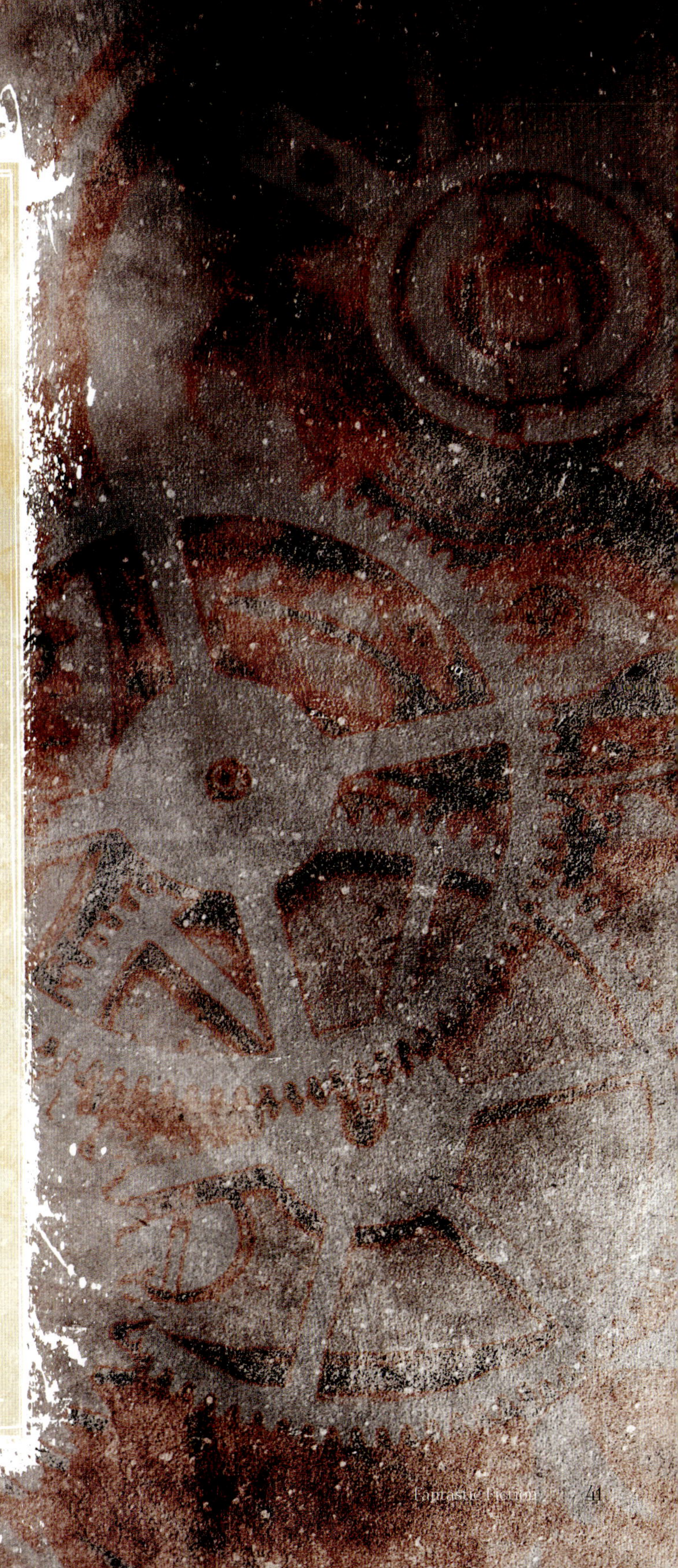

'The punk in steampunk is partly nineteenth century adventure, which was not self conscious, crossed with twentieth century characters who are self-conscious.'

Tim Powers

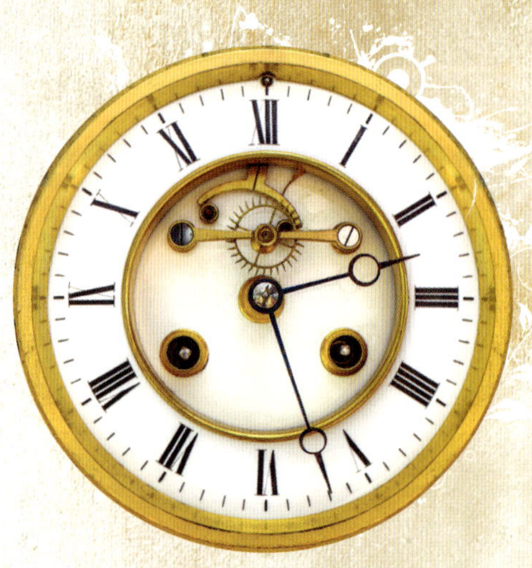

Digging Up the Past

Jeter's compadre, James P. Blaylock's first published story was ***The Ape Box Affair*** (1978), but ***The Digging Leviathan*** (1984) is his first proper steampunk novel. It concerns Jim Hastings, a teen living in 1960s San Francisco who is inspired by Edgar Rice Burroughs' ***At the Earth's Core*** (1914) to build a device to tunnel to the centre of the world. Despite its relatively modern setting, there are references to Jules Verne a-plenty, and the tetchy characters with one rose-tinted eye on the past would become core to steampunk's ideology.

The Pressure Builds

As the 1980s steamed forwards, Blaylock, Powers and Jeter continued writing about their obsessions. Powers took to the high seas with ***On Stranger Tides*** (1987), which became the inspiration for the 2011 ***Pirates of the Caribbean*** film of the same name. Jeter's ***Infernal Devices*** (1987) defined the view of a clandestine, steam-powered version of Victorian London in which a watchmaker is drawn into a world of clockwork twins and characters who speak fluently in twentieth-century American. Meanwhile Blaylock's ***Homunculus*** (1986) introduces a set of characters obsessed with a dirigible losing altitude over England's capital city.

Coining the Phrase

Between them the trio had defined steampunk without even realizing it, but it was Jeter who came up with the phrase. Keen to prove he had been the first of the friends to write

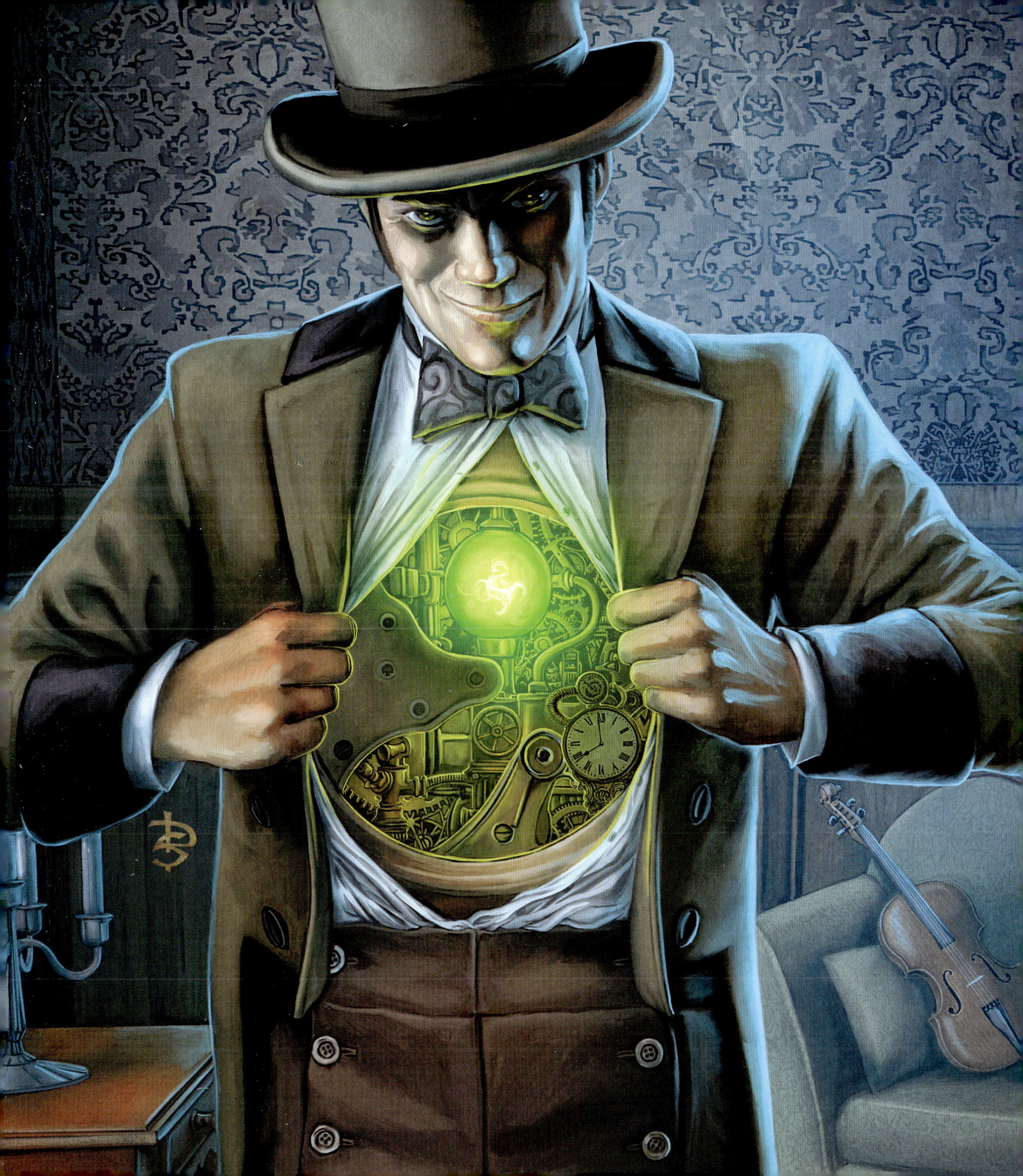

a 'gonzo-historical' novel, he forwarded a copy of ***Morlock Night*** to the influential science fiction magazine ***Locus***, accompanied with a letter. 'Personally, I think Victorian fantasies are going to be the next big thing, as long as we can come up with a fitting collective term for Powers, Blaylock and myself,' he wrote. 'Something based on the appropriate technology of the era; like "steam-punks", perhaps.'

The Other 'Punks

Popular 1980s science fiction sub-genre cyberpunk was similarly inspired by Philip K. Dick, but it's almost the antithesis of steampunk, obsessed with the then-nascent world of computing and the intangible nature of virtual reality rather than the more practical nature of steampunk's machines. Cyberpunk heroes William Gibson (***Neuromancer***, 1984) and Bruce Sterling (***Islands in the Net***, 1988) merged their genre with steampunk with ***The Difference Engine*** (1990). It imagines a Victorian society ruled by Charles Babbage's titular early computer, which in turn allows cyberpunk's key traits (hackers, artificial intelligence) to enter the steampunk world.

The Millennium of Steam

Gibson and Sterling's established audience found themselves engaging with a whole new perspective on science fiction, and ***The Difference Engine*** helped steampunk transform from a cult literary movement to a mainstream ideology. It made sense, too: a dominant theme of science fiction of the time was the then-upcoming turn of

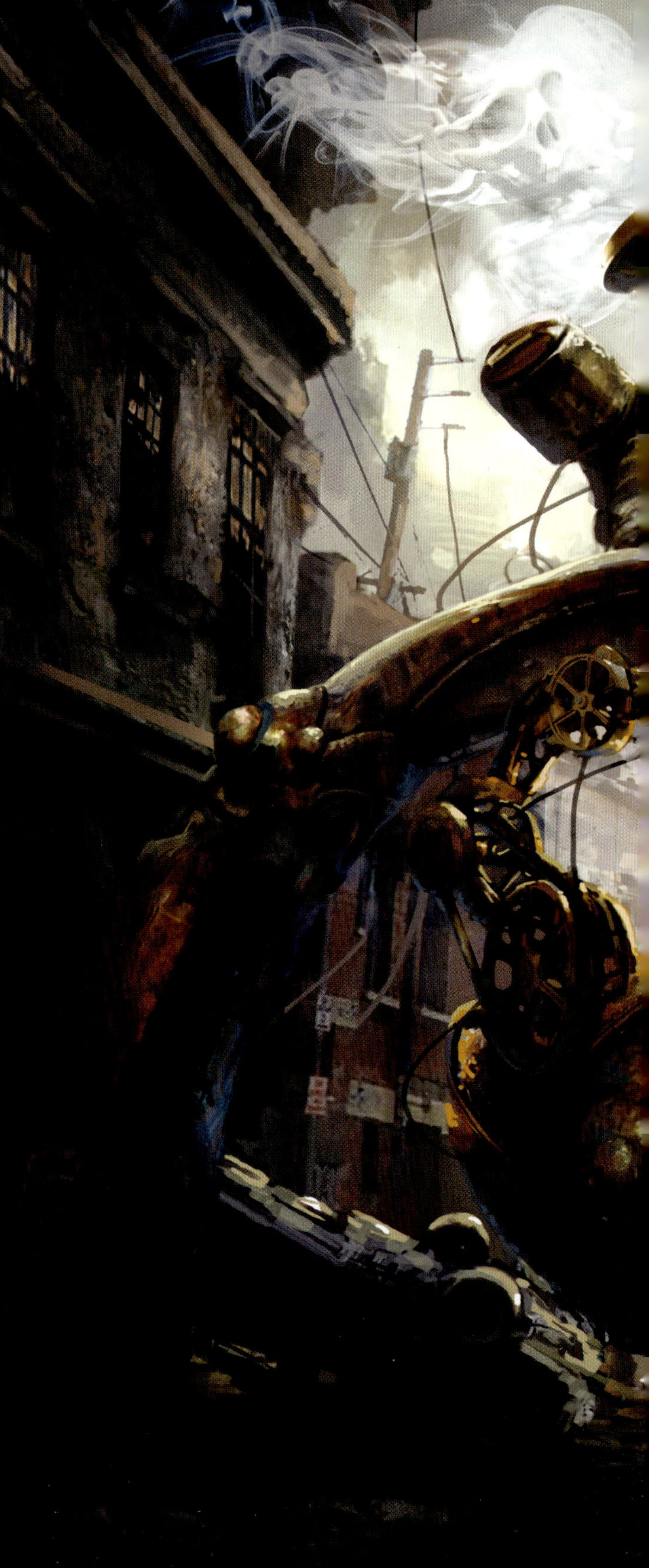

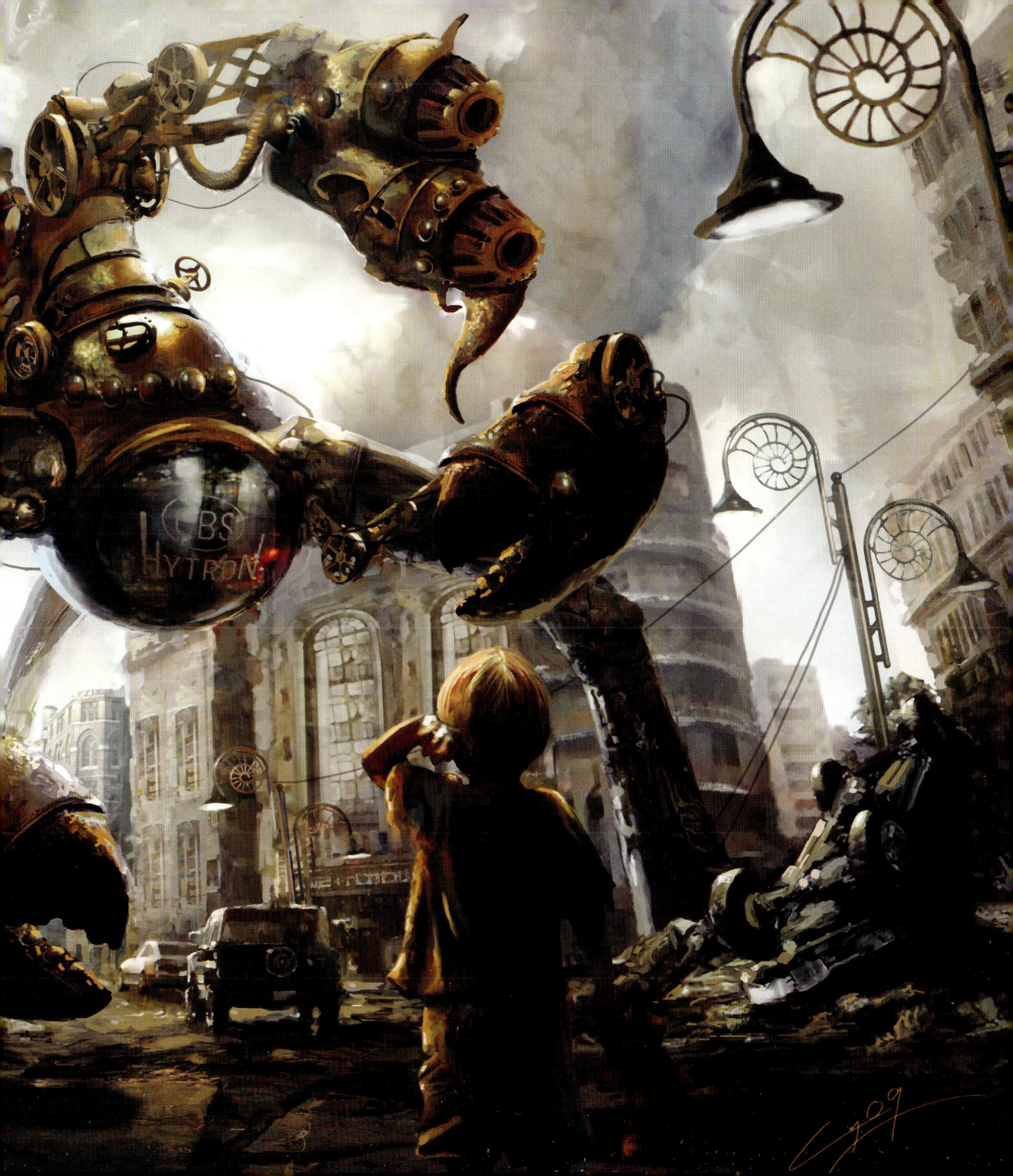
CBS
HYTRON

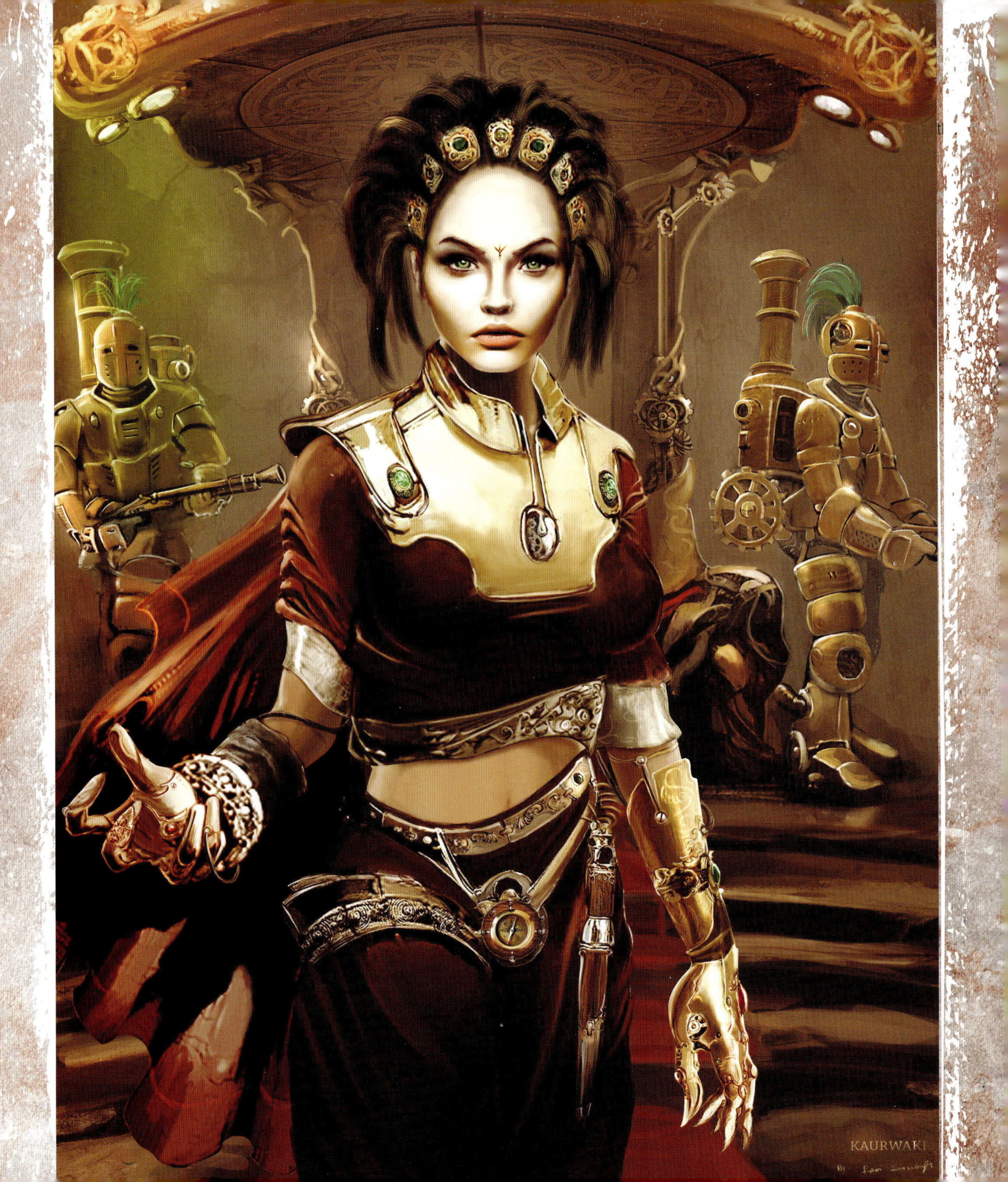
KAURWAKI

millennium, and looking back to the previous turn of the century could assuage worries about computers taking over, the second coming of Christ and the potential end of the world. Fortunately, none of these fears were realized.

Carry On Steampunking

The establishment of steampunk also meant that second-generation writers could put their own spin on the sub-genre. Paul Di Filippo's short story collection ***The Steampunk Trilogy*** (1997) almost spoofs Jeter, Blaylock and Powers' work with its tales of Queen Victoria being replaced with a giant newt, and a Swiss nudist tramping through the countryside. They're certainly not the best steampunk stories ever written, but the fact that they exist (and they include the word 'steampunk' in the title) is testament to the movement's growth. As steampunk progenitor G.K. Chesterton pointed out, the test of a religion is whether or not it can laugh at itself – and that was now true of steampunk.

Diamonds Are Forever

While Di Filippo toyed with steampunk's tropes, other authors were twisting the sub-genre into new and interesting forms. Neal Stephenson's ***The Diamond Age, or a Young Lady's Illustrated Primer*** (1995) may be set in a nanotechnologically augmented future, but its society subscribes to Victorian values and ideals. It depicts Nell, a working-class girl, as she works her way up the social ladder thanks to her accidental discovery of a 'primer' book.

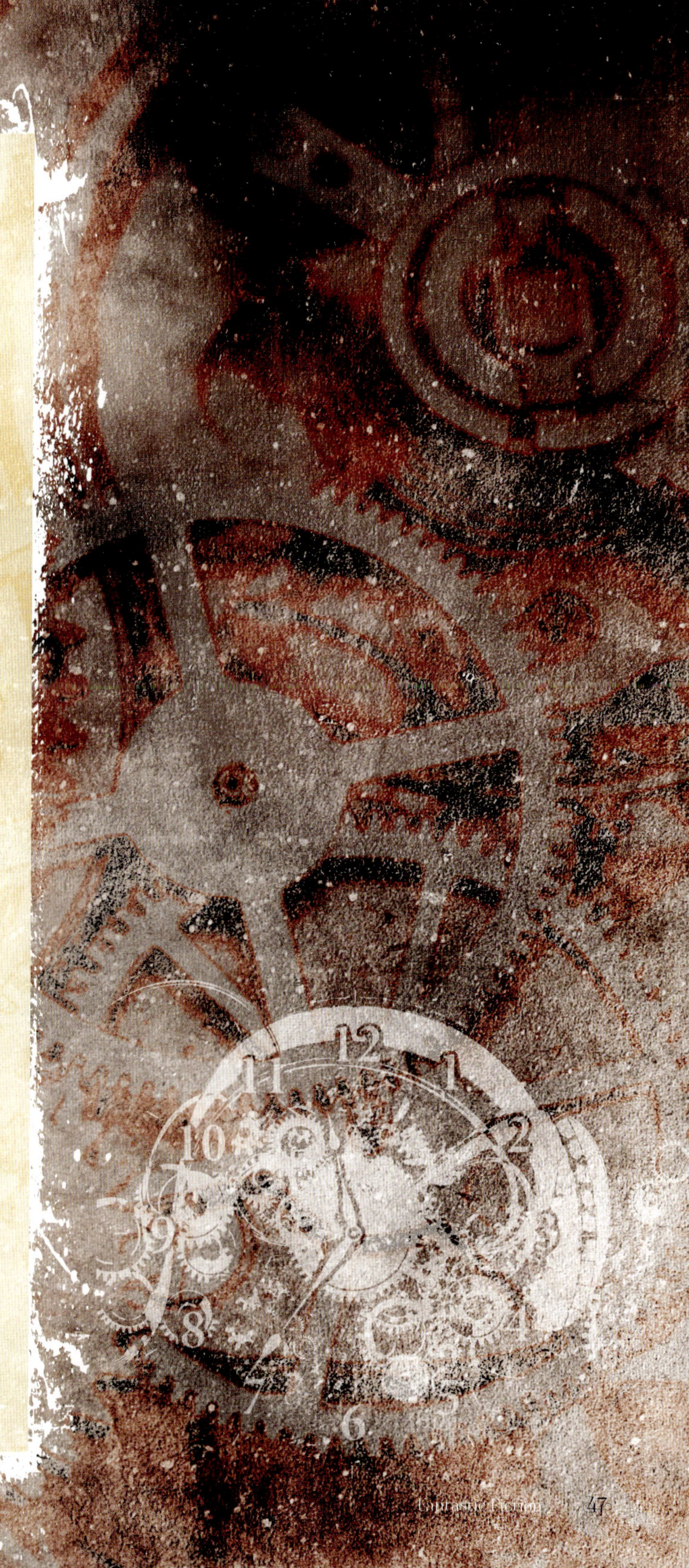

A middle-class and an upper-class girl also have access to 'primers', and through these characters Stephenson is able to explore class in a manner similar to Charles Dickens' ***Great Expectations*** (1861).

'Personally, I think Victorian fantasies are going to be the next big thing, as long as we can come up with a fitting collective term for Powers, Blaylock and myself ...Something based on the appropriate technology of the era; like "steam-punks", perhaps.'

K.W. Jeter

Britain Fights Back

Ironically for such a British-focused movement, steampunk's prime proponents had largely been Americans. However, the mid-1990s saw the Brits reclaim their rightful throne with a trio of writers – Stephen Baxter, Kim Newman and Christopher Priest – successfully experimenting in the sub-genre. While these writers weren't as close-knit as Blaylock, Powers and Jeter, they each had their own take on Britain's history combined with an intimate knowledge of the country's culture – something the original three freely admitted they lacked.

Time Travellers, Vampires and Magicians

Stephen Baxter's ***The Time Ships*** (1995) follows H.G. Wells' ***The Time Machine*** with a tale of the Time Traveller attempting to defeat the Morlocks (again!) by visiting both past and future, and it was authorized by Wells' descendants. Film buff Kim Newman's ***Anno Dracula*** (1992) posits a subtle change in history: Queen Victoria marries Dracula, giving Newman the excuse to fill his novel with everyone from Jack the Ripper to Lewis Carroll. Meanwhile, two nineteenth-century magicians battle with archaic technology in Christopher Priest's

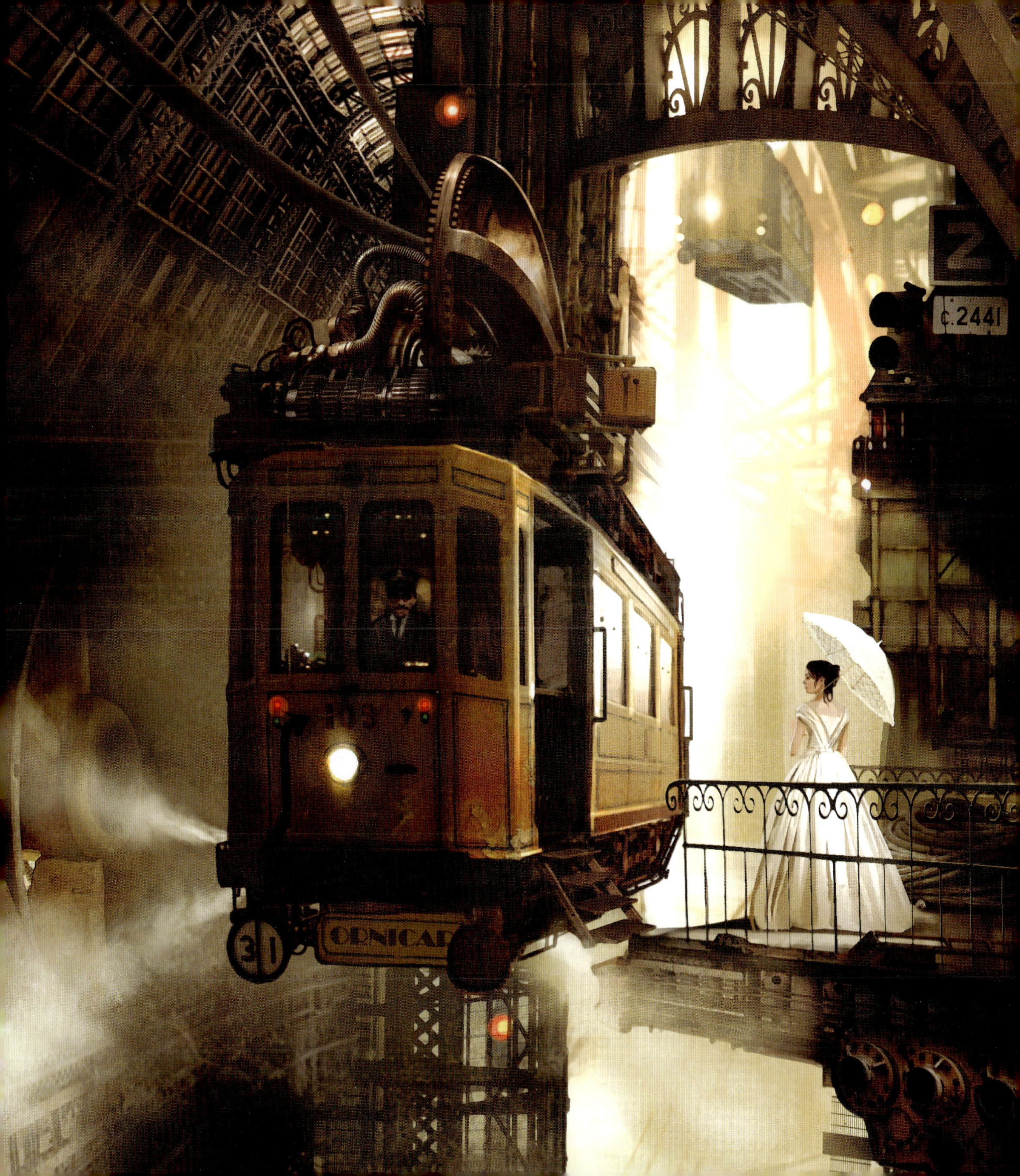
Z
C.2441
31
ORNICAR

The Prestige (1995), which was subsequently adapted into Christopher Nolan's 2006 movie.

A Tale of Two Cities

Born in London in 1971 to an American mother, China Mieville is perhaps the Anglo-American author who united steampunk's US beginnings with its UK settings. His novel ***Perdido Street Station*** (2000) is considered one of the best efforts in the sub-genre, taking place in the London-like city of New Crobuzon in a parallel world. Mieville draws on the movies ***Blade Runner*** and ***The City of Lost Children*** for influence, but it's the vividly imagined denizens that make ***Perdido Street Station*** stand out. Previously steampunk heroes were pulpy and typecast, but Mieville fills in backstories and rounds out characters – both human and otherwise.

Architecture and Mortality

Strange cities certainly took a hold on steampunk in the early 2000s. Philip Reeve's ***Mortal Engines*** (2001) applies Darwinian thought to the evolution of cities themselves, with capitals rebuilt as a huge vehicles travelling through a post-apocalyptic landscape and even devouring other settlements. While the deserted and scorched earth may not sound like the most upbeat of places, it's a wonderful adventure with lots of steampunk elements such as hot air balloons and air pirates, and it was followed by ***Predator's Gold*** (2003), ***Infernal Devices*** (2005) and ***A Darkling Plain*** (2006).

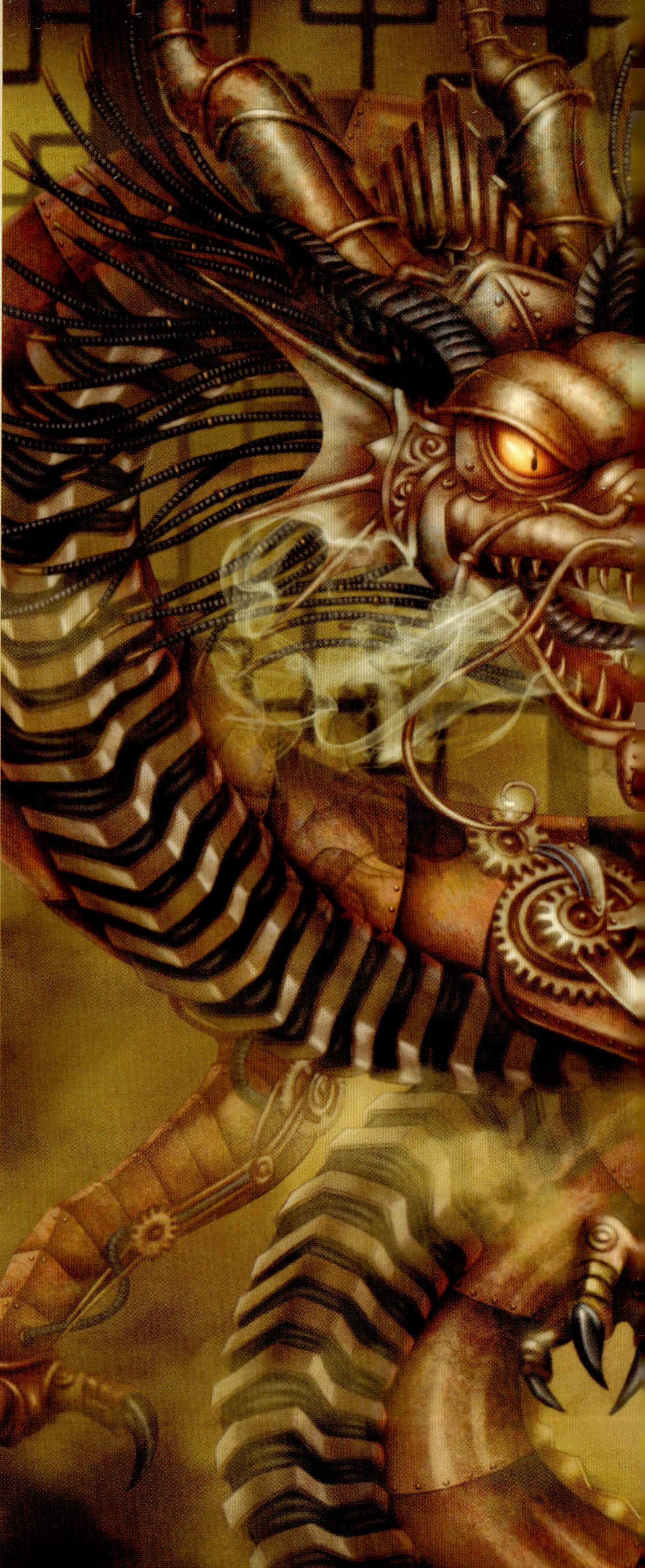

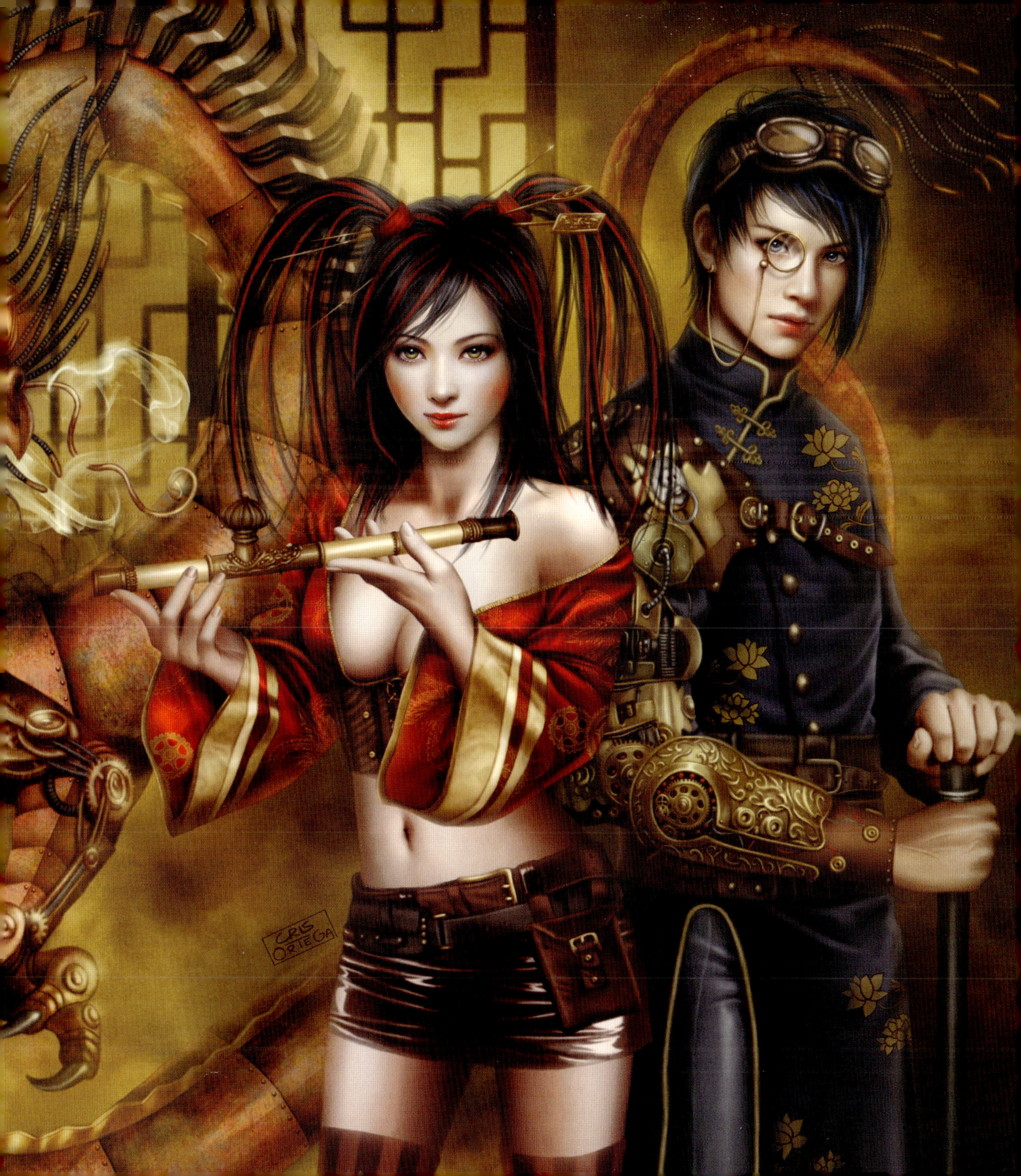
CRIS
ORTEGA

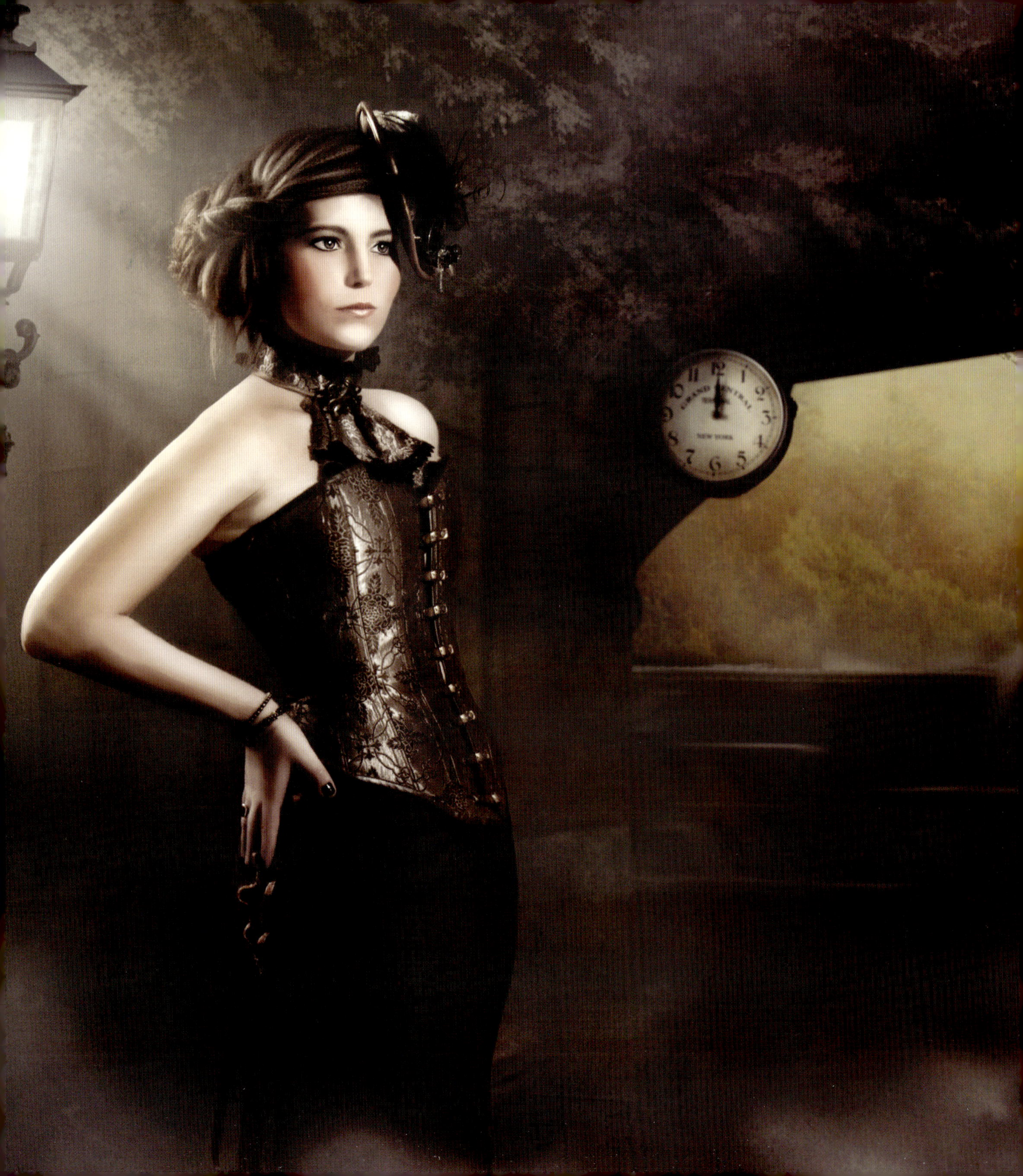

Cruse Ships

Kenneth Oppel's ***Airborn*** (2004) is a tribute to swashbuckling adventures such as Robert Louis Stevenson's ***Treasure Island*** with a minor twist: the ships travel through the sky rather than the sea. Set at the beginning of the twentieth century, it follows Matt Cruse, a cabin boy, as he falls in love with a girl obsessed with mythical panther-sized creatures who spend their whole lives in the air. It ends in true Stevenson style with a piratical confrontation on a desert island. It's a Boys' Own adventure with a nice sense of Victorian enthusiasm for then-emerging technology.

On the Hunt

Stephen Hunt's incredible six novels cover just about every facet of steampunk, beginning with ***The Court of the Air*** (2007) and ending with ***From the Deep of the Dark*** (2012). Hunt tackles different genres with each book, and puts a steampunk spin on everything. The first novel introduces a Dickensian pair of orphans (Molly Templar and Oliver Brooks) on the run after Molly witnesses a murder. It's packed to the brim with the things we know and love about steampunk: steam-powered machines, mechanical men, magicians and mutants. That the characters take a back seat to the setting doesn't really matter: like Tolkien before him, it's Hunt's rich tapestry of a world that keeps us intrigued.

'I may be a werewolf and Scottish, but despite what you may have read about both, we are not cads!'

Gail Carriger, Soulless.'

Violent Femmes

While steampunk contains some strong and well-rendered female characters, it's mostly a boys' game of outlandish adventures and damsels in distress. A handful of female steampunk authors are an exception to this rule, though. Russian author Ekaterina Sedia's ***The Alchemy of Stone*** (2008) takes place in a London-esque city state, but casts Maddie, a clockwork female automaton in the lead role. In turn, this allows Sedia to critique the patriarchal nature of society in general, and provide insight into the mechanization of manual labour as workers revolt against the machines which have taken their jobs.

Less Ordinary

Meanwhile, Gail Carriger's ***Parasol Protectorate*** series, beginning with ***Soulless*** (2009), creates a compelling cocktail of steampunk, gothic horror and gender politics. Her heroine, Alexia Tarabotti, lacks a soul, which means she can take on the werewolves and vampires which inhabit this particular version of Victorian London. While science fiction's females tend to be male characters rewritten for female roles, Tarabotti is established from the ground up as a female. She's also a dab hand with her umbrella, which is stuffed with gadgets and weapons – although she prefers to just stab assailants in the head with it.

Warlords

Scott Westerfeld's ***Leviathan*** (2009) takes place in an alternative version of the First World War with the German Central Powers using huge, steam-driven machines to take on the British, who toy with Darwin-inspired genetic manipulation to create fearsome beasts of war. There is a twist in line with Carriger and Sedia's novels, though: the protagonist, Dylan Sharp, is in fact Deryn Sharp, who's disguised herself as a boy in order to access the British forces' giant airship. Westerfeld followed up ***Leviathan*** with two more books featuring Deryn: ***Behemoth*** (2010) and ***Goliath*** (2011).

A Mann's World

Bringing everything full-circle are the Newbury and Hobbes series by George Mann, beginning with 2008's ***The Affinity Bridge***. Mann has worked on ***Doctor Who*** and ***Sherlock Holmes*** audiobooks, so he knows the intricacies of great characters – something which is evident in his novels' leads. Sir Maurice Newbury is a gentlemanly 'Investigator for the

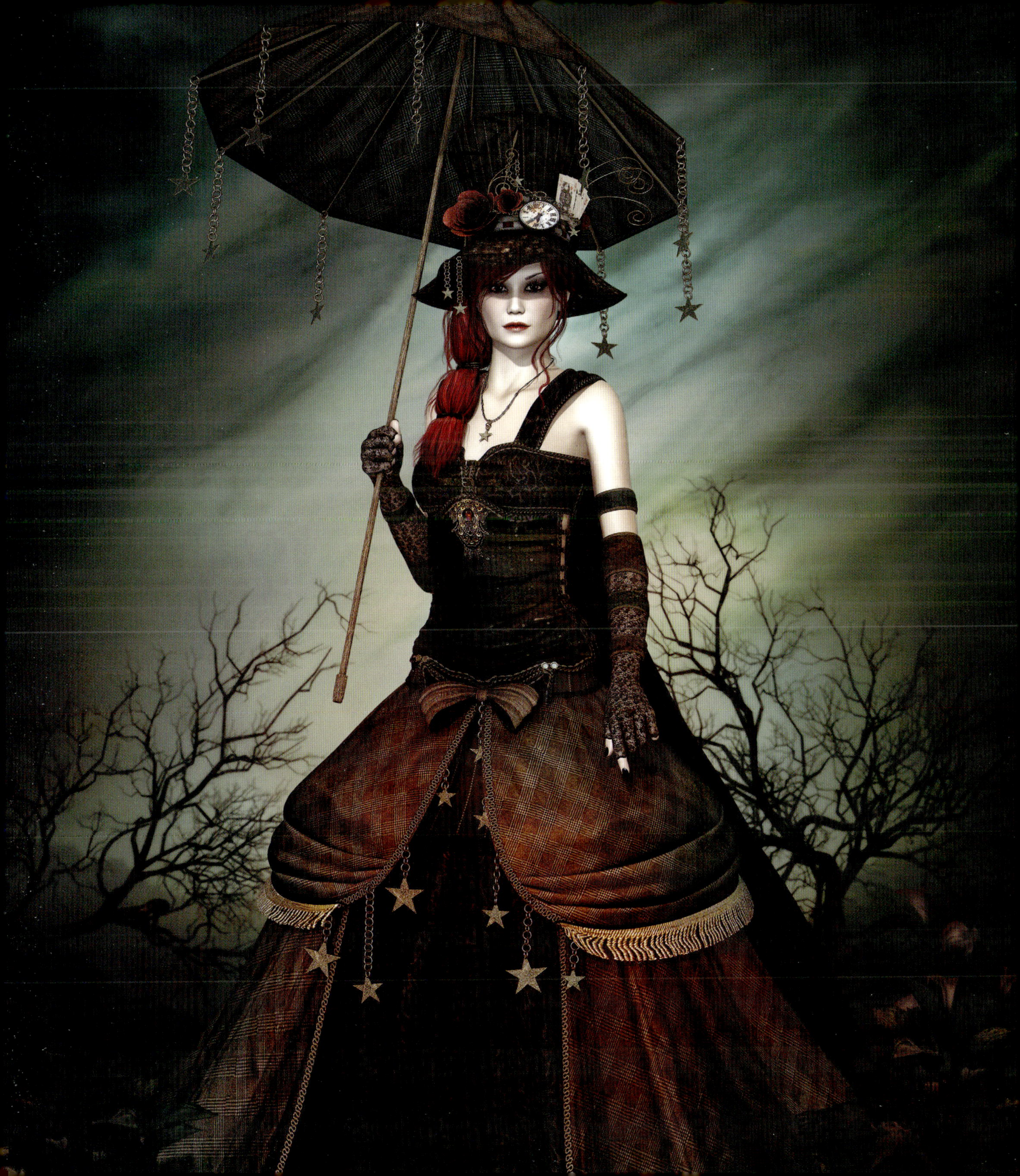

Crown' paired with the rather more hotheaded Miss Veronica Hobbes, who carries her own secret agenda. It's an affectionate tribute to steampunk's roots, with enough airships and automatons to please ardent fans of the sub-genre.

A Falksen Hero

A true Renaissance (or should that be Industrial?) man, G.D. Falksen has become a modern steampunk icon. As well as writing a number of short stories and blogs for Tor.com, he's also become a go-to expert in the field. His debut novel, ***Blood in the Skies*** (2011) is a fast-paced adventure set in a rebuilt world two hundred years after its destruction in 1908. The central character, Elizabeth Steele, is a kind of female take on Indiana Jones, equally capable of piloting an aeroplane and taking on the evil sky pirates. While light on deeper commentary, it's still a fun and enjoyable read.

Steampunk Anthologies

This collection of novels is merely the tip of the iceberg as far as steampunk is concerned, and recently a huge number of novels have been published in the sub-genre. A great primer for all things literary and steampunk are Ann VanderMeer and Jeff VanderMeer's anthologies, which include essays and excerpts from the field's greatest practitioners. The first, published in 2008, includes work by Paul Di Filippo, James P. Blaylock and Michael Moorcock, as well as new and unestablished authors. Each is compelling in its own right, and it is fitting testament to just how malleable steampunk can be in the hands of talented authors.

'Philip K. Dick didn't so much mentor me and Blaylock and Jeter as simply hang out with us. We each did give him a manuscript at some point and said, basically, "What do I do with this?"'

Tim Powers

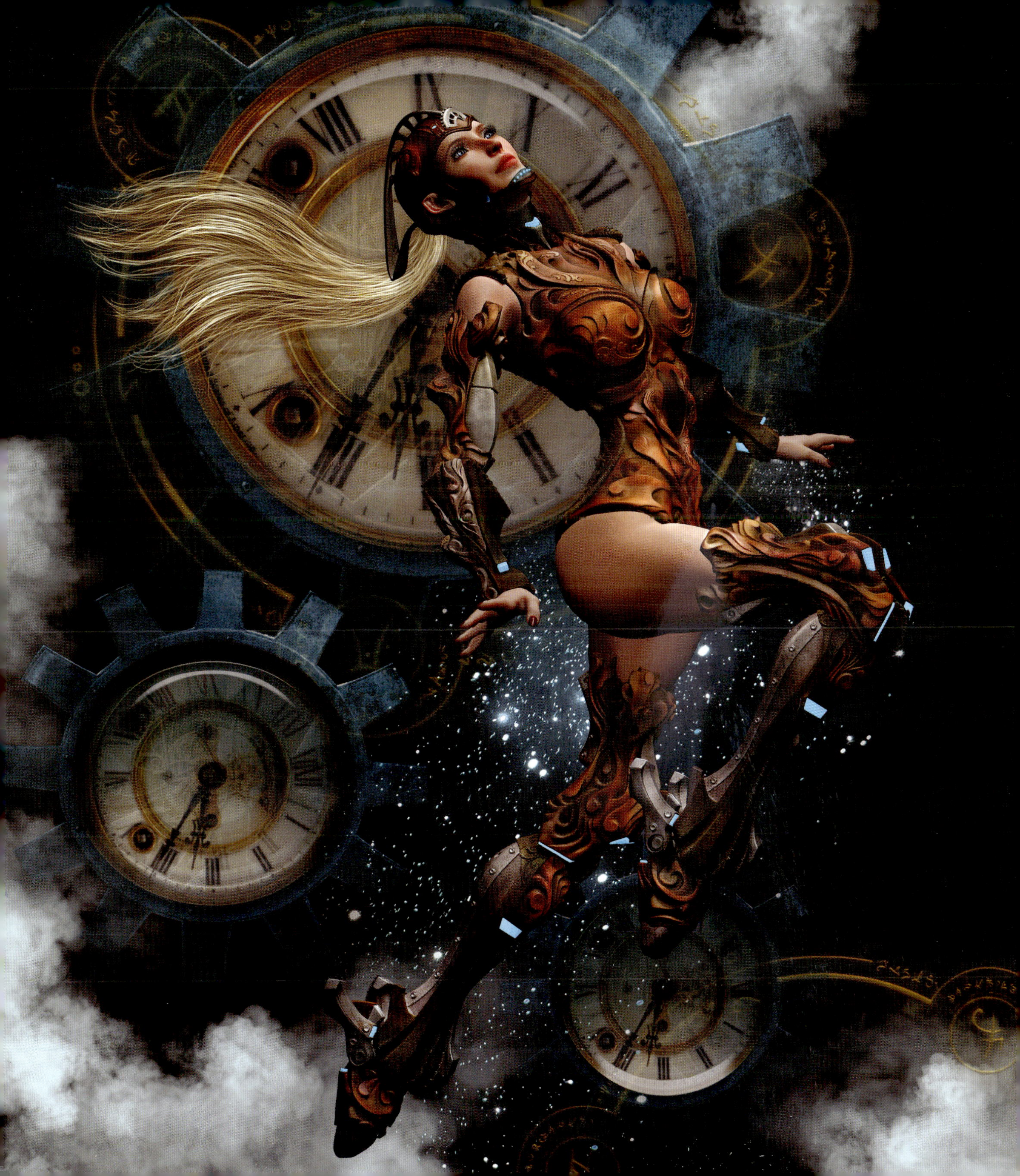

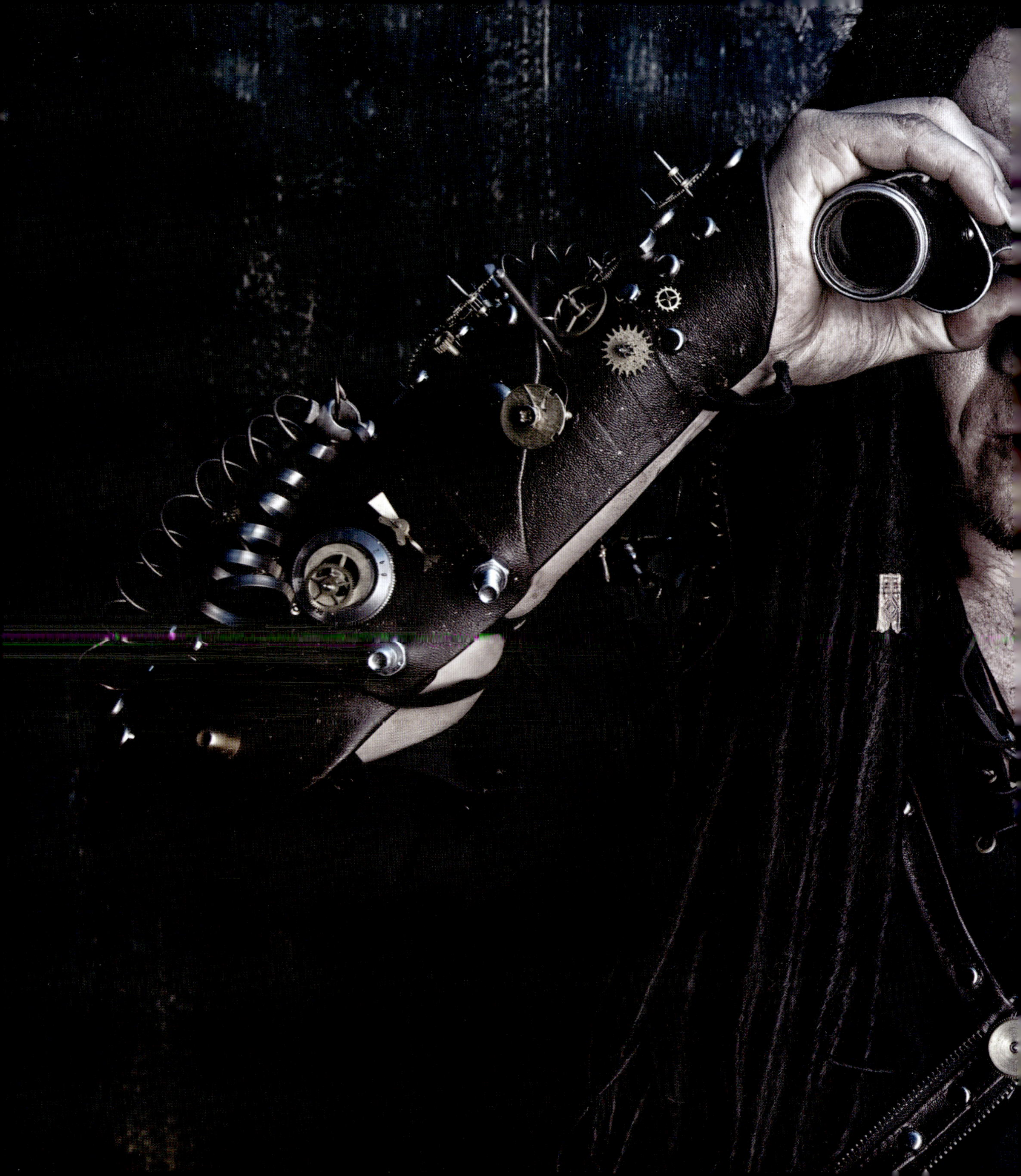

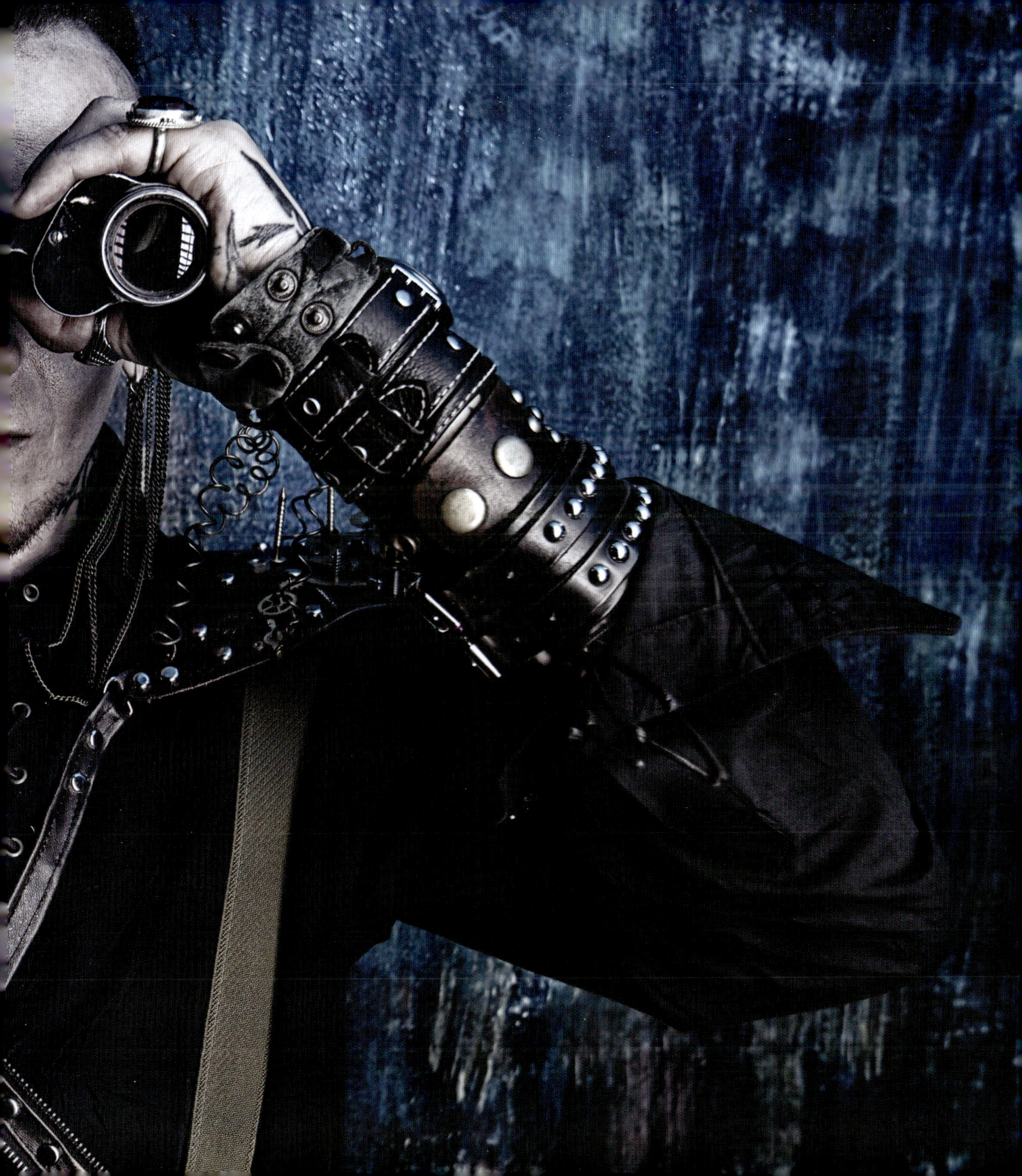

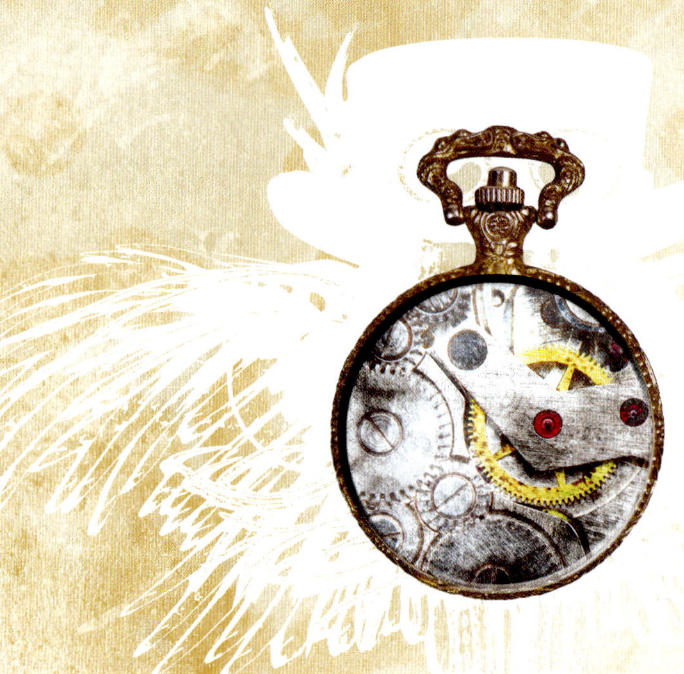

Steampunk On Screen

There's something very steampunky about cinema itself. The medium was invented in the Victorian era, and early projectors and cameras were intricate, archaic devices with hundreds of moving parts. Television, which became popular in the 1930s, was similarly magical and mysterious, consisting of valve-based electronic parts rather than the more crude mechanics of a projector. The crucial difference was – and still is – that the television found its way into the home, whereas cinemas replaced theatres as entertainment venues. Both devices inspired whole new mediums – and steampunk played a part right from the very beginning.

Sparkling Jules

A glut of Jules Verne adaptations in the 1950s and 60s reimagined the author's works with grand steampunk machines. ***20,000 Leagues Under the Sea***'s (1954) submarine, the ***Nautilus***, beautifully combines organic, aquatic shapes with industrial design, and ***Five Weeks in a Balloon***'s (1962) titular dirigible basket takes the form of a steam-powered unicorn. Adaptations of H.G. Wells' ***The Time Machine*** in movie-form, such as in 1960 and 2002, feature very steampunky aesthetics in the form of the machine itself. ***Chitty Chitty Bang Bang***

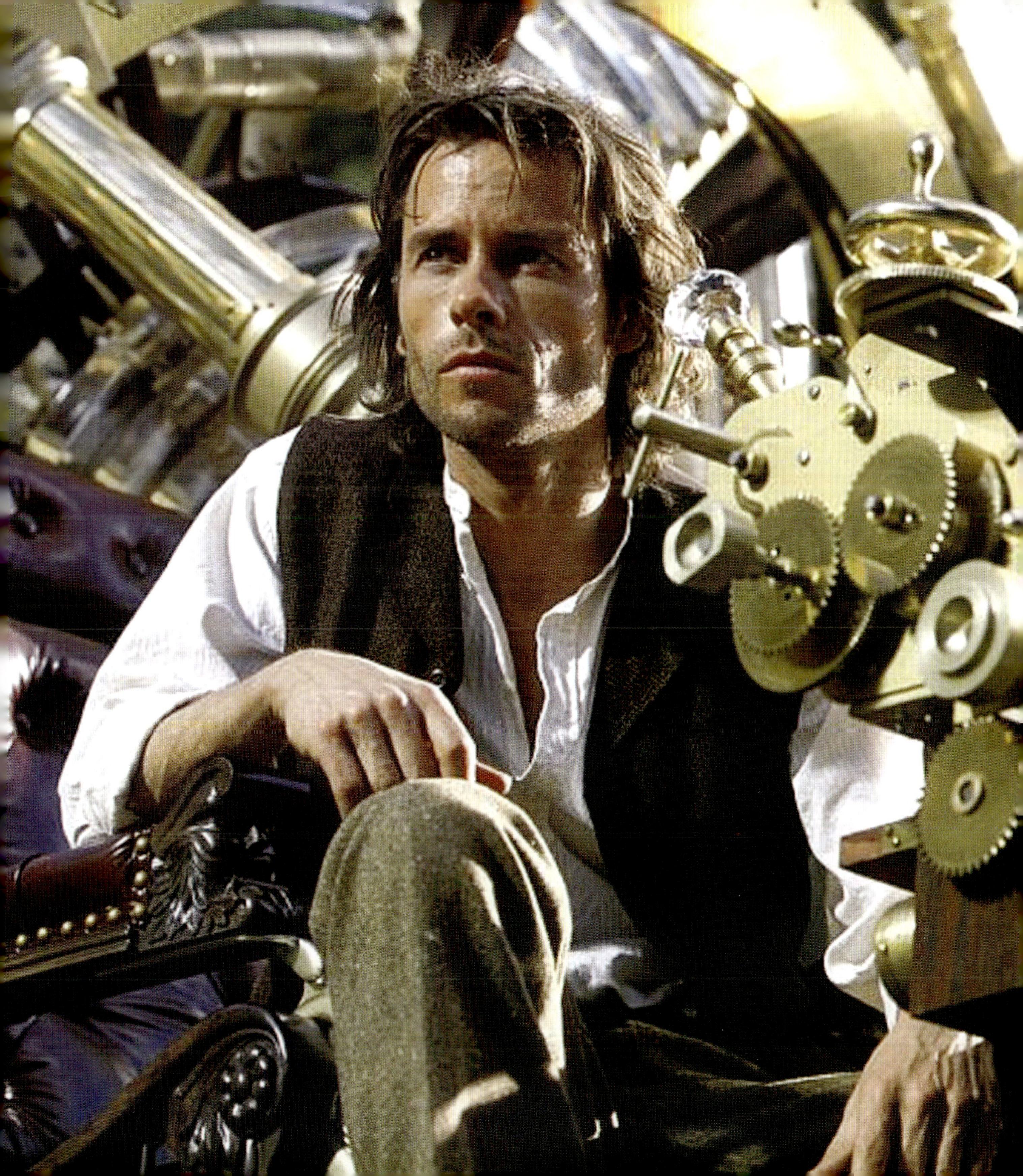

> *'I wish I'd never invented that infernal time machine. It's caused nothing but disaster.'*
>
> Doc, Back to the Future III

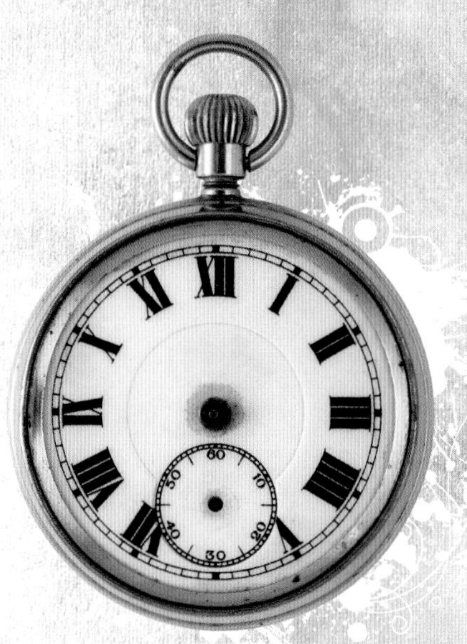

(1968) – based on a novel by Bond scribe Ian Fleming – features a flying car which was the epitome of retrofitted early-1900s technology and cemented a certain vision of the Edwardian era and its imaginary hijinks.

Wild At Heart

Meanwhile, the small screen was host to the TV series 'The Wild Wild West' (1965–69). Like shows 'The Man from U.N.C.L.E.' and 'Mission: Impossible', it was commissioned on the success of the James Bond films, but 'The Wild Wild West' had a novel twist: it was set in the frontier times of America. James West (Robert Conrad) is the series' equivalent to Bond, with Artemus Gordon (Ross Martin) filling Q's shoes and providing a wonderful array of nineteenth-century mechanical gadgets – including West's iconic sleeve-guns, a steam-powered tank and – somewhat ironically – a television.

Get Surreal

Before coming to prevalence as a director, Terry Gilliam was responsible for the surreal animations in TV series 'Monty Python's Flying Circus' (1969–74), which themselves exhibited some steampunk qualities. ***The Adventures of Baron Munchausen*** (1988) continued his love of the weird and wonderful with Munchausen's tall tales of escaping in a hot air balloon made of women's underwear, and bumping into the Roman God Vulcan. It's Gilliam at his most deranged and unrestrained, and it's helped along amicably by Dante Feretti's retro production design.

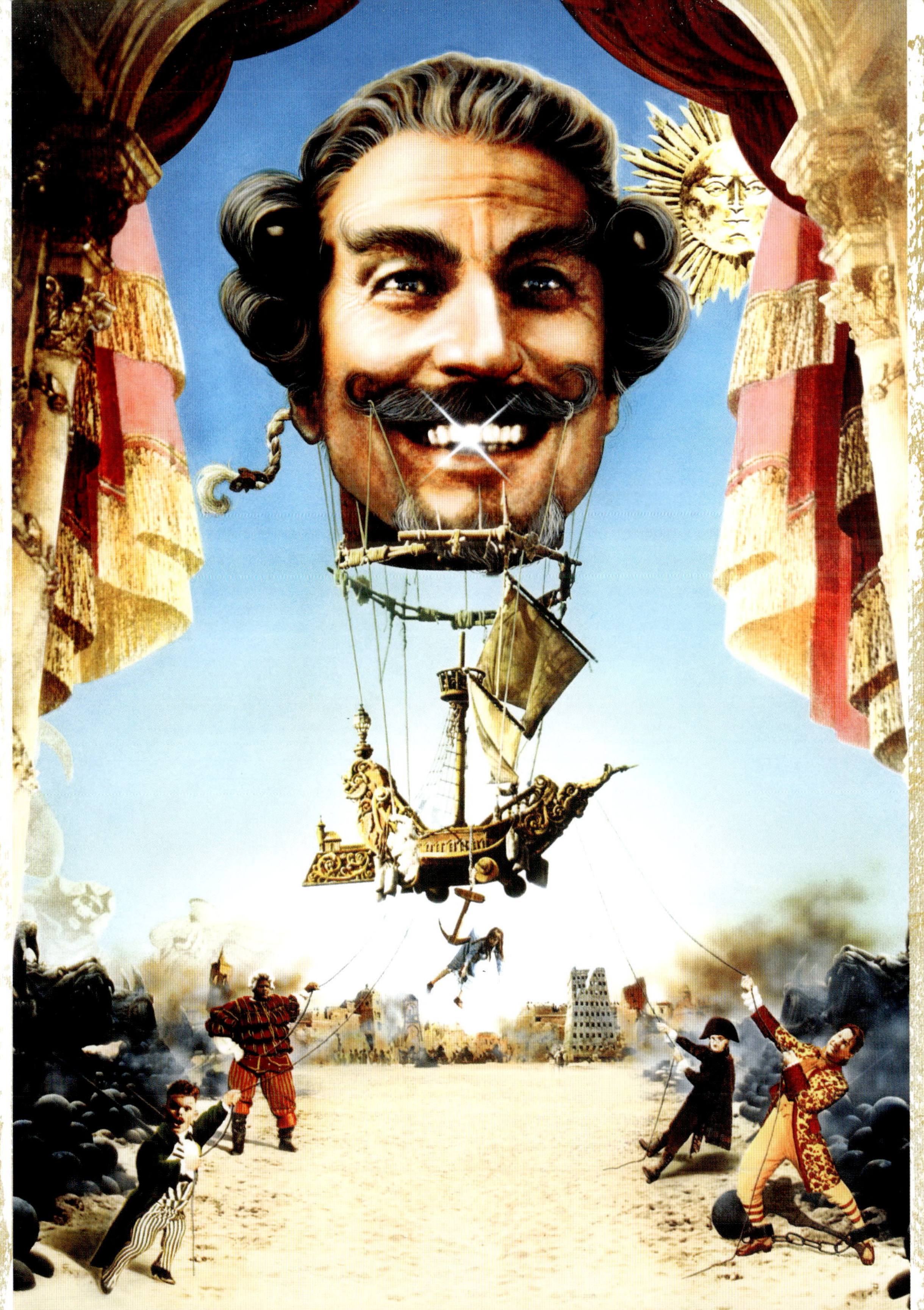

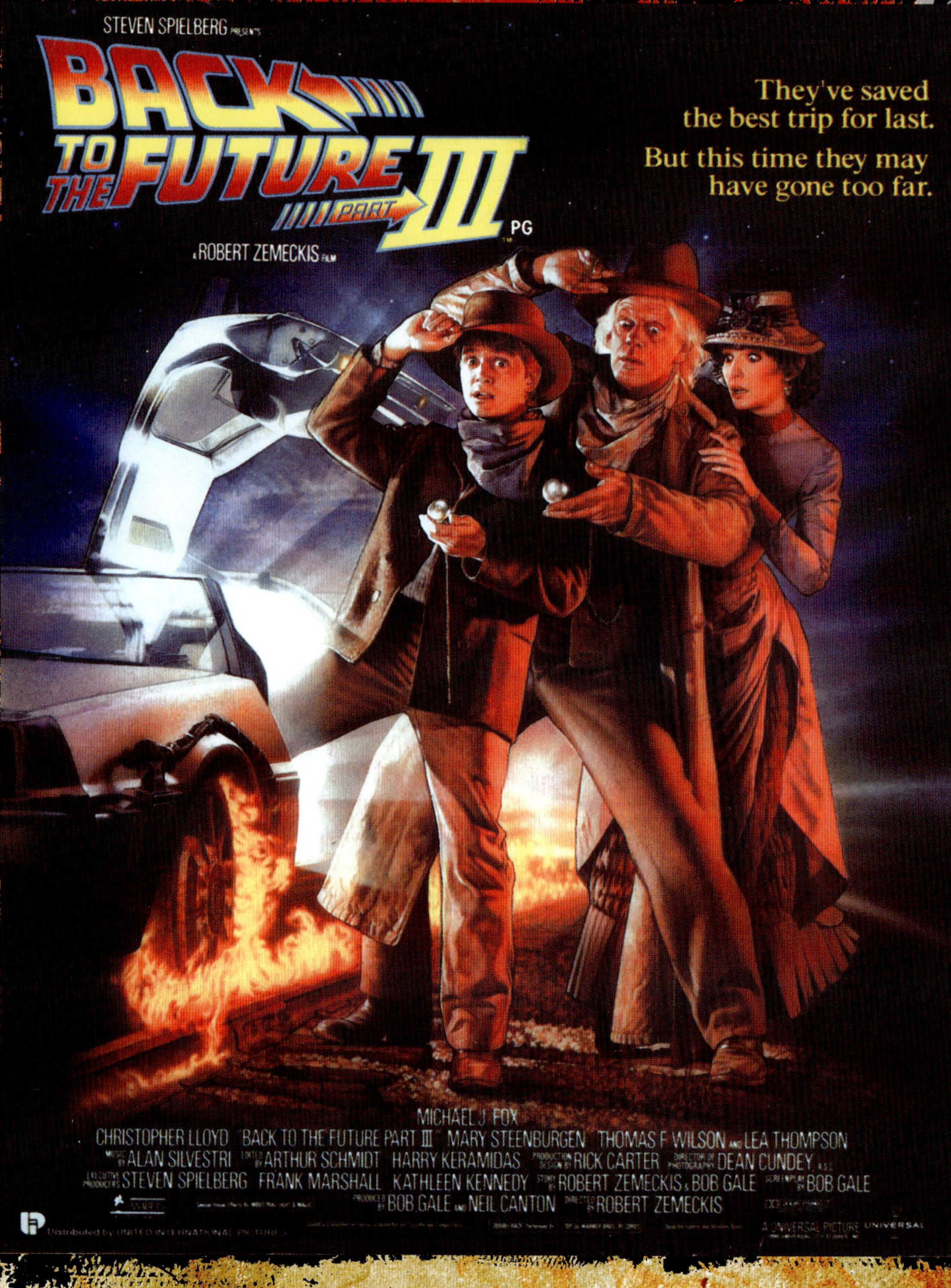

STEVEN SPIELBERG PRESENTS
BACK TO THE FUTURE PART III
PG
A ROBERT ZEMECKIS FILM
They've saved the best trip for last.
But this time they may have gone too far.
MICHAEL J. FOX
CHRISTOPHER LLOYD "BACK TO THE FUTURE PART III" MARY STEENBURGEN THOMAS F. WILSON AND LEA THOMPSON
MUSIC BY ALAN SILVESTRI EDITED BY ARTHUR SCHMIDT HARRY KERAMIDAS PRODUCTION DESIGN BY RICK CARTER DIRECTOR OF PHOTOGRAPHY DEAN CUNDEY
EXECUTIVE PRODUCERS STEVEN SPIELBERG FRANK MARSHALL KATHLEEN KENNEDY STORY BY ROBERT ZEMECKIS & BOB GALE SCREENPLAY BY BOB GALE
PRODUCED BY BOB GALE AND NEIL CANTON DIRECTED BY ROBERT ZEMECKIS
A UNIVERSAL PICTURE UNIVERSAL

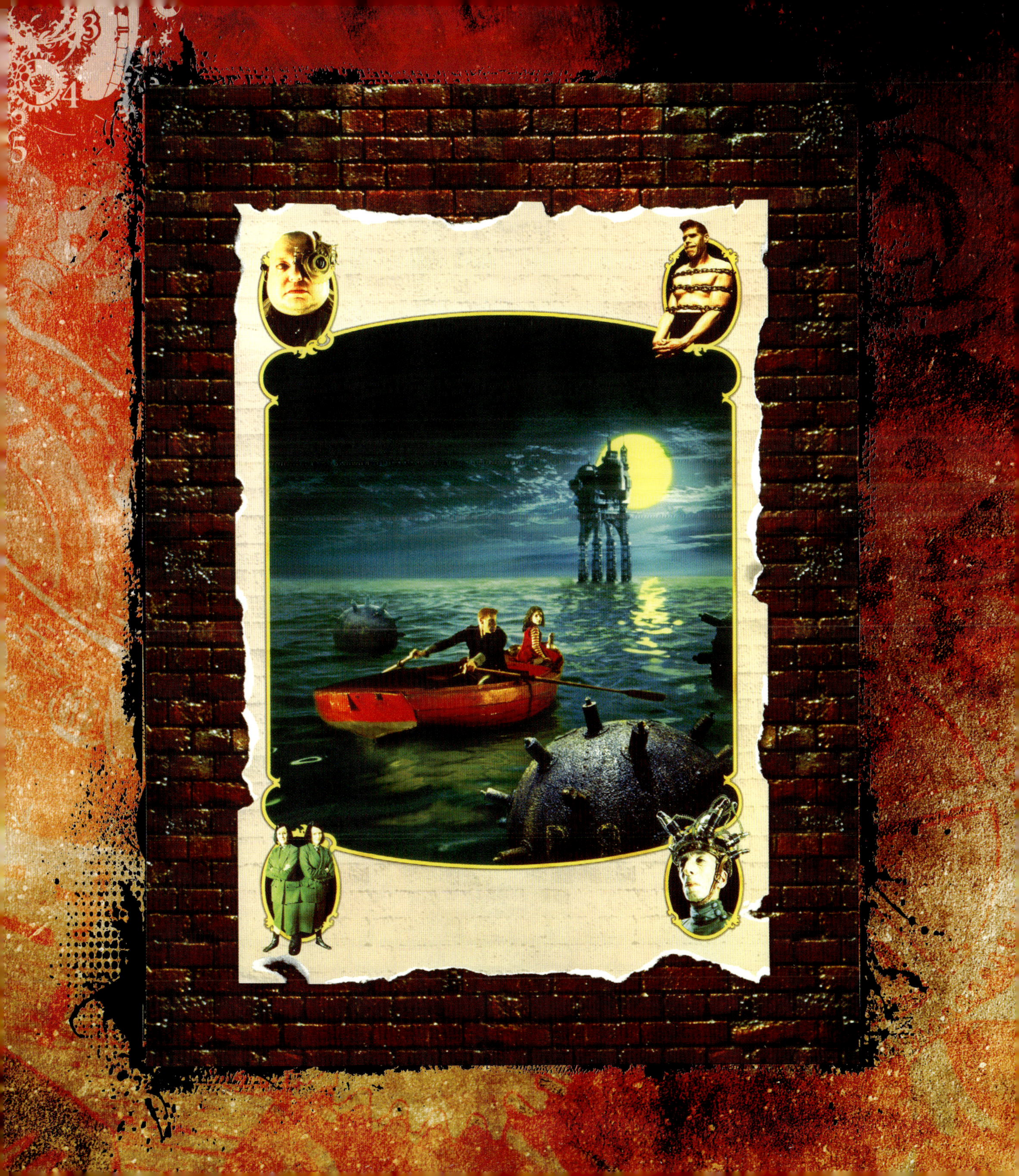

1.21 Gigawatts

The joy of the ***Back to the Future*** films (1985–90) lies in their combination of mind-bending time travel with 1980s coming-of-age comedy. In the final part of the trilogy, Christopher Lloyd's Dr Emmett 'Doc' Brown is stranded in 1885, but he lacks the series' time-travelling DeLorean. How will he get back to the future? By building a very steampunk train with all the necessary equipment to jump forward one hundred years, where he introduces his two sons – knowingly named Jules and Verne. If that's not enough, the train can also fly.

The Dream Team

Co-directed by ***Amélie*** and ***Delicatessen*** director Jean-Pierre Jeunet, ***The City of Lost Children*** (1995) paved the way for the steampunk movies which followed. The out-there plot deals with a mad scientist (Daniel Emilfork) who captures children in order to steal their dreams – while hatching plans with a talking brain in a jar. The industrious design sets the film on an ocean rig, and Victorian-style designs and costumes feature heavily throughout, including the brain's gramophone-like apparatus and the scientist's headwear, which injects dreams directly into his noggin. It's a dark and twisted film, but one which puts steampunk's decrepit aesthetic to great use.

Brisco Business

'It's kind of Jules Verne meets "The Wild Wild West",' 'Brisco County, Jr' (1993–94) star Bruce Campbell told ***Starlog***

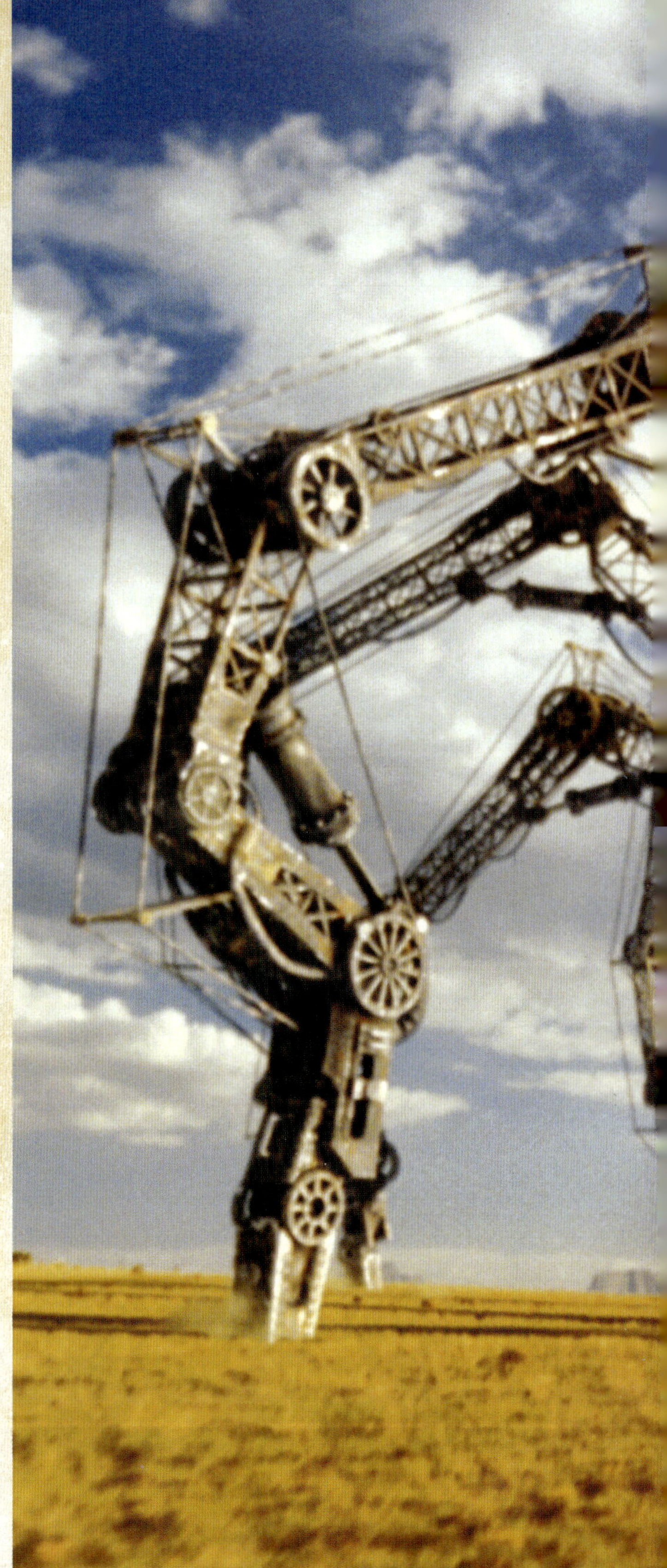

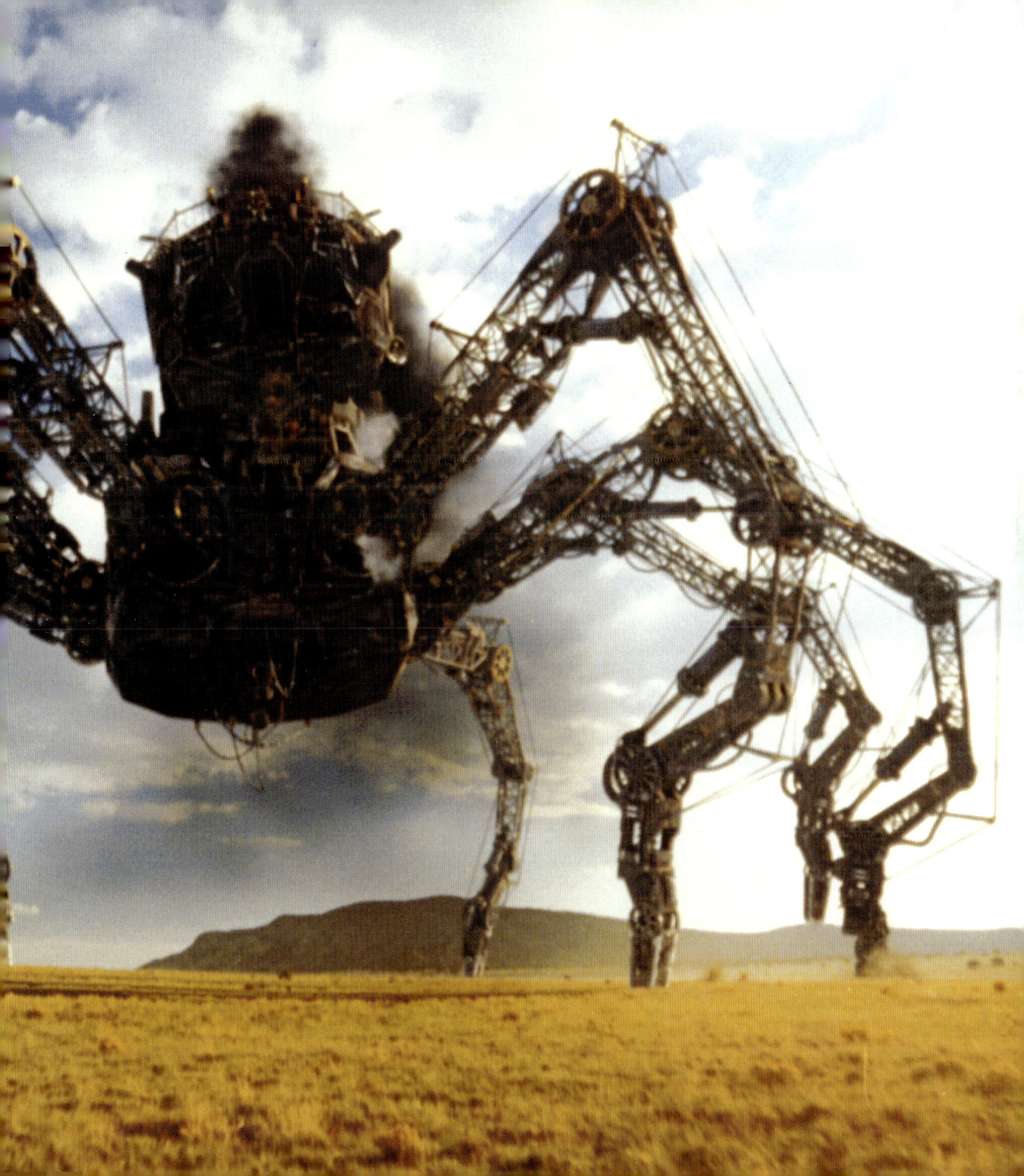

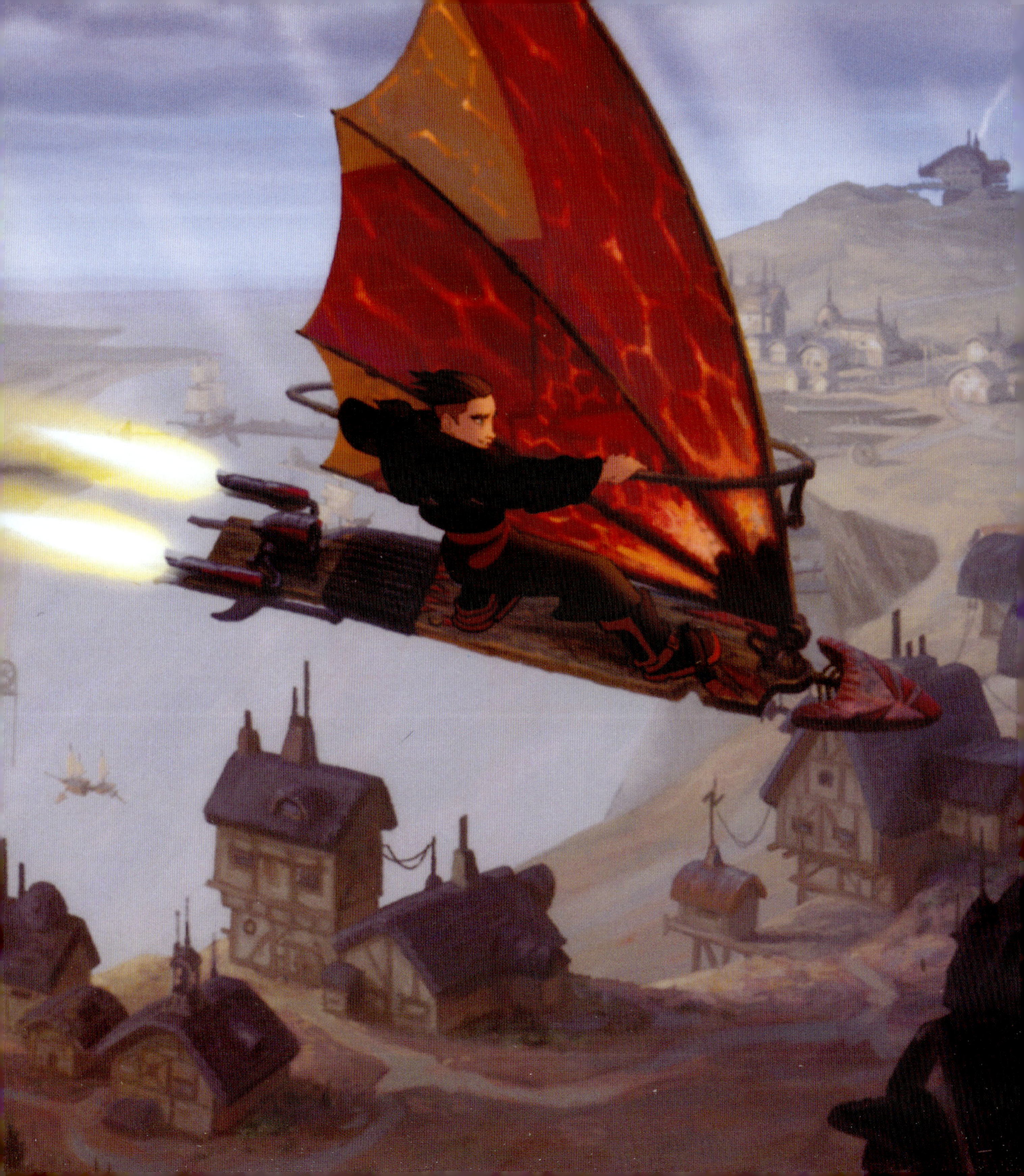

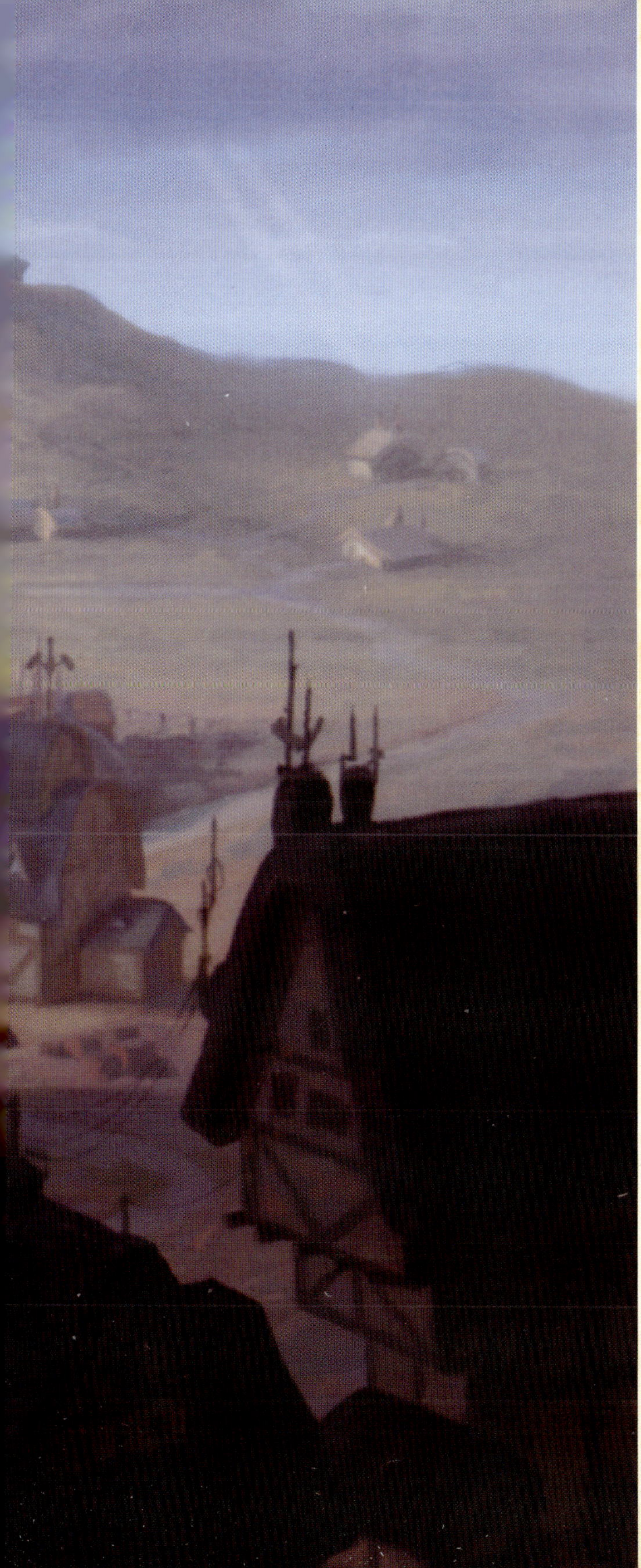

magazine. The TV series featured Campbell as the titular character, who attempted to find the outlaws responsible for the death of his father. At the same time, Chinese miners uncovered a mysterious orb from the future which granted people special powers. It was purposefully anachronistic, with a fire-breathing rocket train and a wagon-cum-steam-powered-tank. Although well received by critics, dwindling audience numbers ensured its swift cancellation after just one season.

Mild Mild West

A spin-off from the popular 1960s TV series, 'Wild Wild West' reunited ***Men in Black*** star Will Smith with director Barry Sonnenfeld. Smith played secret service agent James West, and was joined by Kevin Kline as inventor and scientist Artemus Gordon. The film's a treat for the eyes – if not the brain – and it features a whole host of madcap steampunk inventions. Among them is Kenneth Branagh's legless baddie Dr Loveless, who uses a giant mechanical spider to hold the entirety of American to ransom. No, really.

Treason and Treasure

Relocating Robert Louis Stevenson's 1883 pirate adventure ***Treasure Island*** to outer space may have offended purists, but ***Treasure Planet*** (2002) is packed with imaginative shots and hilarious visual jokes. If you've ever picked up Stevenson's classic you'll know the plot: 17-year-old Jim Hawkins battles with Long John Silver over the location of some long-lost treasure. While the pirates are replaced with robots and the islands with

'Allow me to introduce myself. Rodney Skinner, gentleman thief. Now, I thought invisibility would be a boon to my work. Well, you can imagine, it was my undoing. Once you're invisible, it's bloody hard to turn back.'

Rodney Skinner, The League of Extraordinary Gentlemen

planets, the coming-of-age story remains thankfully untainted. The film's designers chose to make it 70 per cent traditional and 30 per cent sci-fi, which gives it its unique galleonpunk aesthetic.

Ordinary Boys

Based on Alan Moore's comic of the same name, ***The League of Extraordinary Gentlemen*** (2003) was a critical and commercial flop – but its rich world has ensured a lasting legacy among Steampunk fans. It pitches Sir Henry Rider Haggard's hero, Allan Quatermain (Sean Connery), alongside other fictional Victorian heroes, including ***Twenty Thousand Leagues Under the Sea***'s Captain Nemo, ***Dracula***'s Mina Harker and Robert Louis Stevenson's Dr Jekyll, as they fight a mysterious, and similarly fictional, villain. While juggling so many great characters may have led to its downfall, the Nemo's retooled ***Nautilus*** is a fabulous steampunk invention.

Steam … Everything

Steamboy (2004), Katsuhiro Otomo's follow-up to legendary cyberpunk adventure ***Akira*** (1988), takes place in an alternative version of 1863 Europe where just about everything has 'steam' in its title. Anna Paquin voices Ray Steam (told you), who receives a Steam Ball, which is an engine capable of immense power. However, Ray's disfigured father has other plans for the incredible forces contained within the ball, and wishes to use it to control his Steam Castle. As with ***Akira***, ***Steamboy*** is a visual feast set

A ROGUE · A SCIENTIST · A SPY · A HUNTER · A VAMPIRE · A BEAST · AN IMMORTAL

LXG

THE LEAGUE OF EXTRAORDINARY GENTLEMEN

THE POWER OF SEVEN BECOME A LEAGUE OF ONE

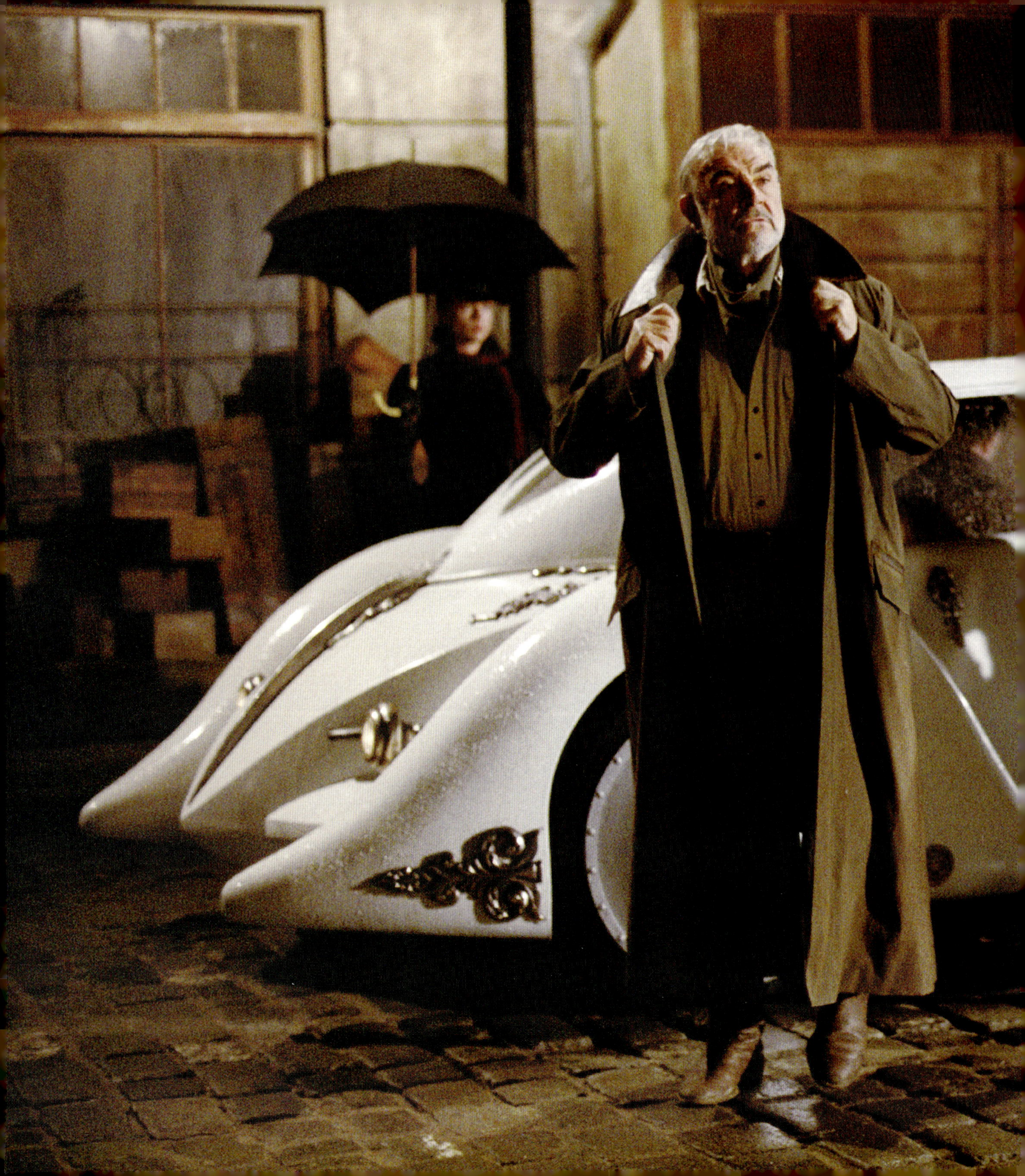

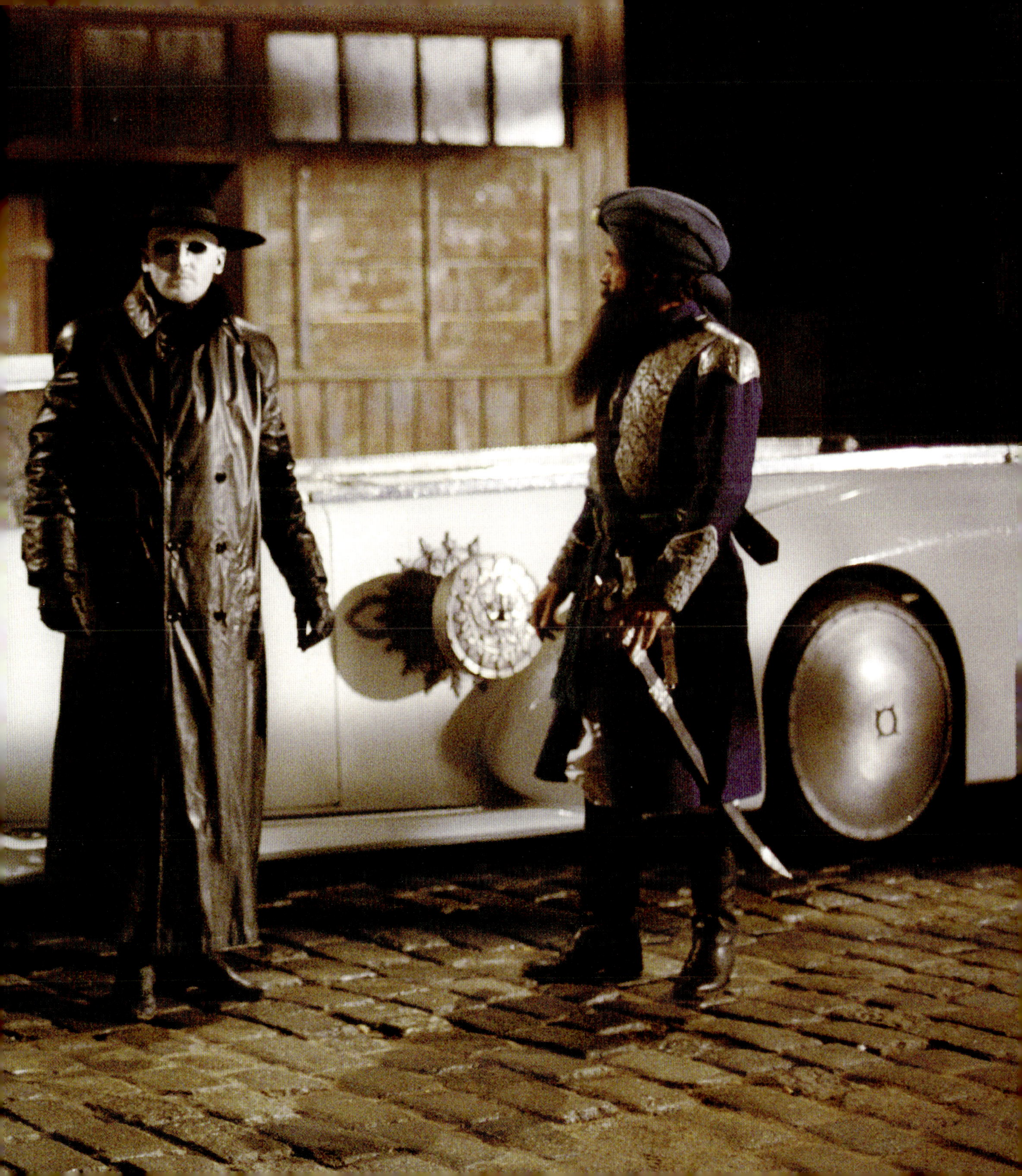

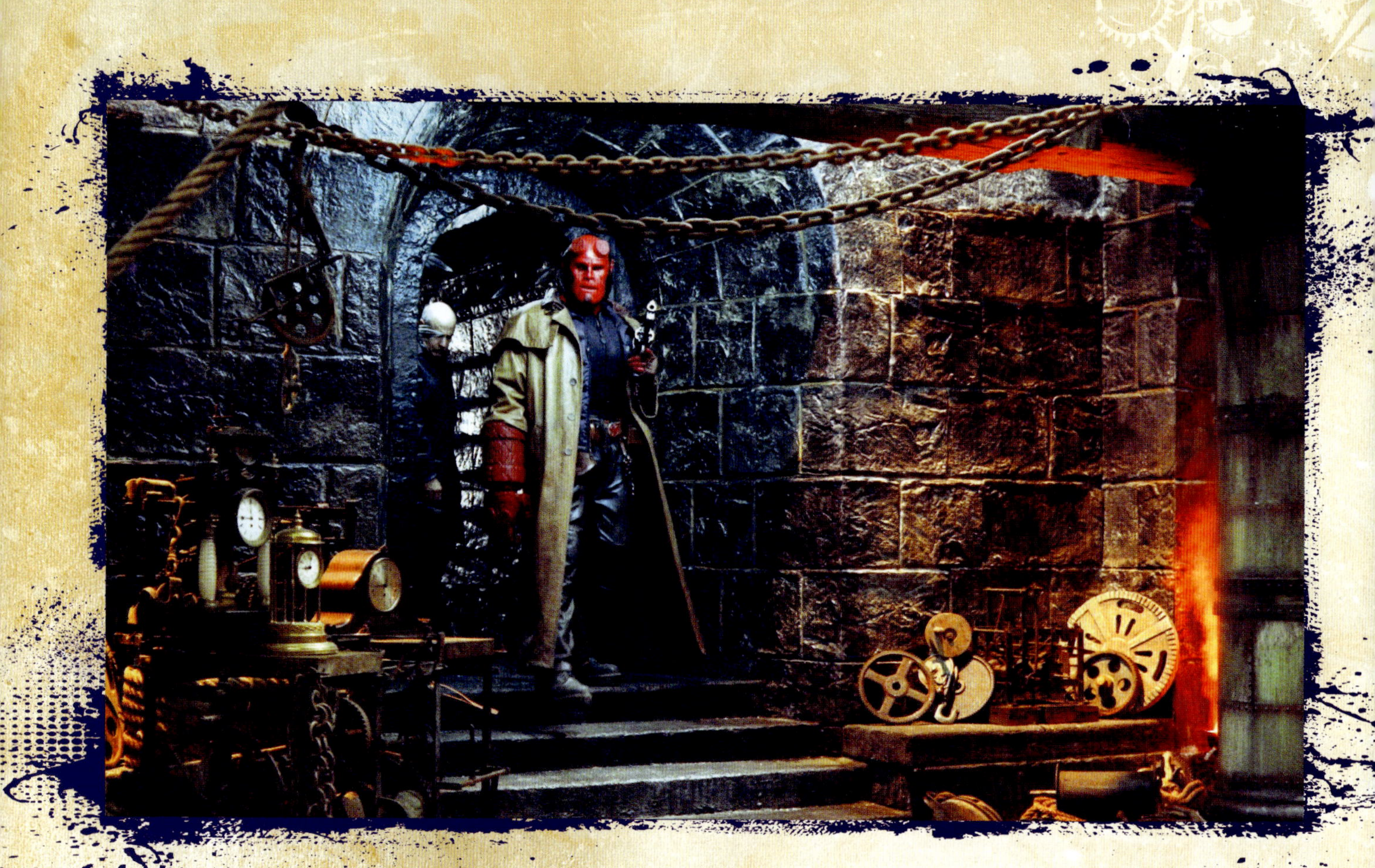

in an exotic re-imagining of the real world, and one which frequently highlights the parallels between British and Japanese life and culture.

Sophie's Choice

Like ***Steamboy***, ***Howl's Moving Castle*** (2004) provides a Japanese perspective on Western society of yore – in this case, it's an adaptation of Diana Wynne Jones' book set in Wales. It follows 18-year-old heroine Sophie as she tracks down Howl, a wizard who has turned her into a 90-year-old woman. His moving castle is a brilliant steampunk invention, a floating city in stark contrast to the bucolic countryside, spewing smoke wherever it goes. Director Hayao Miyazaki has dabbled in steampunk before with ***Laputa: Castle in the Sky*** (1986) and ***Princess Mononoke*** (1997), both of which are highly recommended.

Straight To Hell

A seven-foot-tall adolescent demon may not be your ideal blockbuster movie protagonist, but Guillermo del Toro's adaptations of Mike Mignola's comic books handle the big red 'un with enough chutzpah that you end up forgetting

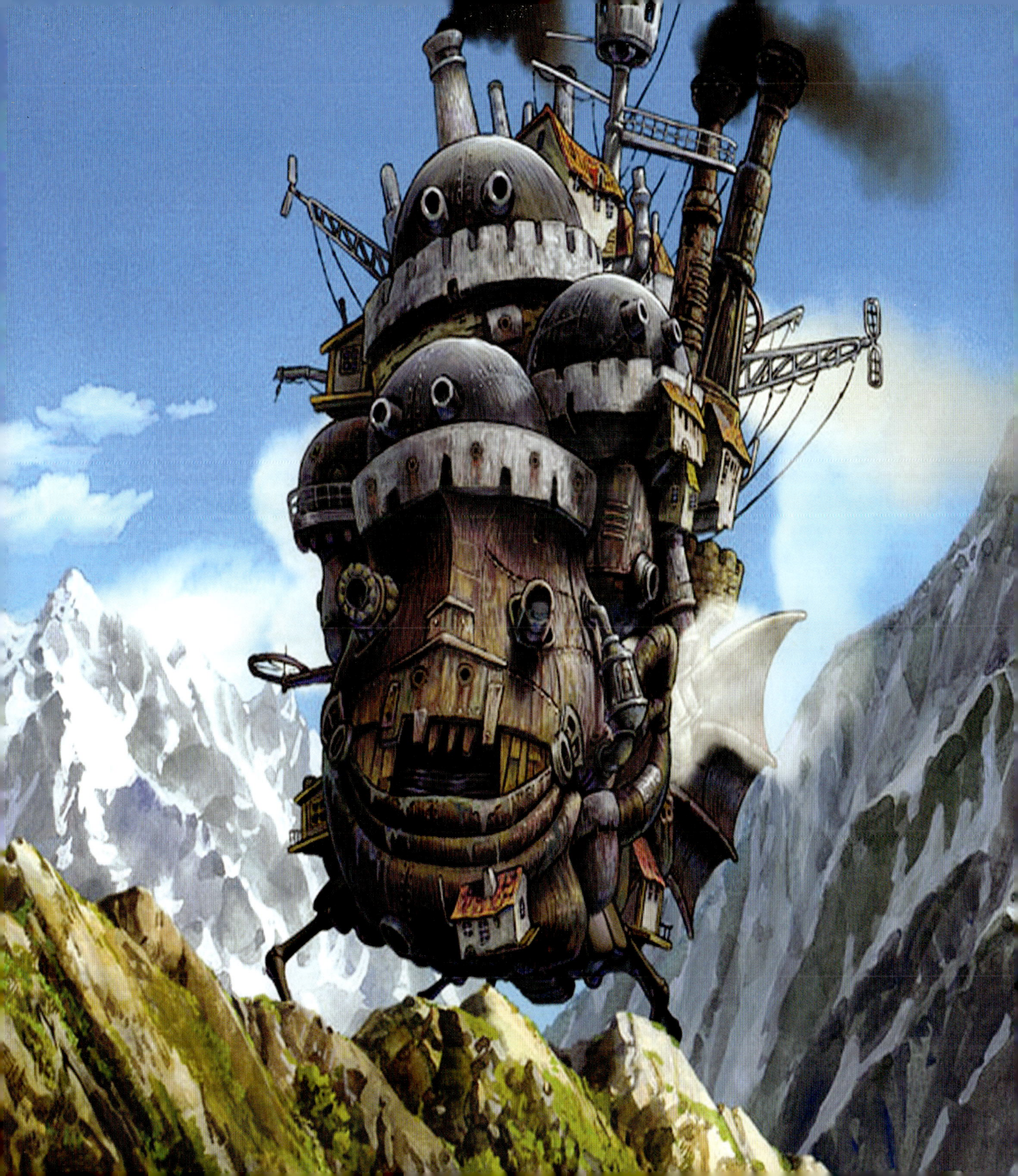

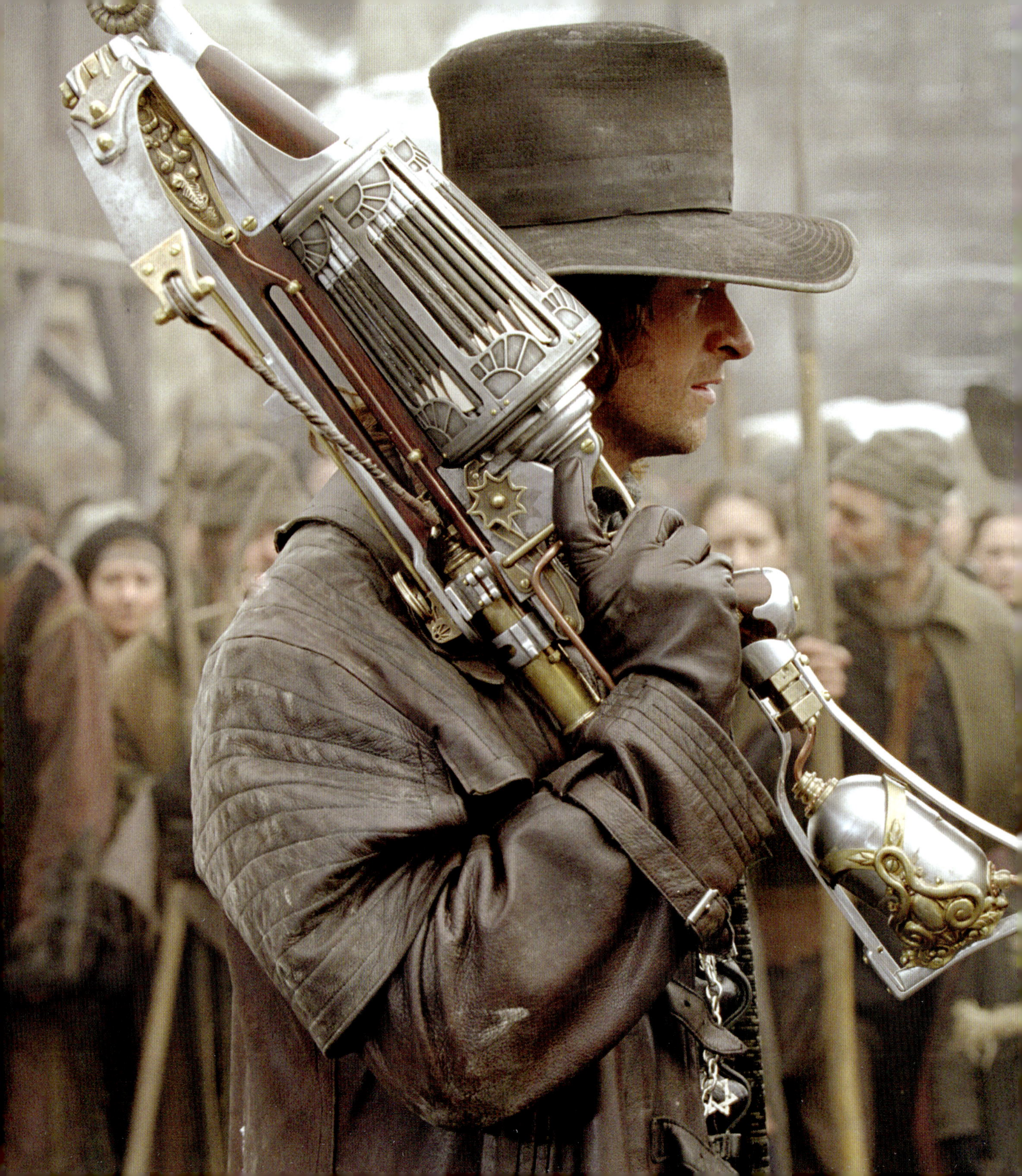

how ridiculous the entire scenario is. Despite ***Hellboy***'s (2004) twenty-first century setting, there are loads of imaginative Steampunk designs on display. Nazi antagonist Kroenen, who met with an unfortunate accident during the Second World War, has a clockwork heart, while its sequel ***Hellboy II: The Golden Army*** (2008) adds Johann Kraus to the mix, a disembodied ectoplasmic spirit who resides in an otherworldly steam-powered suit.

The Stakes Are High

Dracula's nemesis receives a comic book-style reinterpretation in Steven Sommers' action movie ***Van Helsing*** (2004). Hugh Jackman makes a nice change from the more mature Van Helsings of yore, and he's joined by Kate Beckinsale in spectacular arse-kicking mode. The film is at its most steampunk in the gadget-laden crypt beneath the church, where Carl (David Wenham) kits out Van Helsing with a variety of vampire and lycan-busting weapons, including a gas-powered crossbow-cum-machinegun. As the film references classic Universal horrors of the 1930s and 40s, Frankenstein's monster makes a rather gruesome appearance, too.

Film Stars

Stardust (2007) has great fun toying with the tropes of traditional fantasy adventures, with Charlie Cox's Tristan Thorn rescuing Claire Danes' otherworldly Yvaine from a trio of witches. Assisting Thorn is Captain Shakespeare, a fierce

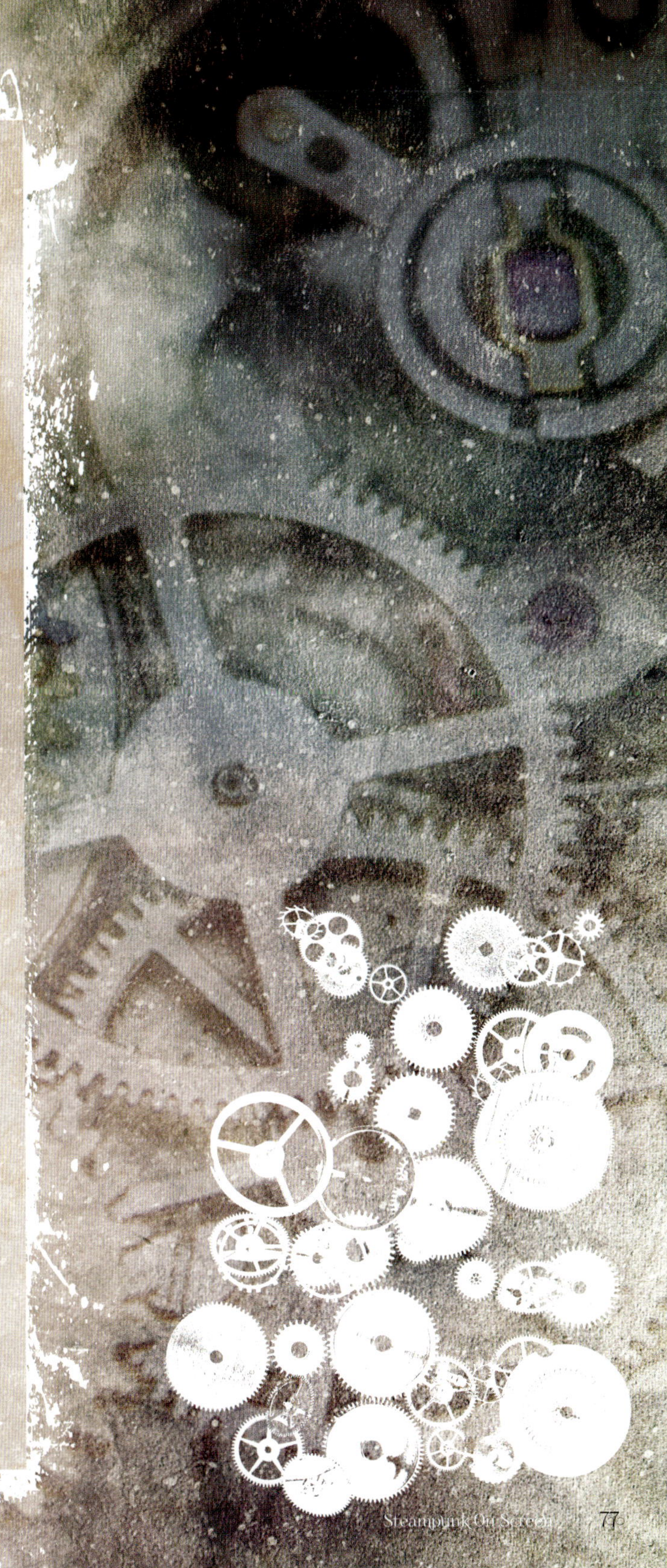

'You know, it was the writings of Jules Verne that had a profound effect on my life. It was when I was 11 that I first read 20,000 Leagues Under the Sea. It was then that I realized that I must devote my life to science.'

Doc, Back to the Future III

pirate of the skies and seas – who just so happens to be played by Robert De Niro in drag. Shakespeare's ship is pure steampunk: it looks like a normal pirate ship, but the sails have been replaced with a huge Zeppelin. That's on top of some bustling, colourful set design and snappily dressed characters who are a world away from ***The Lord of the Rings***' dull plaid.

Uncharted Territory

Despite its marketing as a fantasy film, ***The Golden Compass*** (2007) is steampunk through-and-through: even the titular navigational device is an intricately-designed collection of cogs and dials. The film deals with orphan Lyra Belacqua (Dakota Blue Richards) and her attempts to keep the powerful compass out of the hands of evil. In her journey she encounters airships, archaic cars and armoured polar bears. As with the best steampunk, it deals with corruption in the highest places, and even criticizes religion – although this element was toned down from Philip Pullman's source novel.

Antiques Road Trip

Whereas most steampunk creations only draw upon recent history, TV series 'Warehouse 13', which began in 2009, looks back into the past: to 336 BC, to be precise, when Alexander the Great established Warehouse 1 to store rare and mystical artefacts. The thirteenth incarnation is located in remote South Dakota, and employees Pete Lattimer (Eddie McClintock) and Myka Bering (Joanne Kelly) scavenge the

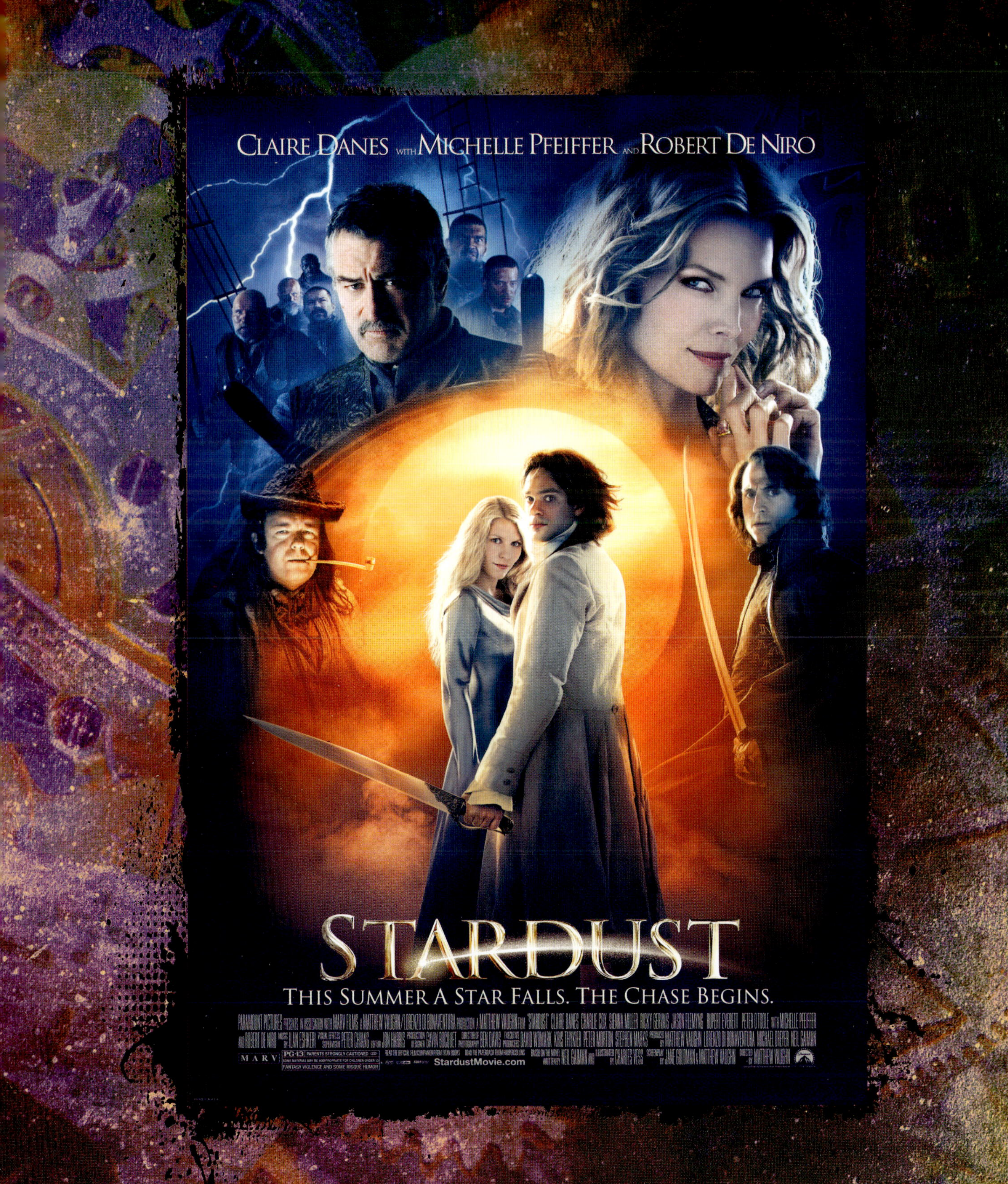

CLAIRE DANES WITH MICHELLE PFEIFFER AND ROBERT DE NIRO
STARDUST
THIS SUMMER A STAR FALLS. THE CHASE BEGINS.
MARV
PG-13 PARENTS STRONGLY CAUTIONED
FANTASY VIOLENCE AND SOME RISQUÉ HUMOR
StardustMovie.com

'It was very like a clock, or a compass, for there were hands pointing to places around the dial, but instead of the hours or the points of the compass there were several little pictures, each of them painted with extraordinary precision…'

Philip Pullman,

The Golden Compass

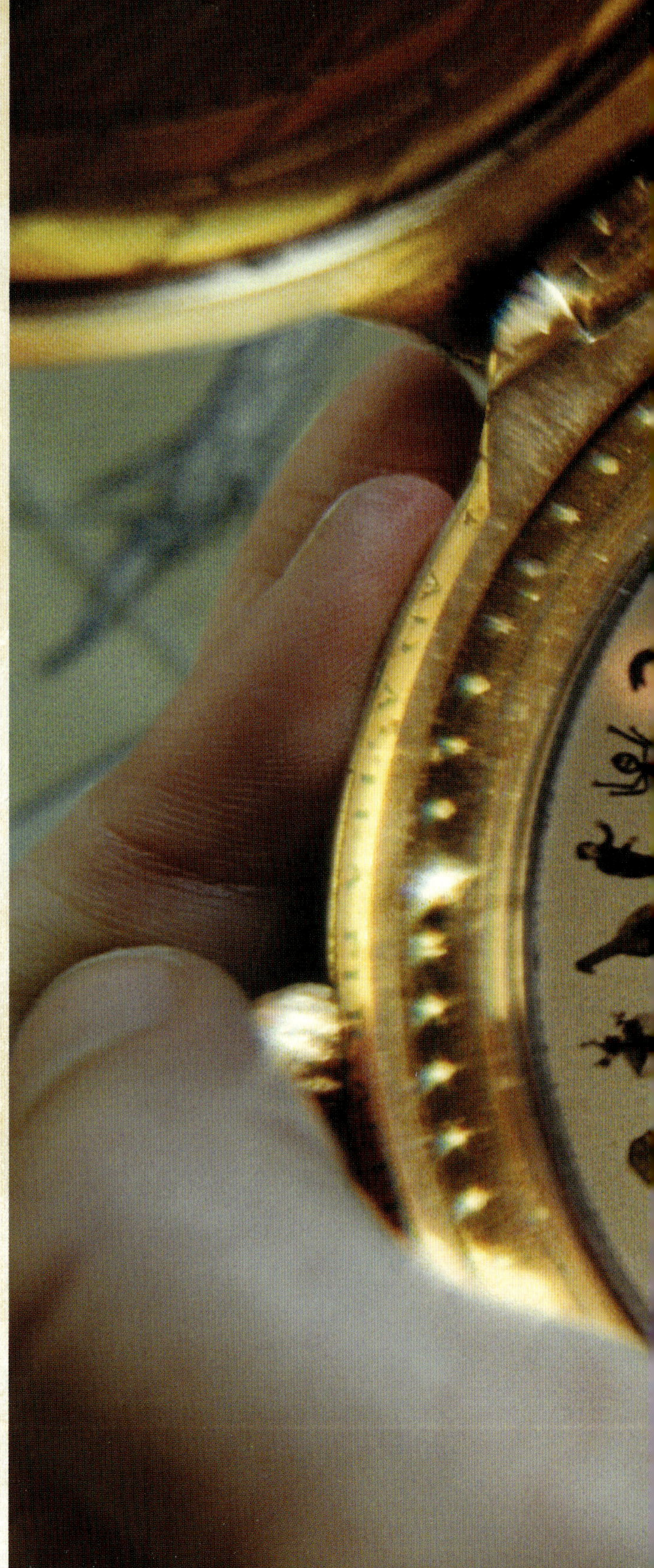

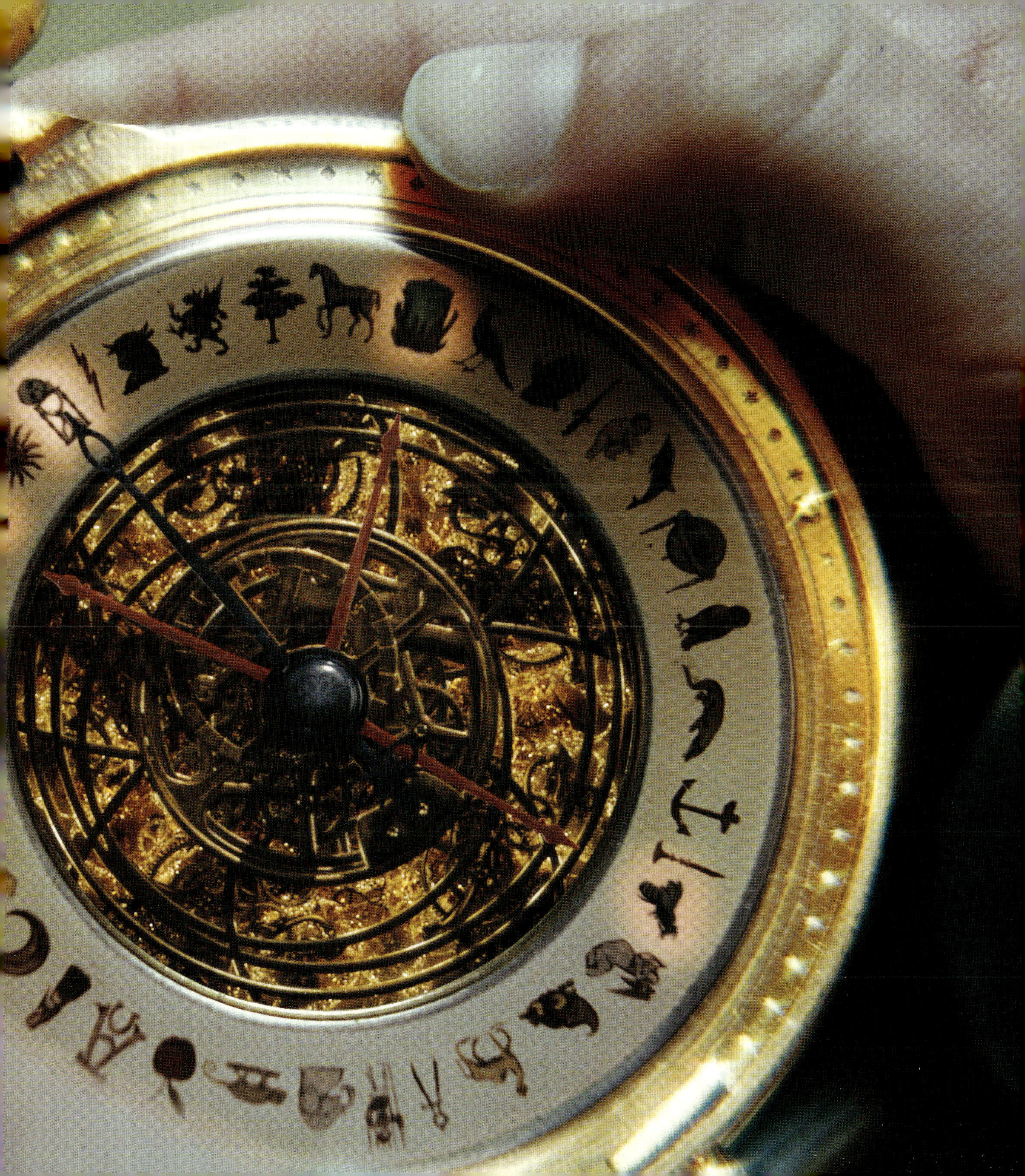

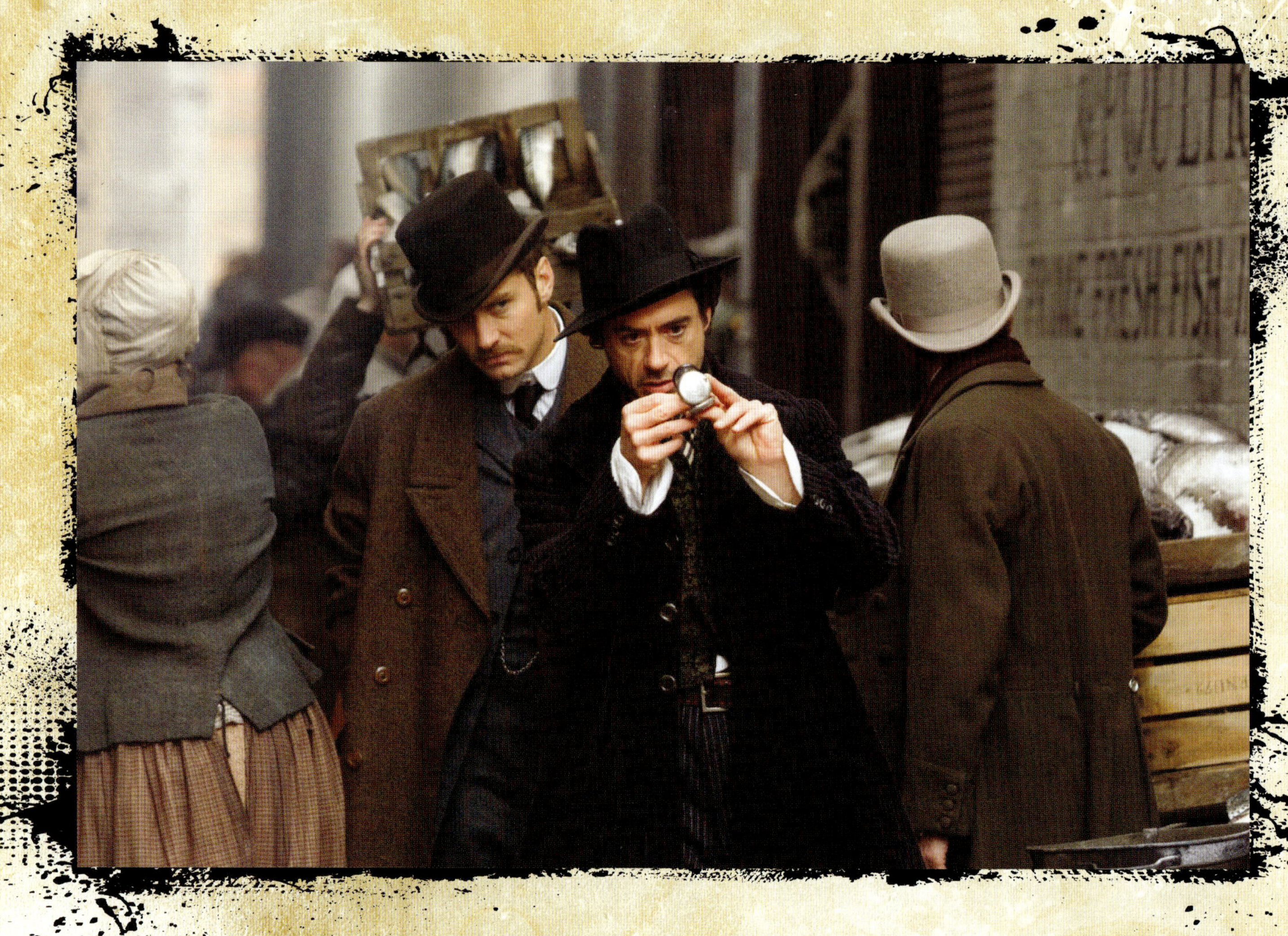

country for priceless antiquities. Thanks to the series' obsession with the past, the entire warehouse takes on a steampunk aesthetic, to the point where you can buy replicas of Myka's typewriter-style PC keyboard on the internet.

Elementary

After some truly woeful films in the early 2000s (***Swept Away***, ***Revolver***), it's good to see mockney director Guy Ritchie find his feet with ***Sherlock Holmes*** (2009), and the 2011 sequel, his rollicking interpretation of Conan Doyle's sharp detective. Robert Downey Jr. takes the lead in an inspired if unexpected piece of casting, and he's admirably backed up by Jude Law's pernickety Dr Watson. While the film keeps itself a little more grounded in reality than other steampunk fantasies, it's the stunning revisionist view of 1890 London that really impresses – Holmes' home is packed with brass curiosities and gewgaws which certainly spark your imagination.

NOOMI RAPACE JARED HARRIS EDDIE MARSAN AND RACHEL McADAMS JENNY BEAVAN HANS ZIMMER JAMES HERBERT SARAH GREENWOOD

ROBERT DOWNEY JR. JUDE LAW

SHERLOCK HOLMES
A GAME OF SHADOWS

DECEMBER 16

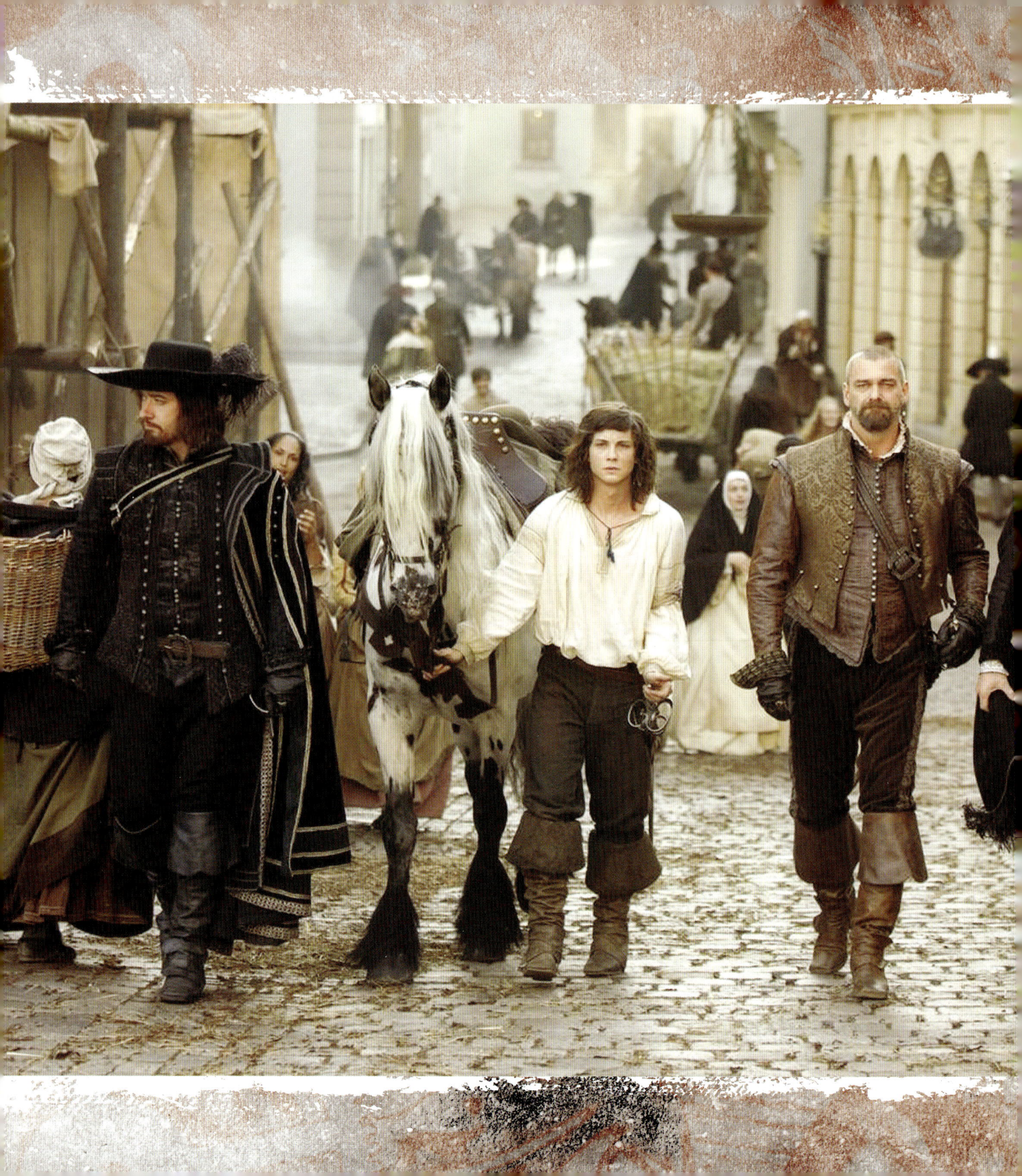

Reynolds Gets Punked

In 2009, American crime series 'NCIS: Los Angeles' attempted a steampunk episode and it was an abysmal failure, enraging fans of the genre by using a hideously inaccurate steampunk bar as a mere backdrop for the proceedings. Fortunately, in the same year crime series 'Castle' got it utterly right with its episode entitled 'Punked'. After a Wall Street broker is shot dead with a 200-year-old lead ball, novelist and amateur detective Richard Castle (Nathan Fillion) is drawn into the world of steampunk fans. Viewers enjoyed the more respectful and enjoyable approach to televisual steampunk, and it's one of the few examples of an outsider entering a steampunk world.

Airship Adventures

Any ***Three Musketeers*** film which opens with the intrepid trio stealing Leonardo da Vinci's airship plans is probably going to upset fans of Alexandre Dumas' classic novel, but Paul W.S. Anderson's 2011 adaptation has enough crazy steampunk ideas to make it rather enjoyable. D'Artagnan (Logan Lerman) may face the usual trials and tribulations to make the three musketeers a foursome, but at least the film's got some crazy mid-air battles and well-executed CG effects to keep things ticking over. The film flopped at the cinema – presumably because viewers were expecting a period drama.

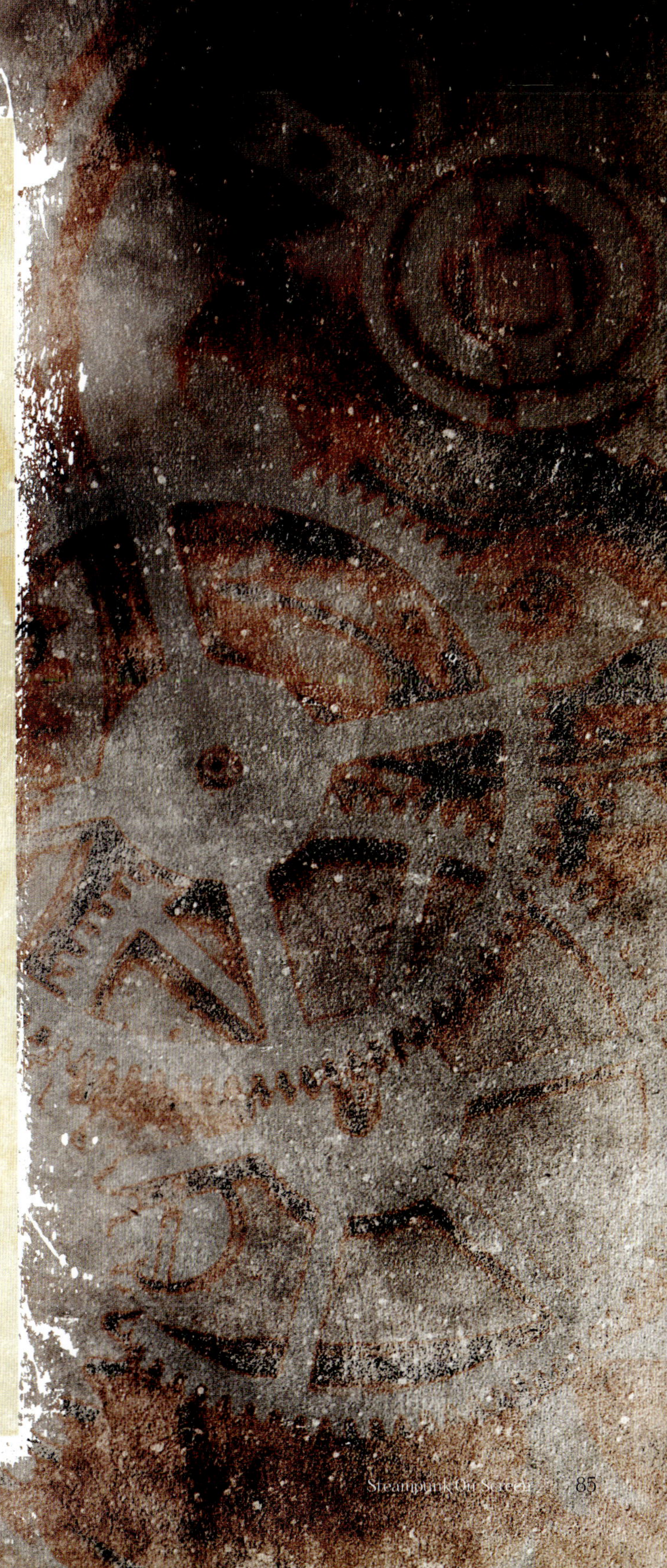

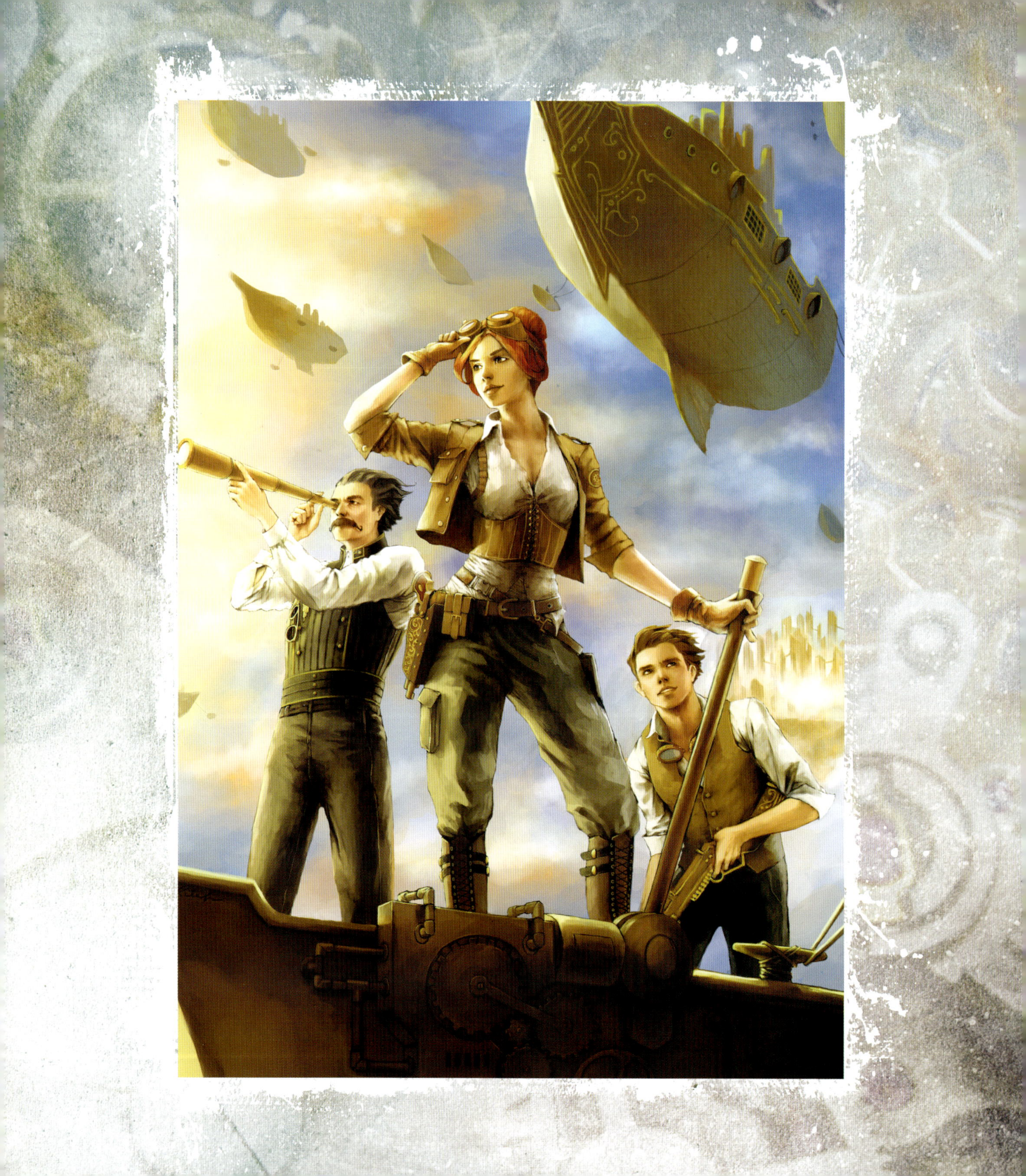

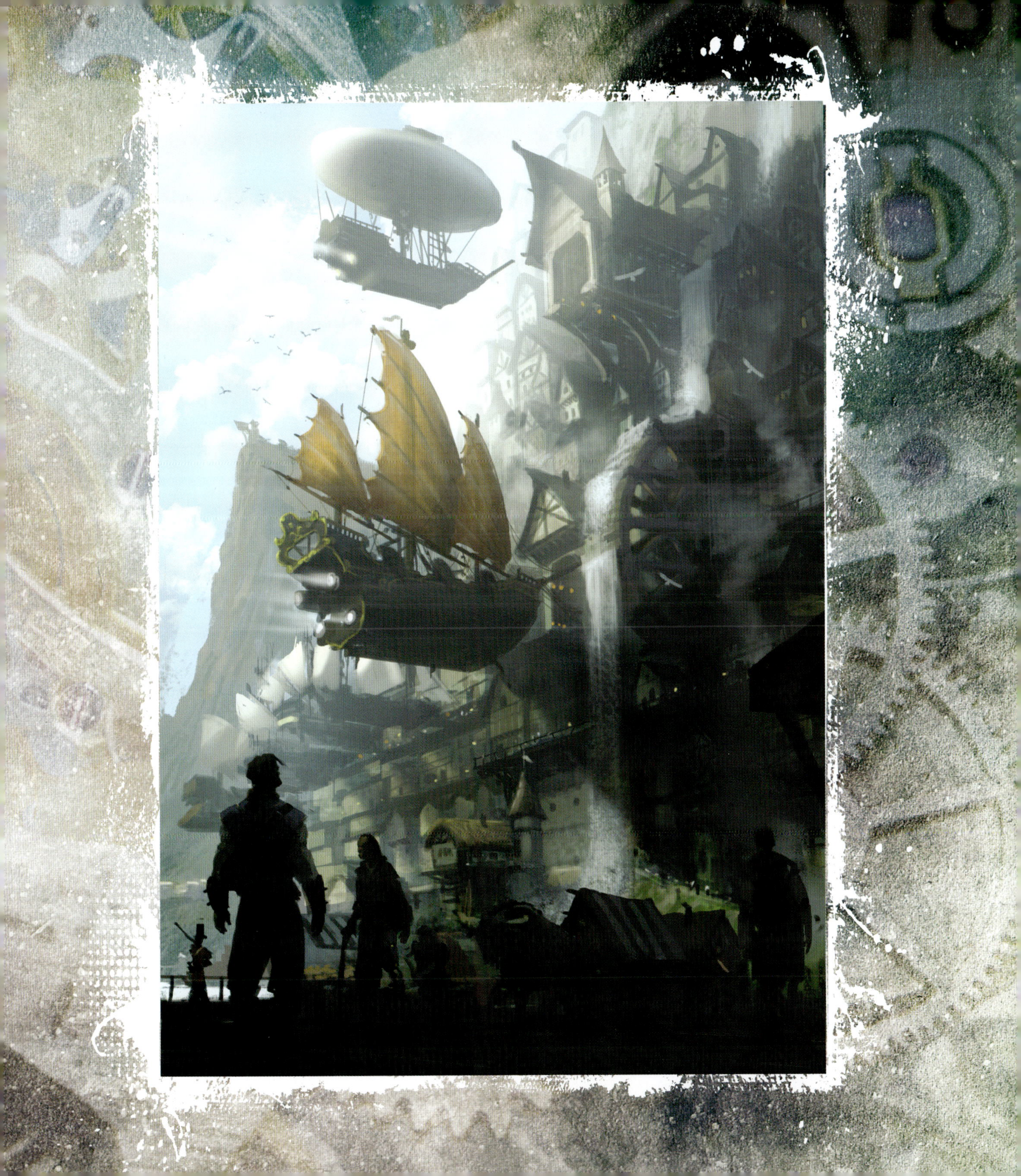

Cabret Act

Hugo (2011) marked Martin Scorsese's first foray into 3D filmmaking, and it was critically acclaimed and became a box-office success. Set in the 1930s, it concerns Hugo Cabret (Asa Butterfield), a 12-year-old boy who lives in Paris's Gare Montparnasse railway station and who wishes to complete his father's work on an automaton. Méliès' ***A Trip to the Moon*** plays a key role in the film, as well as other mechanical and steam-powered inventions, such as Pierre Jaquet-Droz's original writing automaton and the huge trains which revolutionized life in France. It was also Scorsese's touching love letter to cinema's first age.

Rocket Man

Georges Méliès, a historical figure who features heavily in the film ***Hugo***, was himself a filmmaker. He made the 1902 film ***A Trip to the Moon,*** considered one of the first pieces of narrative cinema, and its cannon-propelled spaceship – which iconically plants itself in the moon's eye – could fit into a modern steampunk fantasy. Méliès followed ***A Trip to the Moon*** with adaptations of Jules Verne's ***20,000 Leagues Under the Sea*** and Gottfried August Bürger's ***Baron Munchausen's Dream*** (1911), both of which would reappear as future steampunk movies. From this visionary beginning, steampunk aesthetics and ideas popped up in a large number of science fiction and fantasy movies.

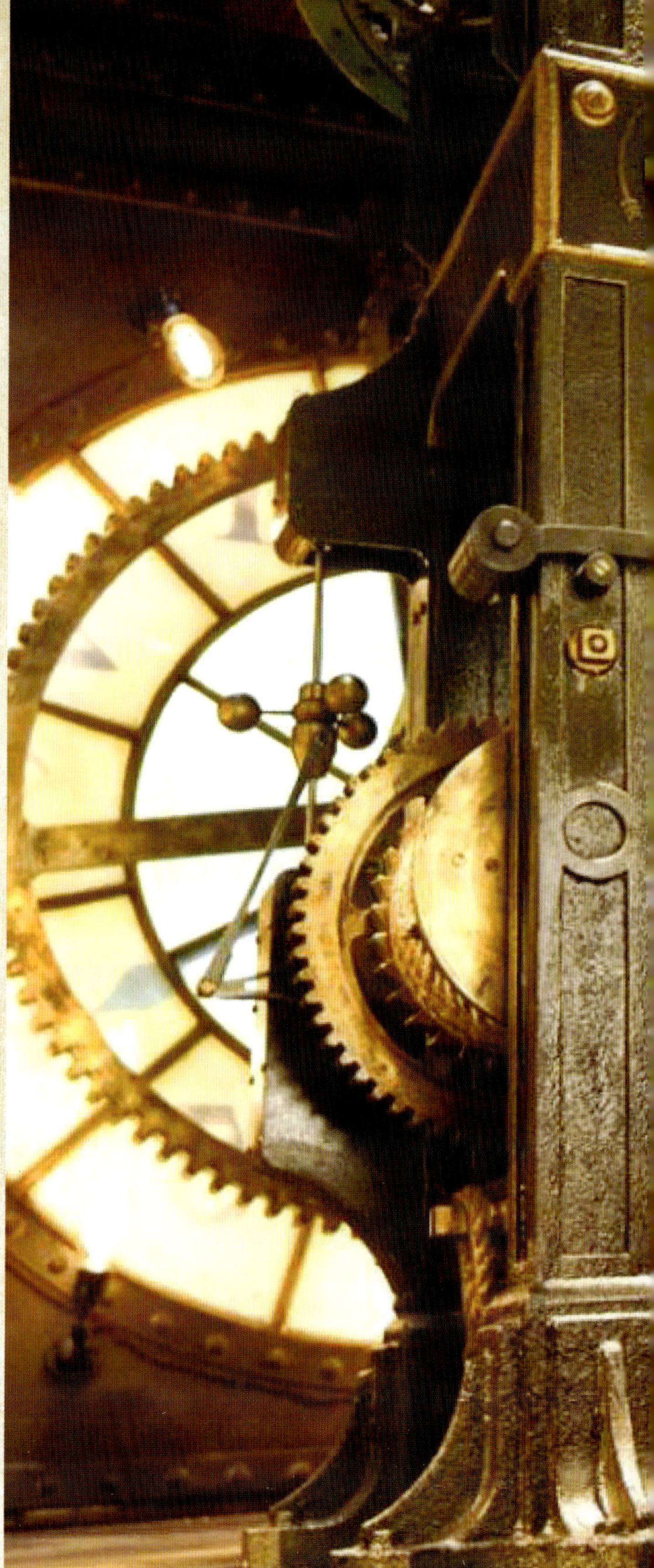

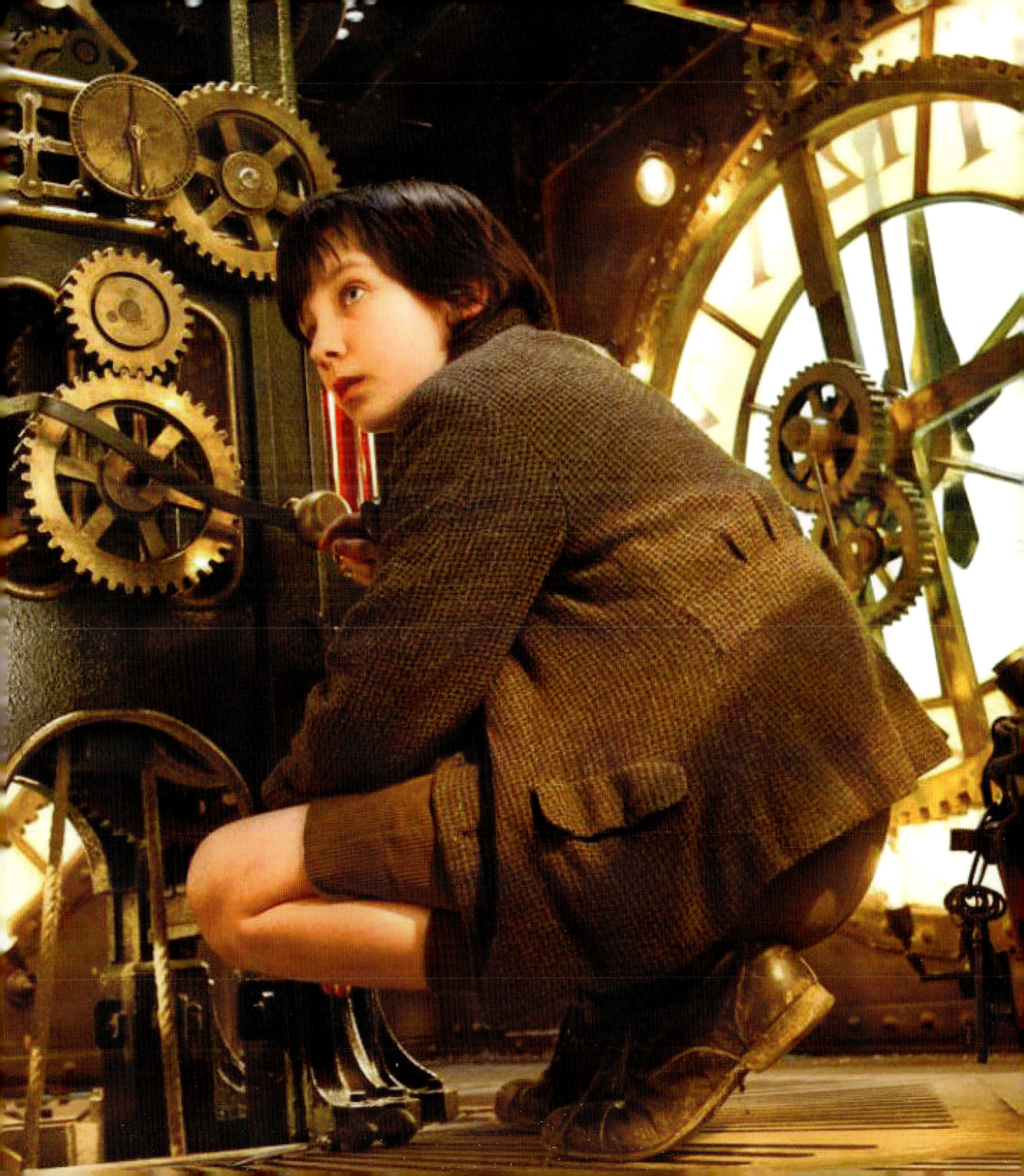

'We've had steampunk movies for just as long as we've had movies…it's just recently been given a name.'

Robert Brown, lead singer of Abney Park

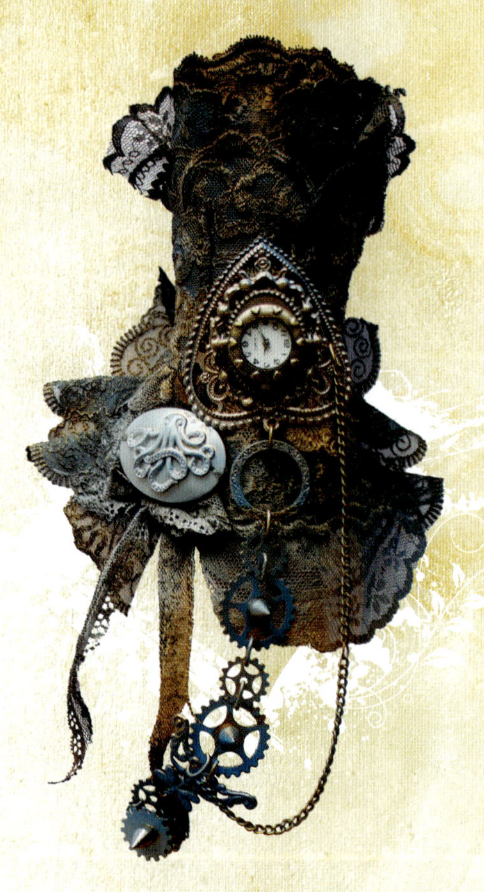

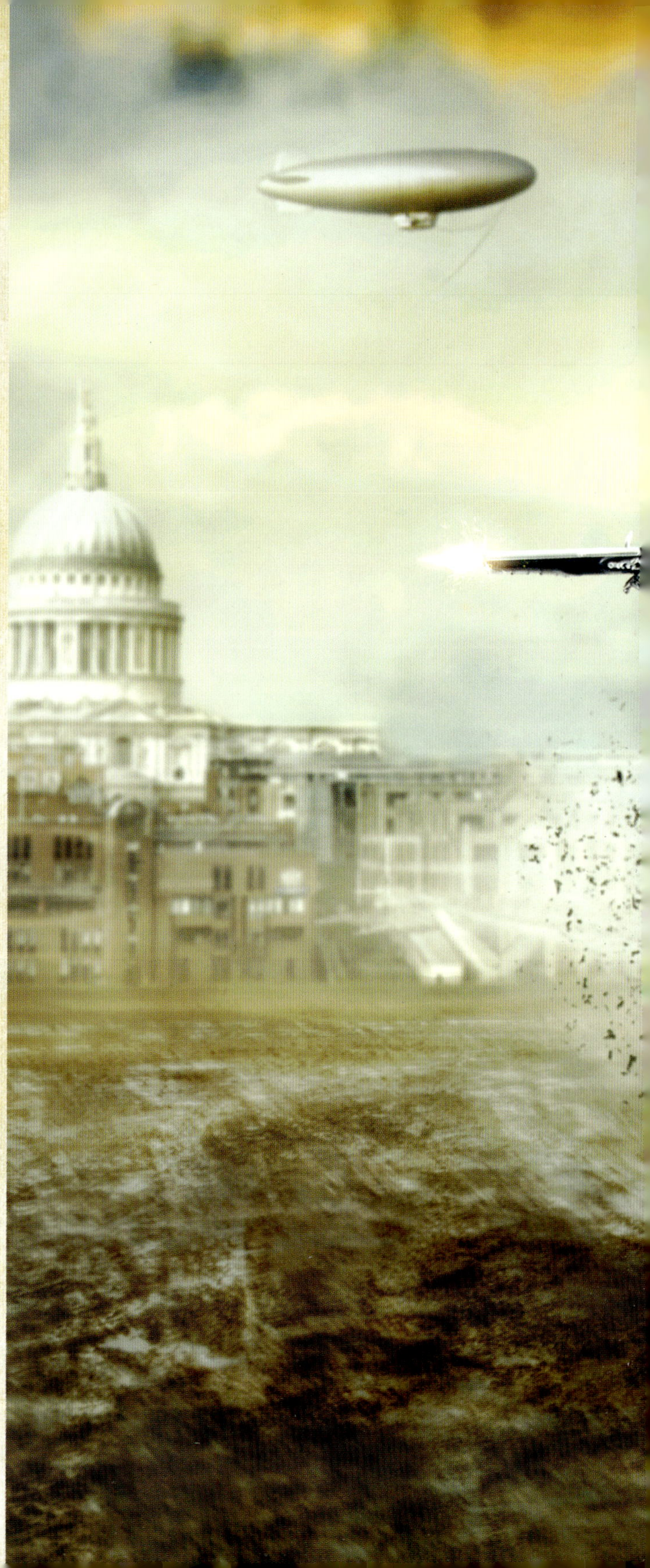

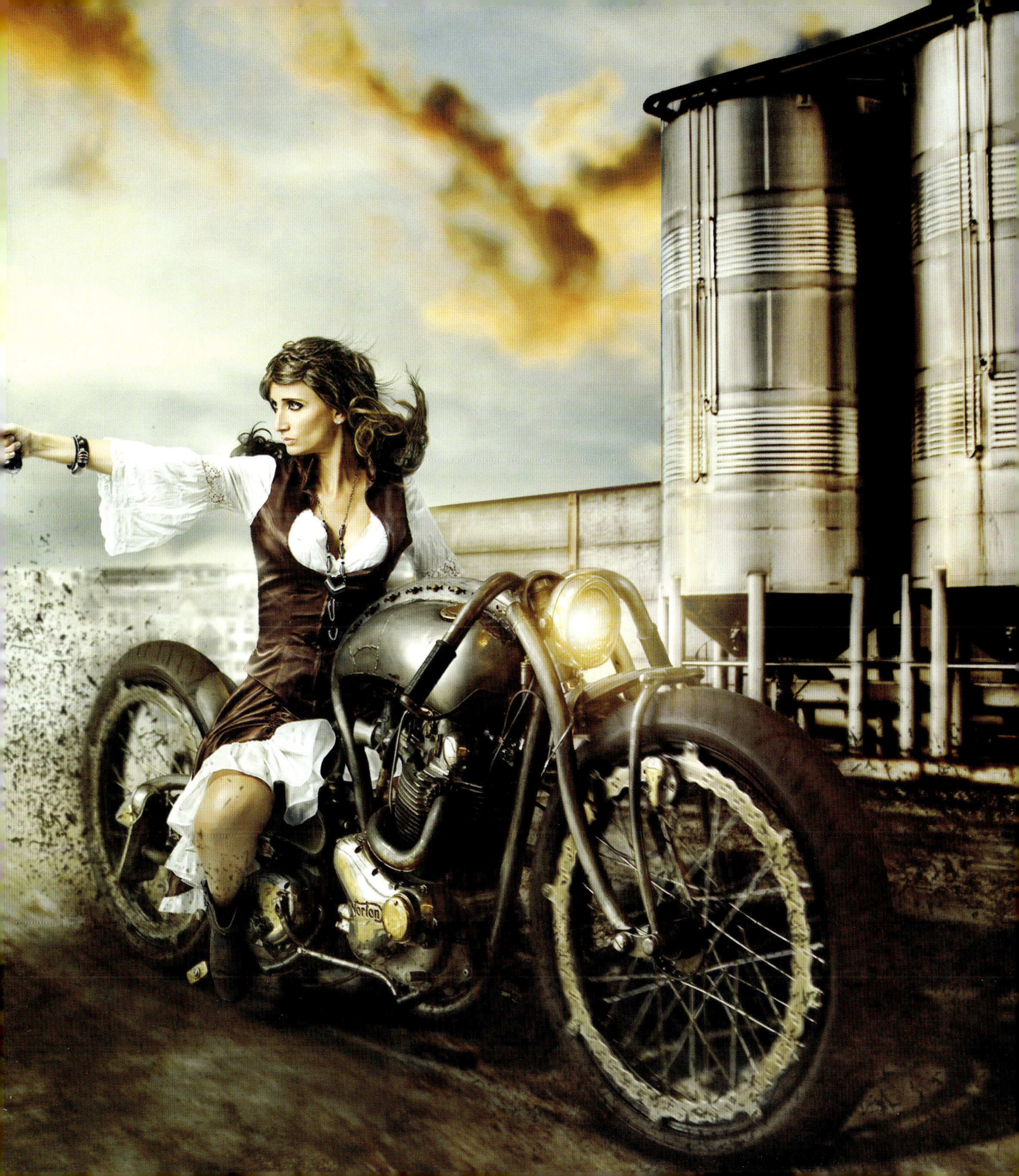
Norton

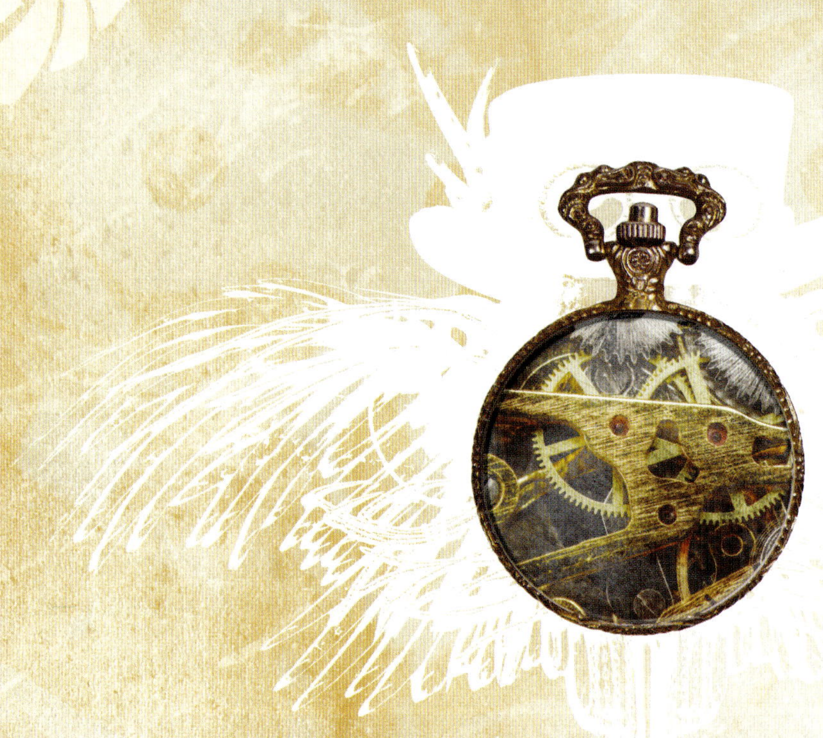

Goggles & Gears: Steampunk Art

Steampunk is an appealing subject for artists as it's so broad and versatile. It covers just about every facet of modern art, including sculpture, painting and digital 3D modelling. For the observer it's equally fascinating – talented artists can create intricate detail in brass and leather, while producing a broader picture. More often than not steampunk art can be used to tell a story, be it in a dramatic painting or a sculpted weapon designed for executing a specific mythical beast. Talented steampunk artists need to draw on a strong knowledge of the genre to create their spellbinding works.

Art History

Like literature, steampunk art builds upon Victorian movements. While the majority of the art of the period concentrated on the wealthy, nudes and wealthy nudes, a handful of artists turned their hands to the darker side of nineteenth-century life. Luke Fildes' painting, ***Applicants for Admission to a Casual Ward*** (after 1908) depicts a queue of sick people standing in the snow, while Gustave Doré's engravings of London show a bleak and congested city with the occasional steam train passing through. The Art Nouveau movement of the turn of the nineteenth century, with its brass and glass flourishes, proved equally influential on steampunk.

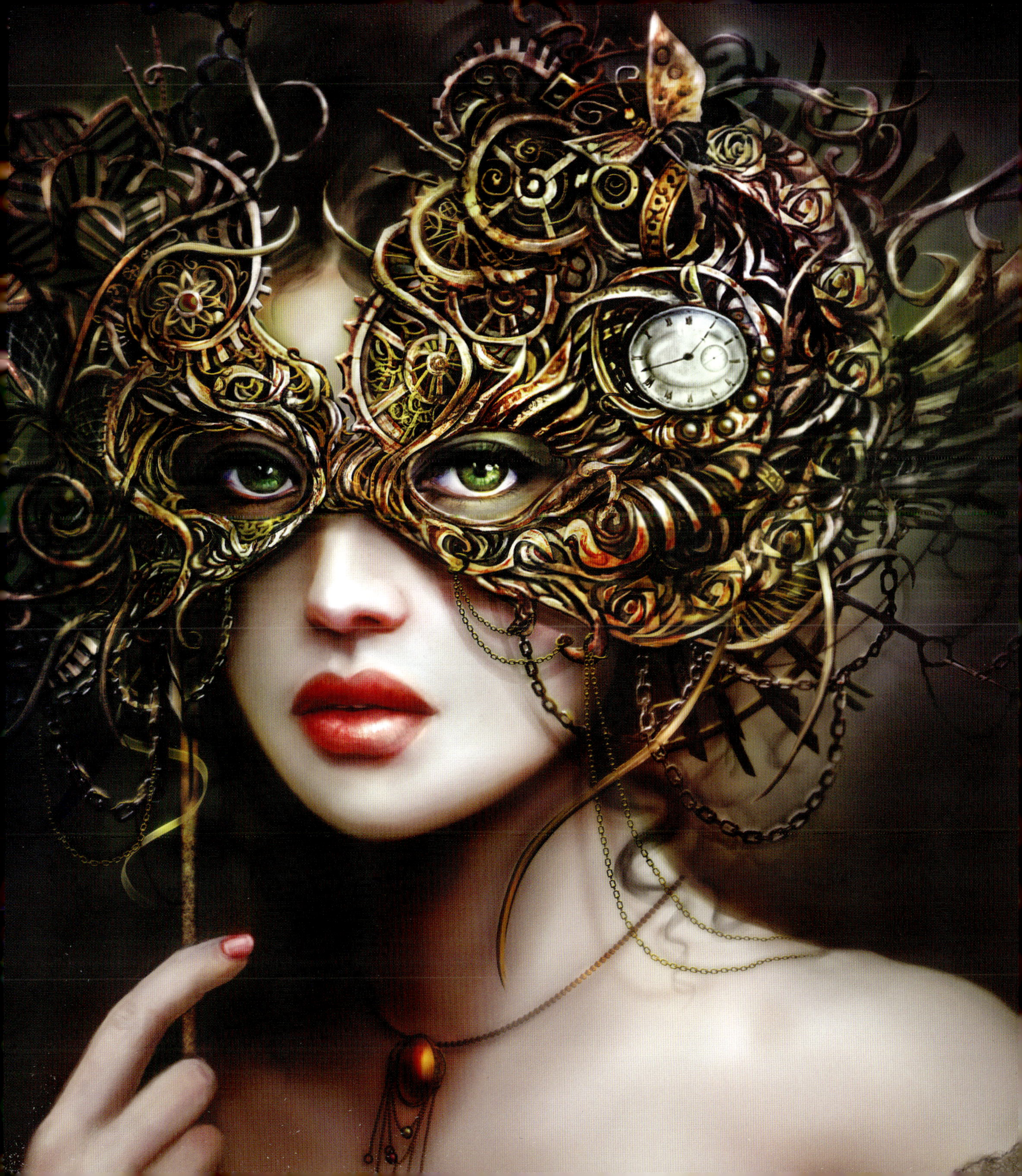

'I'm afraid I really haven't kept up with steampunk literature! I gotta say I love the cover paintings on the books, though!'

Tim Powers

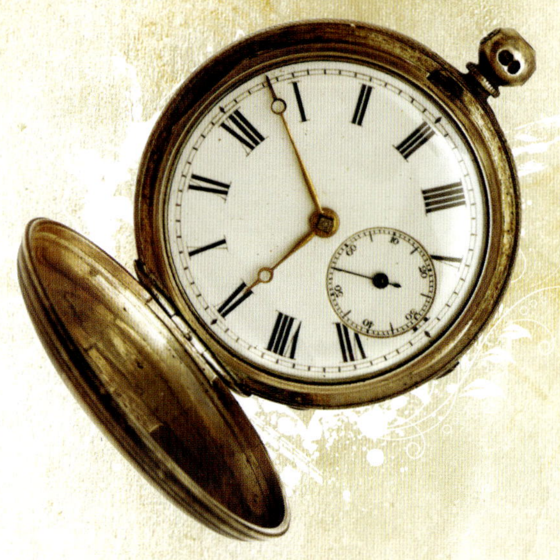

Steampunk Deviations

Leading art website DeviantArt is a great place to see imaginative paintings with a steampunk aesthetic. Brooke Gillette, who has worked as a concept artist and illustrator for games and books, turned her hand to steampunk with ***The Girl with Emerald Eyes*** (*see* page 93), which depicts a woman with an incredibly intricate mask neatly blending organic brassy tendrils with cogs and clocks. Meanwhile, Lindsey Look's ***Portrait of Captain Rackham*** (*see* page 7) shows a heroic-looking gent with a mechanical eye and a raygun.

Propunks

Spanish artist Cris Ortega has made a name for herself in creating wonderful fantasy portraits, and her ***Ex Machina*** (*see* opposite) is beautifully evocative of an imagined bygone time, and nicely contrasts the mechanic and the organic. Brit Jason Juta has created work for popular card games based on the ***Star Wars*** and ***Warhammer*** franchises, and his piece ***Submariner*** (*see* page 38) lavishly recalls Jules Vernes' ***20,000 Leagues Under the Sea*** with its image of a proud captain coming face-to-face with a hideous, Kraken-like monster.

Carréd Away

Benjamin Carré has created some fantastic steampunk pieces, and it is no surprise that he has been used prolifically for cover art. ***The Horns of Ruin*** (*see* page 103) is a powerful visualisation of Tim Akers' book, and his cover

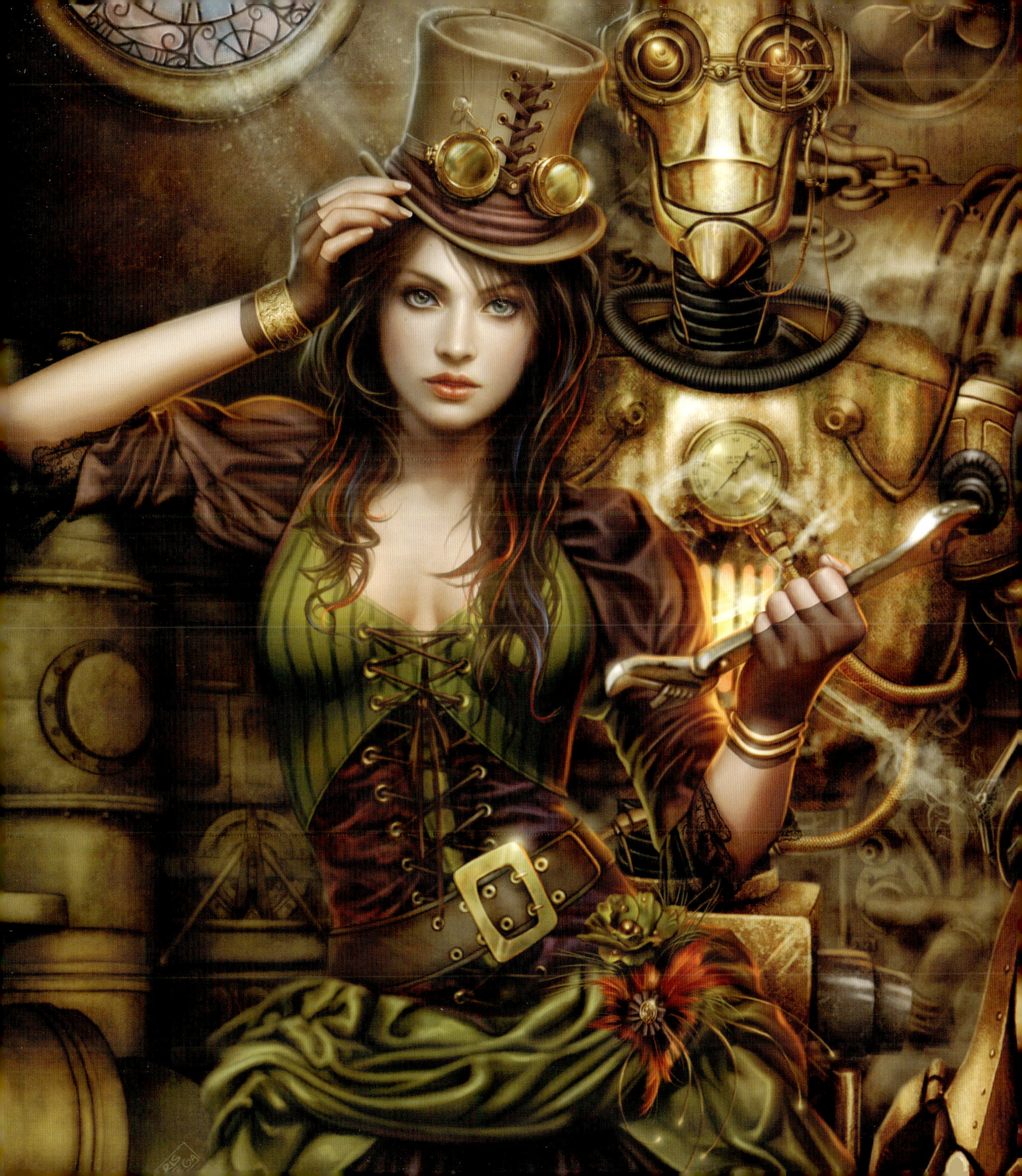

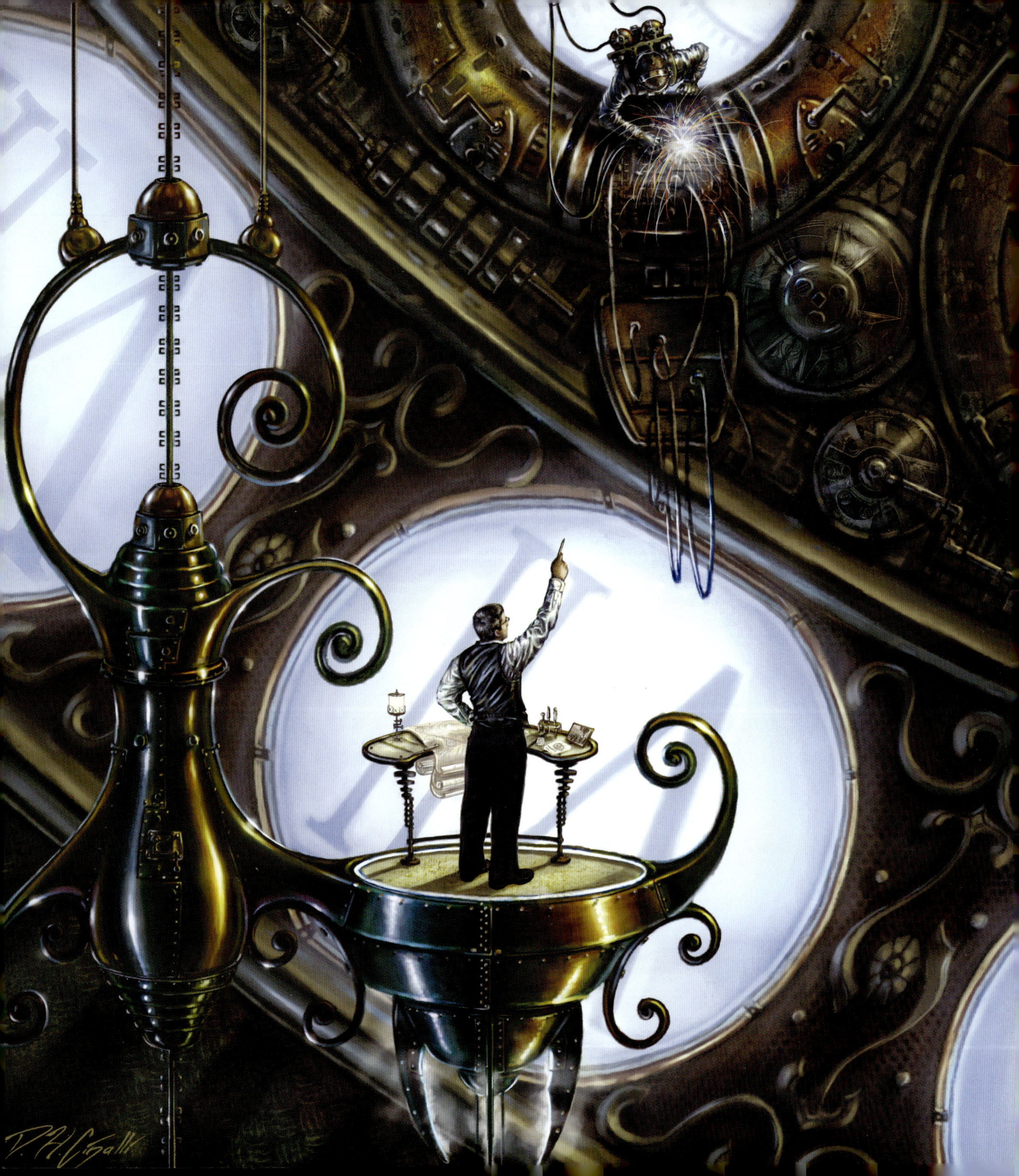

for ***Magies secrètes*** by Hervé Jubert (*see* page 4) draws you straight into the romance of the past. ***The Day the Wires Came Down*** (*see* page 49) has illustrated the front of ***Asimov's Science Fiction*** magazine and is a stunning representation of a steampunk city. Created for Cubicle 7's RPG ***Victoriana***, the fantastic piece of artwork ***Marvels of Science and Steampunk*** (*see* page 33) creates a wonderful sense of adventure by reflecting an ongoing battle between a clockwork dragon and a steampunk warrior in a heroine's goggles.

Getting Sirois

Douglas A. Sirois specialises in 'Narrative Illustration', so his images use characters and objects to tell a story. While he operates primarily in a fantasy setting, his ***Infernal Devices*** (*see* page 43) – possibly named after Jeter's influential novel – shows a steampunk hero opening his chest to reveal mechanical internal organs, a little like a mechanical Iron Man. Cory Jespersen employs a similar story-telling mechanic with ***Steampunk Goliath*** (*see* page 45), a wonderfully detailed image of a steam-powered scorpion wreaking havoc on an oddly anachronistic city as a young innocent boy clutches his teddy out of either fear or defiance.

Of Time and the City

Metropolises are an ideal setting for steampunk illustrations, and artists can go to town (literally!) on background details.

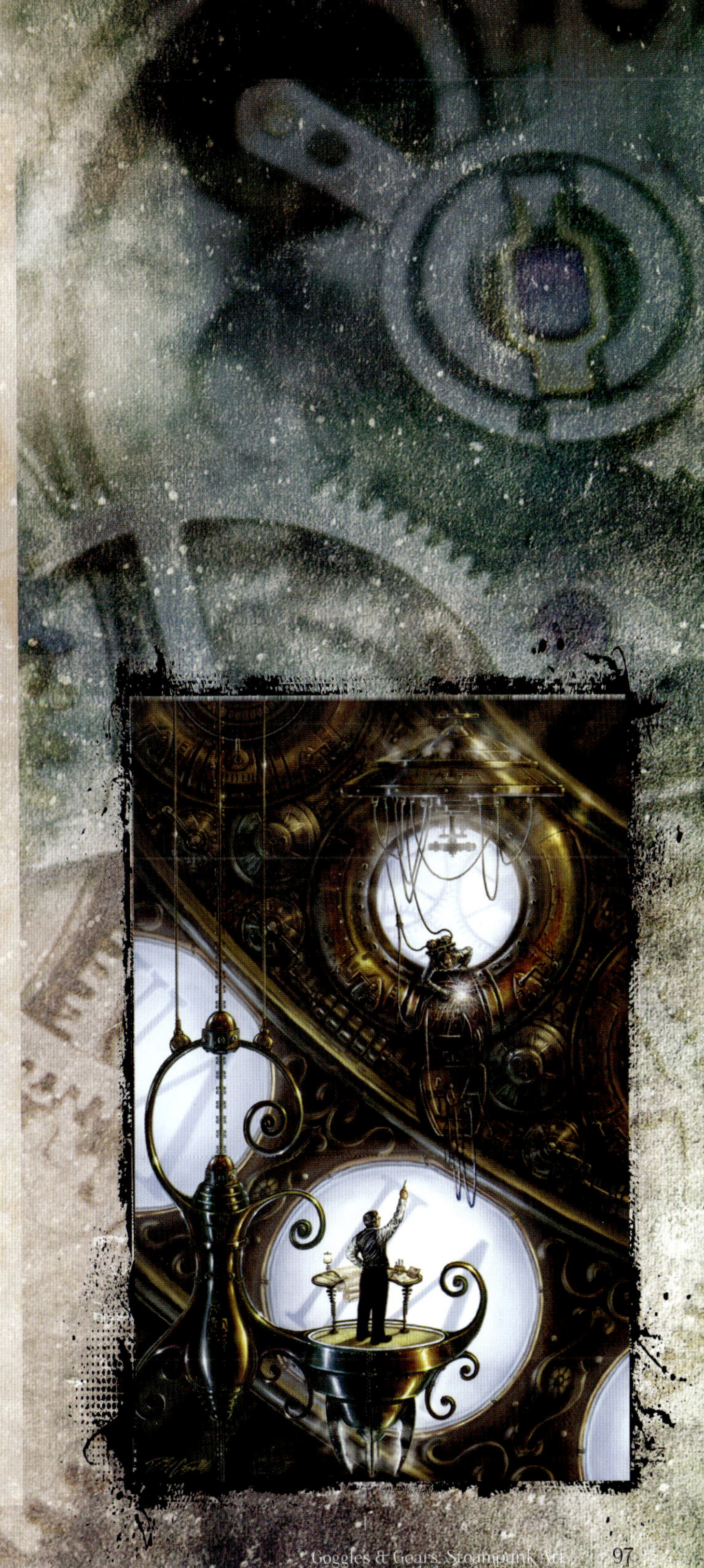

'As they walked, it seemed almost every building had some similar contrivance as decoration, adorning the street in a cacophony of clangs, bangs and whirs. The street's surroundings danced with steam and smoke, the scent of oil and grease its perfume.

A.F. Stewart, Mechanized Masterpieces: a Steampunk Anthology

Visit to Downtown (*see* page 16), by Bernard Bittler, gives us almost every steampunk trope in a single image: an upper-class woman, a bearded warrior and an inverted monorail. The fact that he also includes a steampunk robot which could have been taken from Ridley Scott's ***Alien*** (1979) and a burly biker on a steam-powered Harley only adds to the fun of the image. Meanwhile, Derek Cinalli's ***The Clockmaker*** (*see* page 96) takes a more focussed look at a pair of mechanics working on an enormous piece of clockwork machinery.

Mechanical Beasts

German artist Jenny Lehmann presents some fantastic steampunk femmes with the gorgeous ***Steampunk Lady*** (*see* page 26), as well as her work ***The Cavalry Girl*** (*see* page 12), which tells the story of a young lady who adopts her late father's mechanical horse. Kelley Hensing's ***Mechanical Beast*** (*see* page 104) is calmer but equally brooding - it depicts a ***Sleepy Hollow***-style faceless man riding atop a mechanical ox. The addition of a pair of cheeky monkeys, one of whom appears to be banging a drum, adds a sense of light relief to the somewhat murky proceedings.

Moore Than Enough

Graphic novels are the perfect medium for steampunk, especially when they combine great writing with masterful art. Alan Moore is a master of the form, and frequently credited with taking it to a new, more mature and

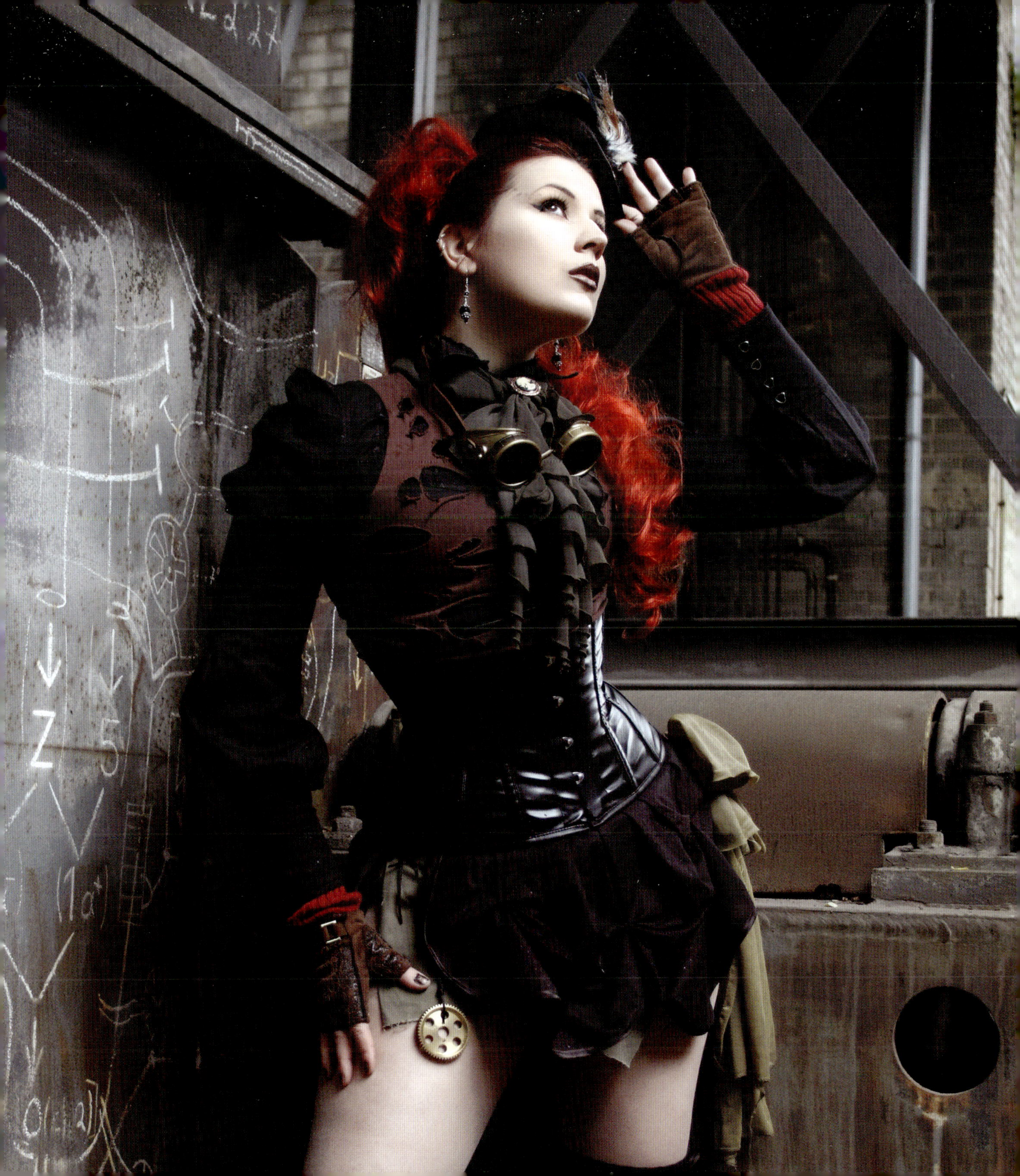

'Many great things have been accomplished by the careful combination of keen minds and ardent spirits.'

G.D. Falksen

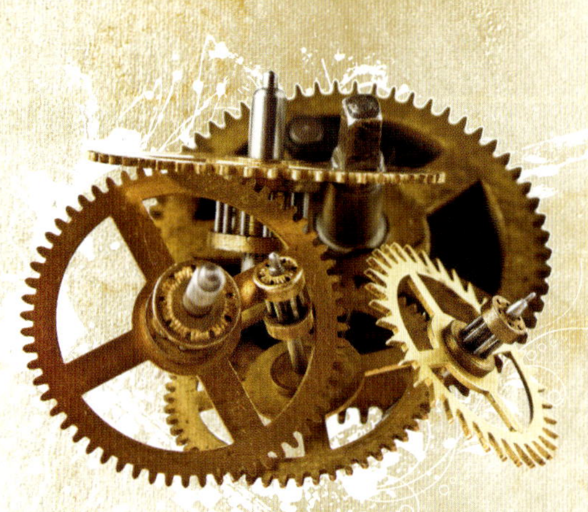

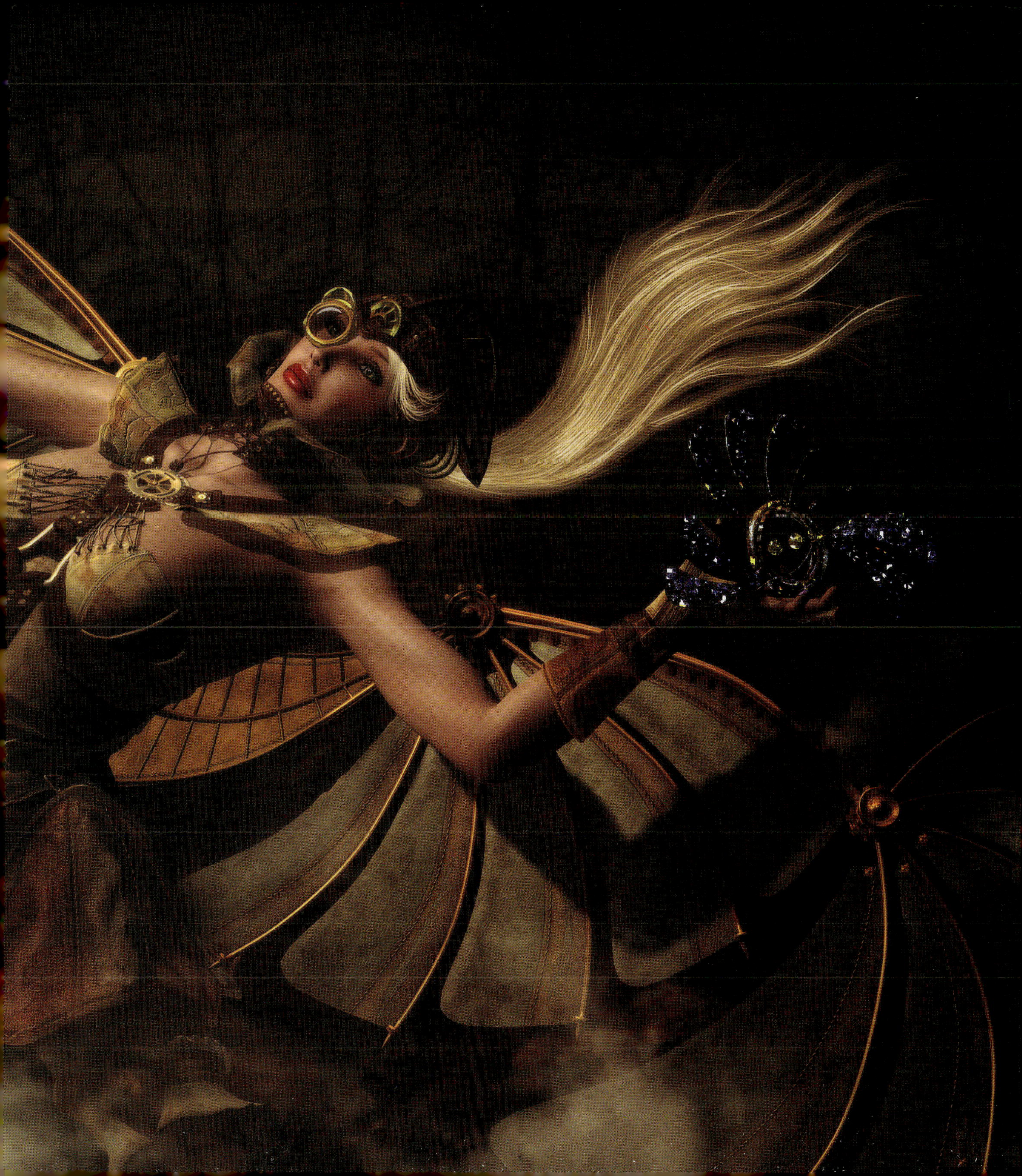

'The clock indicates the moment – but what does eternity indicate?'

Paul Di Filippo,
The Steampunk Trilogy

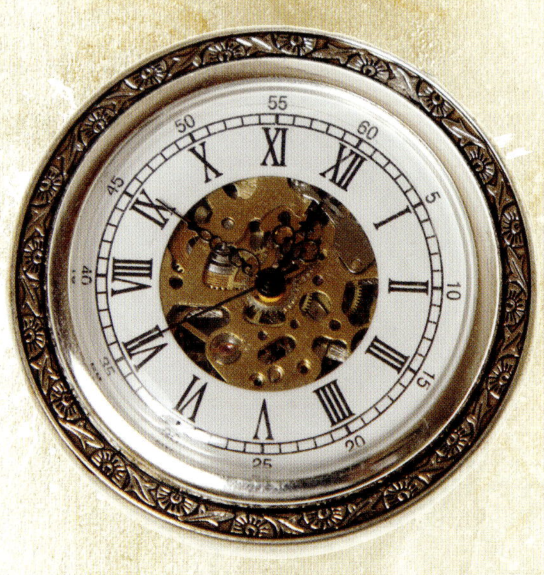

dangerous level. ***Watchmen*** (1986), an anti-superhero comic, frequently goes back in time to an alternative universe where steam and electricity-powered vehicles are commonplace, and even the title refers to Dr Manhattan's obsession with clockwork timekeeping devices. Moore also dabbled in steampunk with Jack the Ripper reimagining ***From Hell*** (1989), set in Victorian London, and ***The League of Extraordinary Gentlemen*** (1999).

The Darker Knight

Batman had already had a darker and more brooding revival with Frank Miller's ***The Dark Knight Returns*** (1986), but the single-issue ***Gotham by Gaslight*** (1989) took the caped crusader into true steampunk territory. Written by Brian Augustyn and illustrated by ***Hellboy*** creator Mike Mignola, it takes place in 1889 and features characters of the time such as Jack the Ripper and Sigmund Freud. It was surprisingly ahead of its time in terms of steampunk, and it's helped along immensely by Mignola's depiction of Gotham's rooftops. A tie-in video game was promised but unfortunately never saw the light of day due to rights' issues.

The Story of O

A brief but hugely important steampunk work, Grant Morrison and Steve Yeowell's ***Sebastian O*** (1993) sits somewhere between Oscar Wilde and ***American Psycho***. Sebastian is a dandy living in a steam-driven version of London, but he's been framed for writing some really

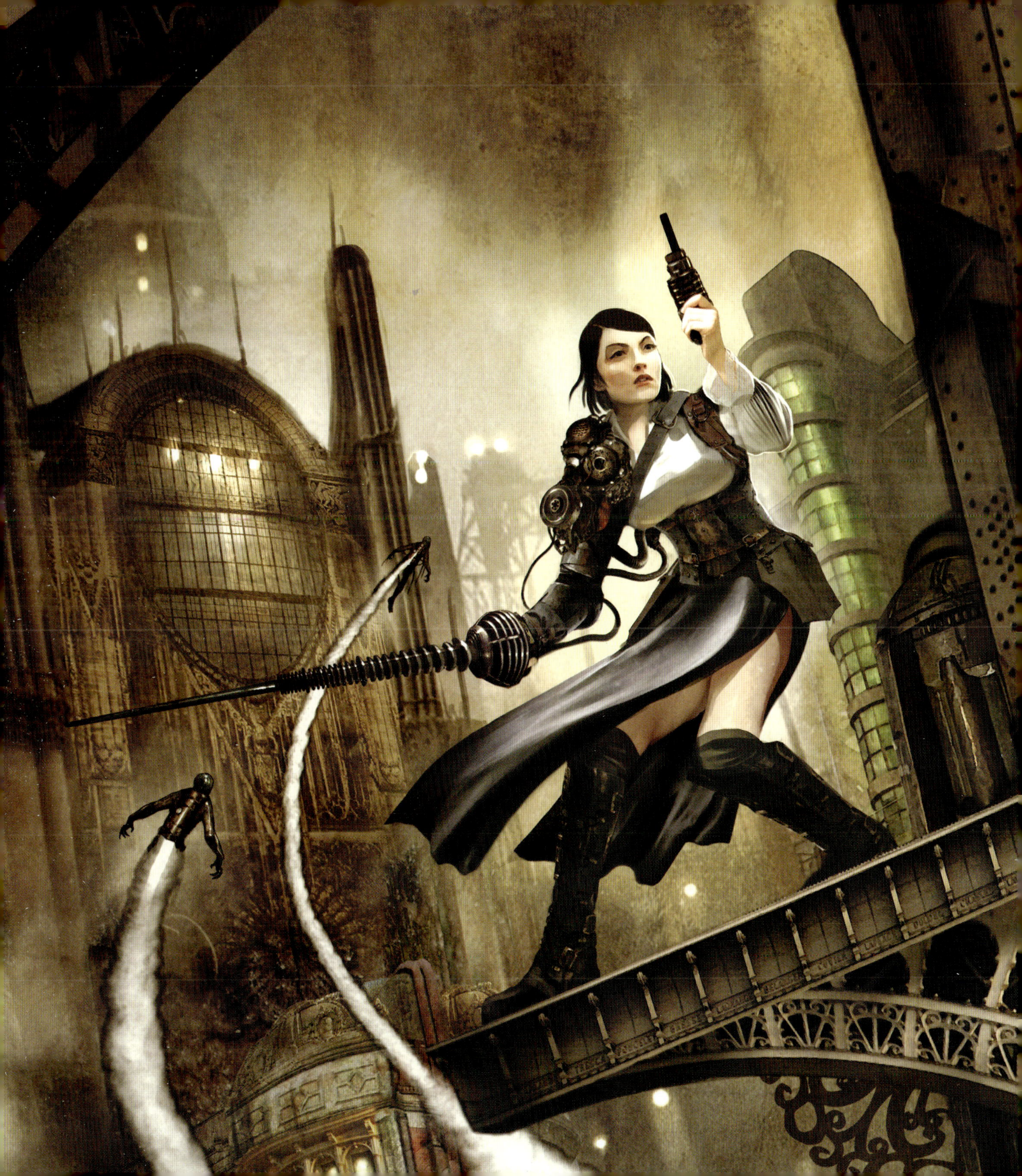

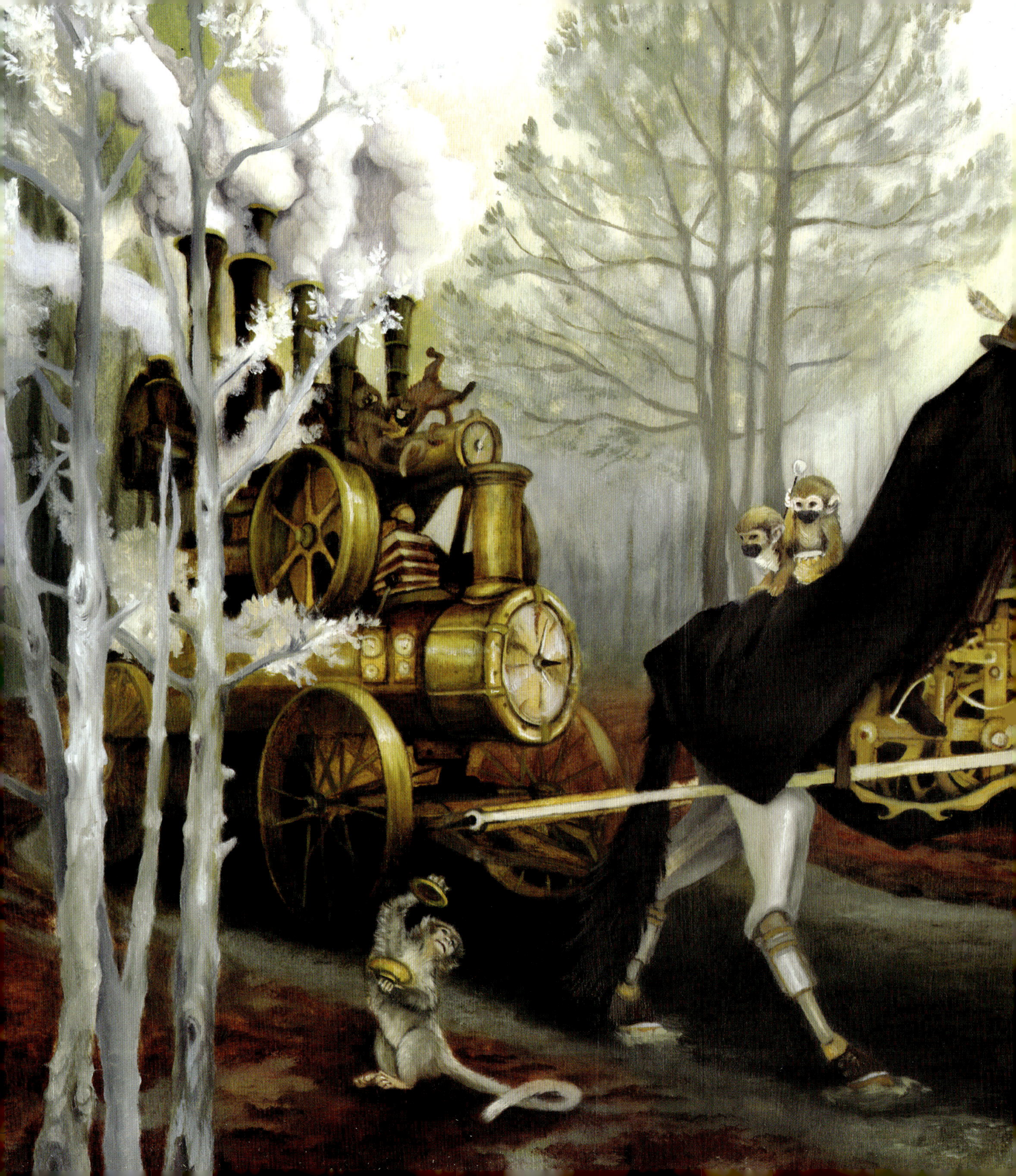

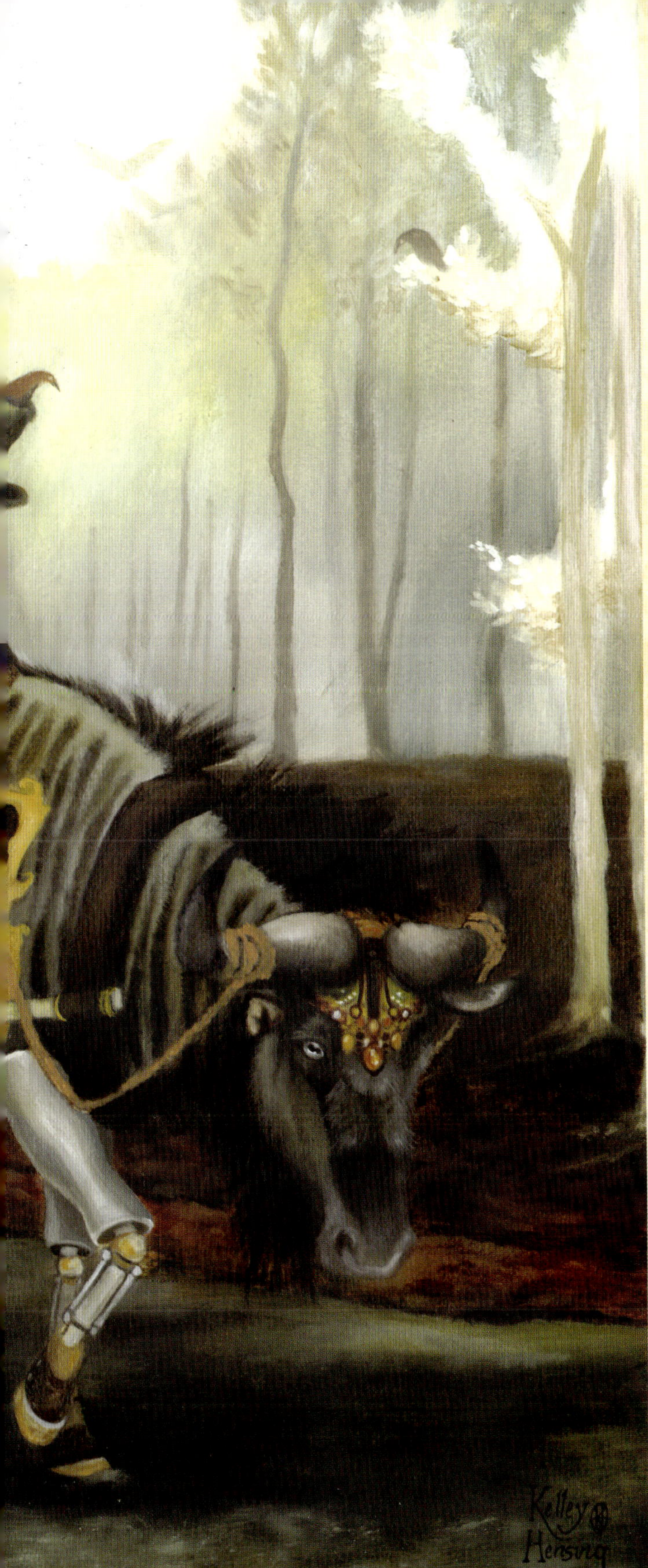

bad poetry. It features with mechanical gardens and clockwork houses-cum-mazes, and it's cleverly written, with a jaw-dropping final twist. While Yeowell's art has dated slightly, it's still a masterpiece of steampunk and proof that graphic novels were in tune with their wordy counterparts in the sub-genre's progression.

From Ellis

Warren Ellis has established himself as one of the finest graphic novel authors in the world, and he's written a couple of books which could definitely be considered steampunk – despite his denial that they fit into the sub-genre. ***Aetheric Mechanics*** (2008), illustrated by Gianluca Pagliarani, depicts an aerial attack on early-twentieth-century London while Holmesian amateur detective Sax Raker investigates a murderer who has apparently disappeared into thin art. ***Captain Swing and the Electrical Pirates of Cindery Island*** (2011), by Ellis and Raulo Caceres, introduces electricity into a steampunk setting with Captain Swing using it to wreak havoc on London.

Steampunk Goes East

Hiromu Arakawa's ***Fullmetal Alchemist*** is one of steampunk's biggest success stories, beginning in Japan as a comic book but spreading around the world through TV series and films. It's rather bonkers, set in an approximation of Europe in the nineteenth century, and featuring a pair of brothers who have lost parts of their

'I tell you all the time, you will never be able to replace me with a brass and steam contraption.'

Maeve Alpin, As Timeless As Stone.

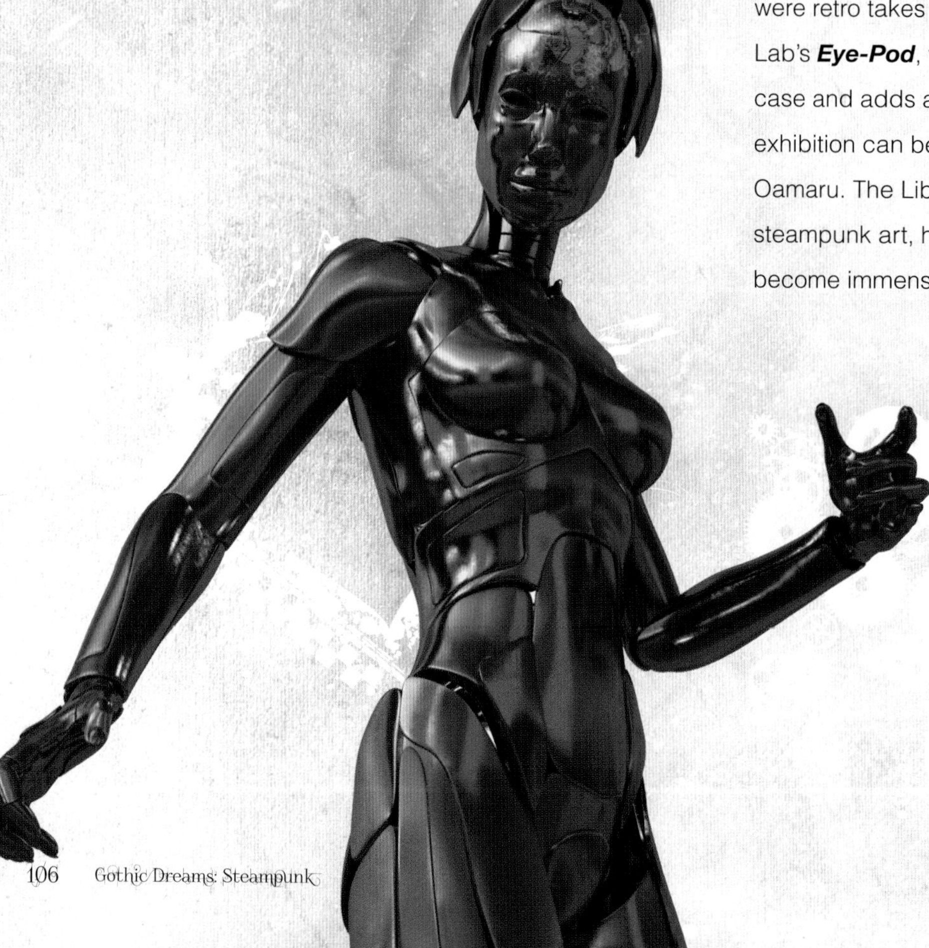

bodies and replaced them with armoured exoskeletons. While it's the titular alchemy that powers the world – rather than steam – there are a lot of steampunk influences, such as an intricate class system and dirigibles in one of the later movies.

Steampunk in the Flesh

As steampunk grew and became a key part of popular culture, exhibitions dedicated to it sprang up around the world. England's esteemed Oxford University – itself the centre of Philip Pullman's steampunky ***His Dark Materials*** trilogy – exhibited steampunk works in 2010. Among them were retro takes on popular items, such as Steam Gear Lab's ***Eye-Pod***, which embeds a music player in an antique case and adds a disembodied eyeball. A more permanent exhibition can be found in the New Zealand town of Oamaru. The Libratory Steampunk Art Gallery hosts steampunk art, hosting events and film screenings, and has become immensely popular.

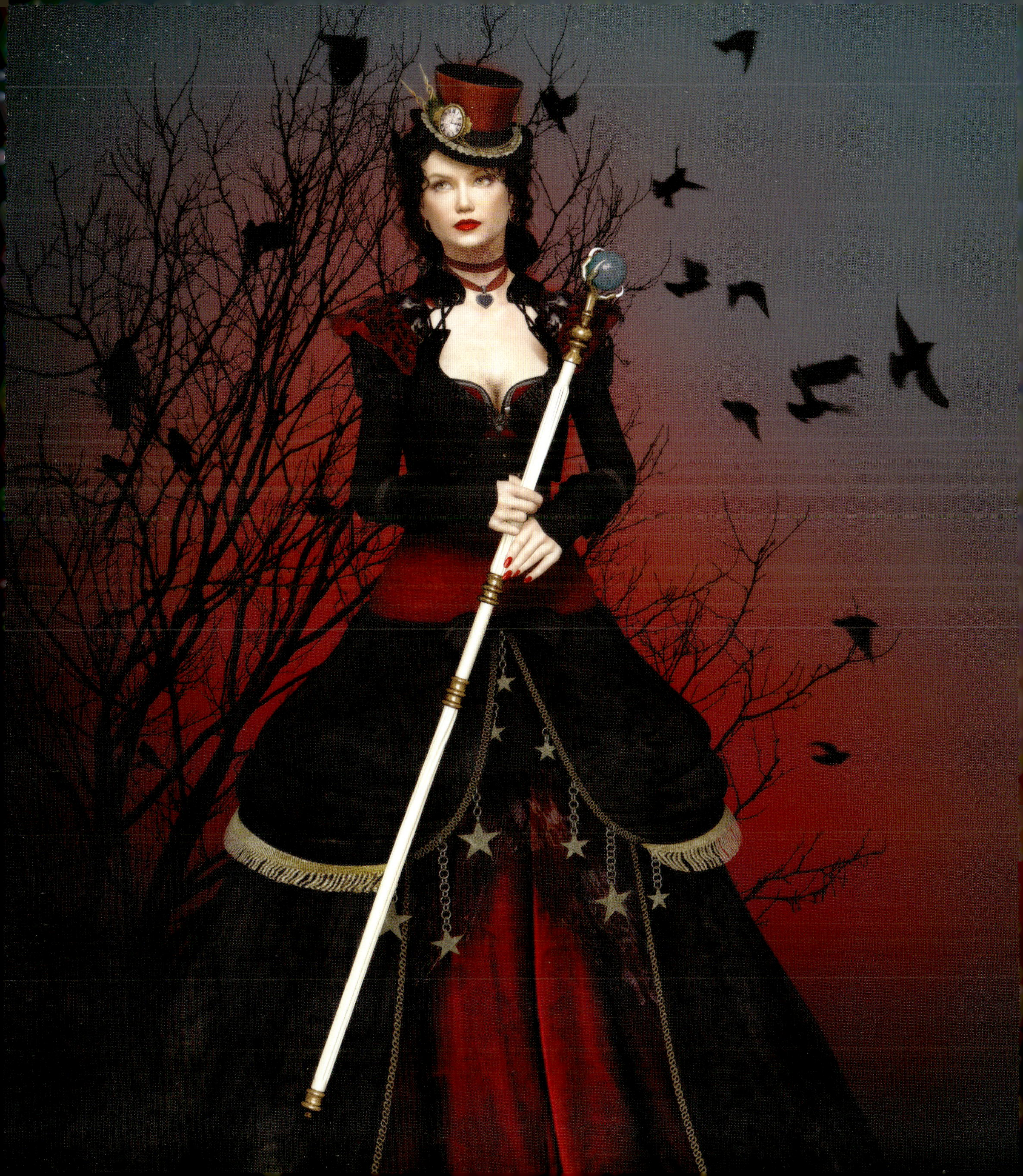

'Today satellite photos make the planet seem so small. Where is the adventure in that? [Steampunk is a] sort of a dream, the way we used to daydream. It's like part of your childhood's just bursting forward again.'

Robert Brown, lead singer of Abney Park

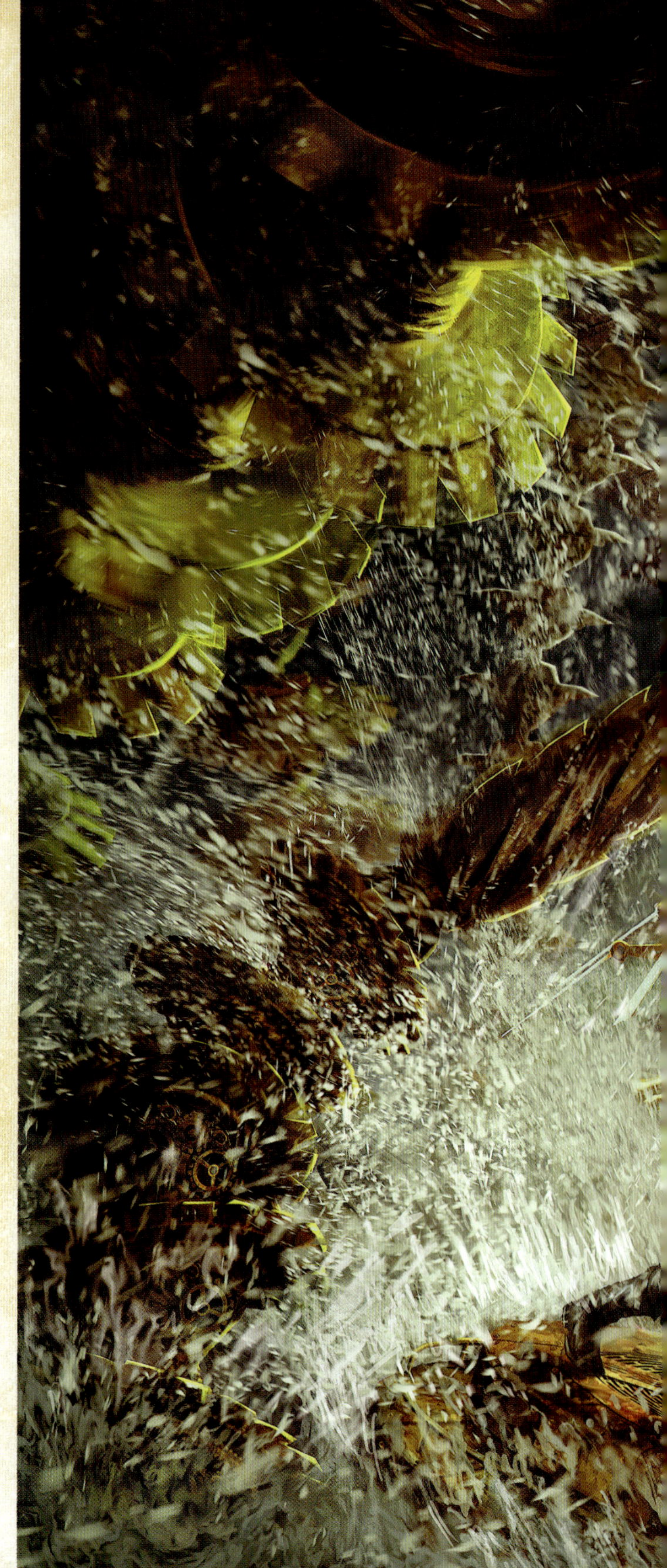

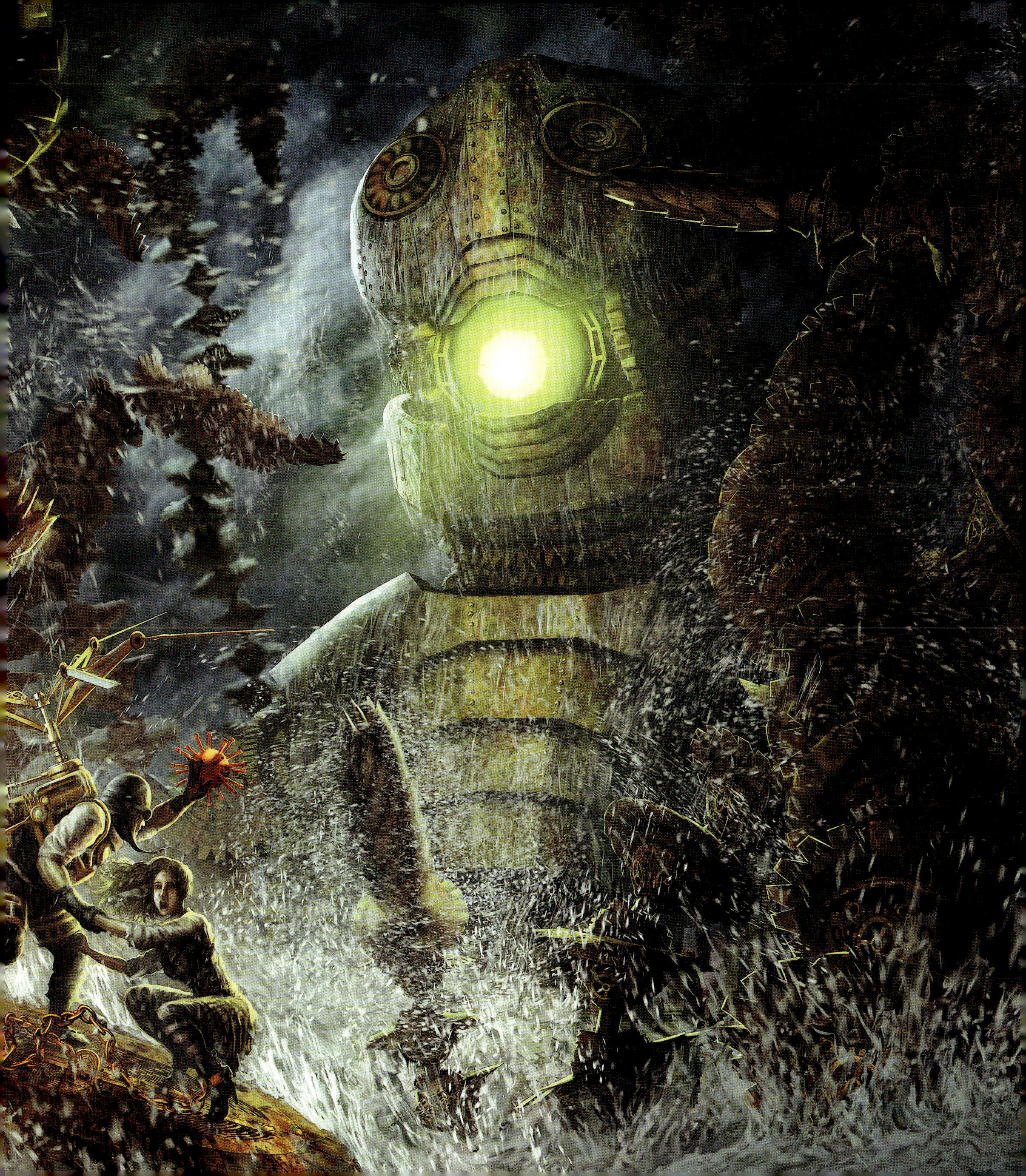

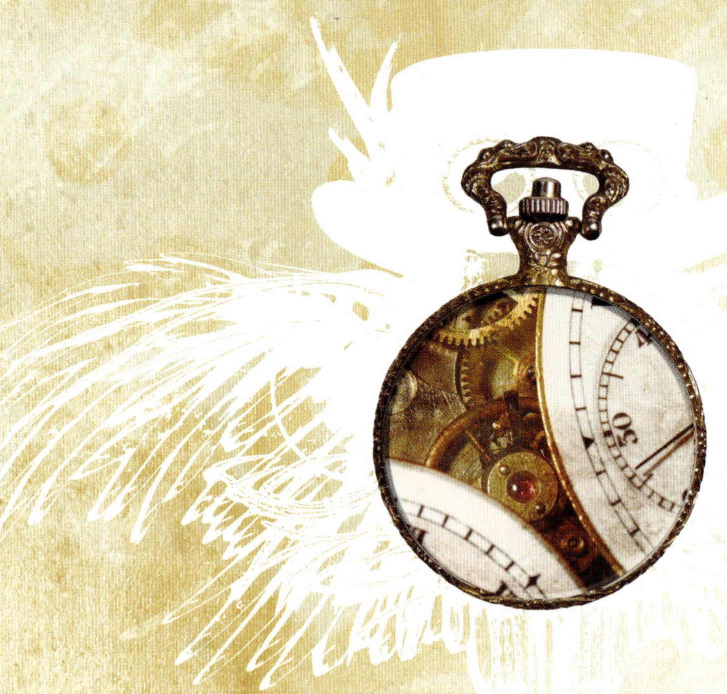

A Clockwork Universe

Steampunk's growth in fashion, literature, film and art slowly began to seep and diffuse into other forms of entertainment and culture. Unlike the goth and punk movements before it, steampunk influenced music rather than music influencing it. Its aesthetic, and its love of the past, makes for striking music videos, and bands have adopted a steampunk look which really stands out in popular music. Games are also the perfect medium for exploring the steampunk universe, especially recently when graphical horsepower allows for intricate and spectacular settings.

Historic Events

As soon as any cultural movement reaches a certain critical mass, it inspires people to get together and share their passions. Steampunk events now take place all over the world, and they are a fantastic way to explore the thoughts and ideas behind the movement, as well as to see some really cool costumes and inventions. The sub-genre's also inspired creative types to construct all sorts of fantastical and odd steampunk objects and gadgets, some of which even serve a useful purpose in the real world.

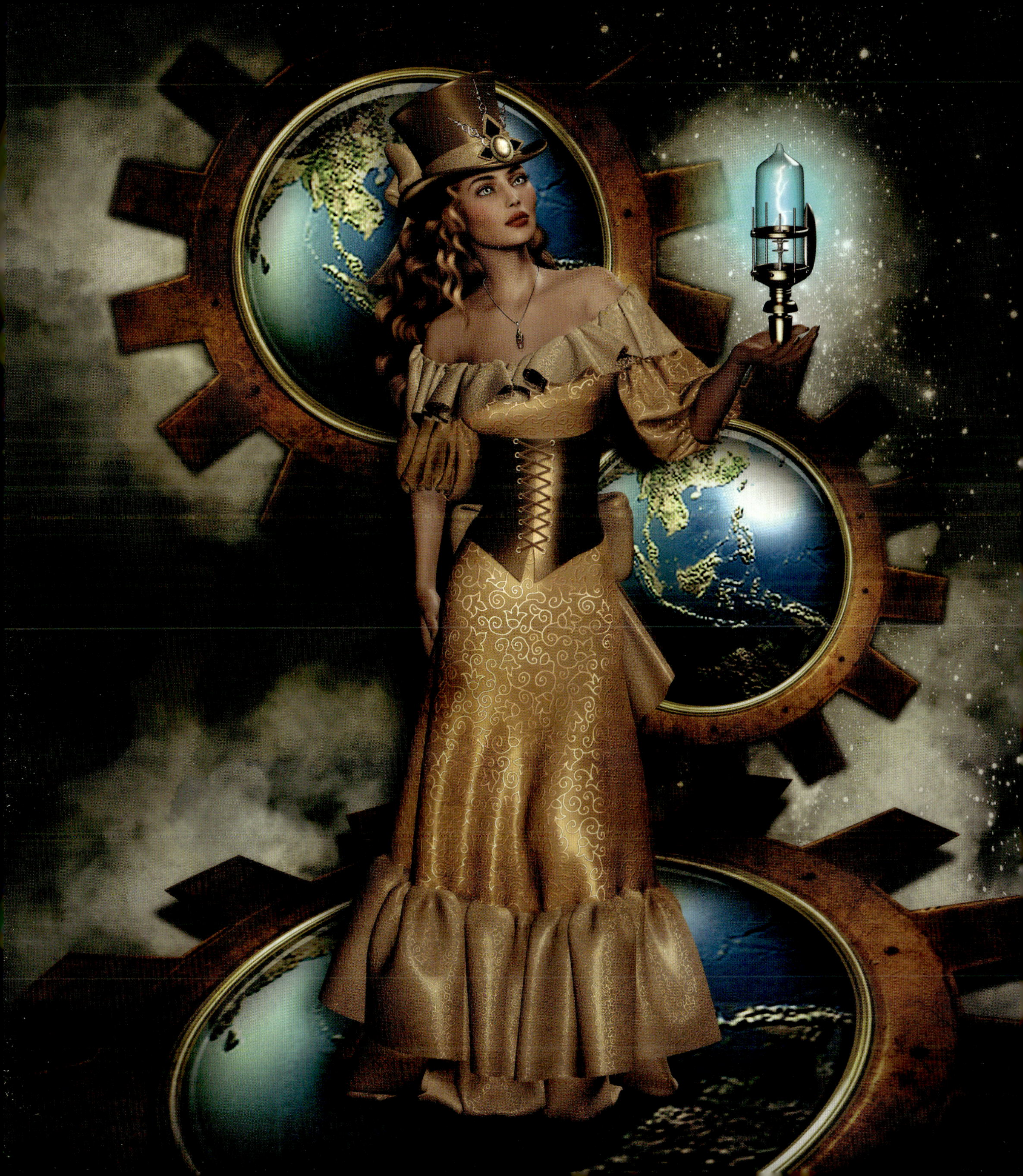

'Steampunk is an opportunity to force us to address those issues of the past, examine what went wrong, what we can do to put it right and make a better world.'

Ann VanderMeer, Steampunk III: Steampunk Revolution

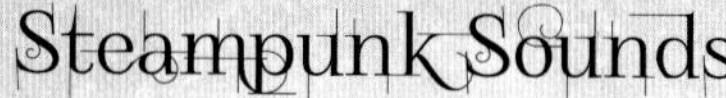

Steampunk Sounds

The 1980s musician, Thomas Dolby, is widely credited as the first steampunk musician, relying on archaic instruments and tape feedback to create a unique soundscape, as well as lyrics which frequently refer to scientific ideas and procedures. Bands Vernian Process and Abney Park, both based on the east coast of America, heavily rely on a steampunk look and mention steampunk ideas in their lyrics. The former takes its name from Jules Verne, while the latter is based on an eighteenth-century cemetery in London. Interestingly, both bands incorporate the goth movement in their work, and modern steampunk is often seen as an offspring from all things black and miserable.

Music Videos

As steampunk grew, more popular acts have jumped on the bandwagon and incorporated its ideas into their music videos. The Smashing Pumpkins' 'Tonight Tonight' (1996) was made as a huge homage to Georges Méliès' ***A Trip to the Moon***, featuring a giant steam-driven airship and Billy Corgan floating on a cloud. Singer Nicki Minaj is turned into a clockwork automaton by David Guetta in the video for the latter's 'Turn Me On' (2011), while Panic! at the Disco's lead singer Brendon Urie dons a top hat and brass goggles for the band's single 'The Ballad of Mona Lisa' (2011).

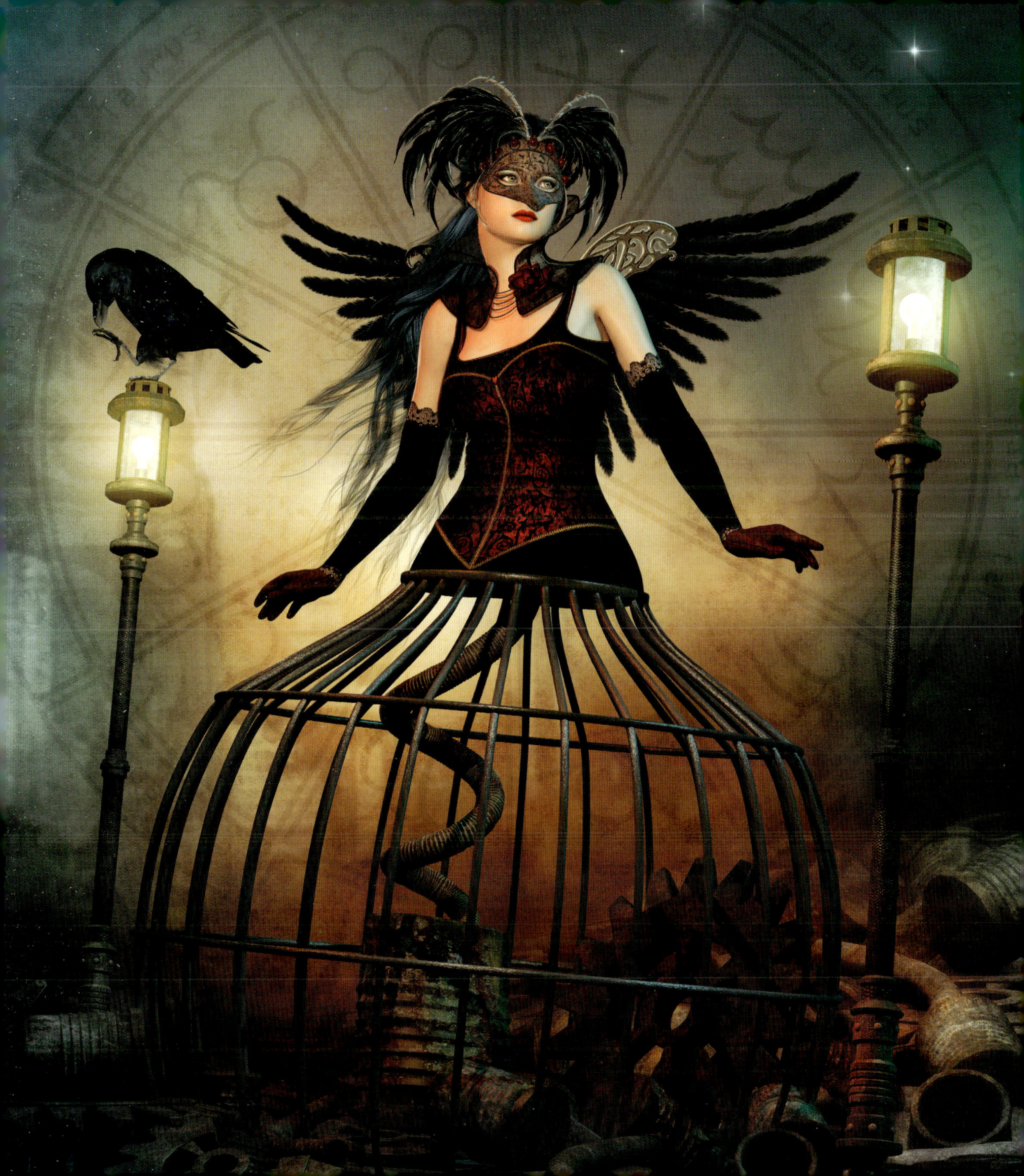

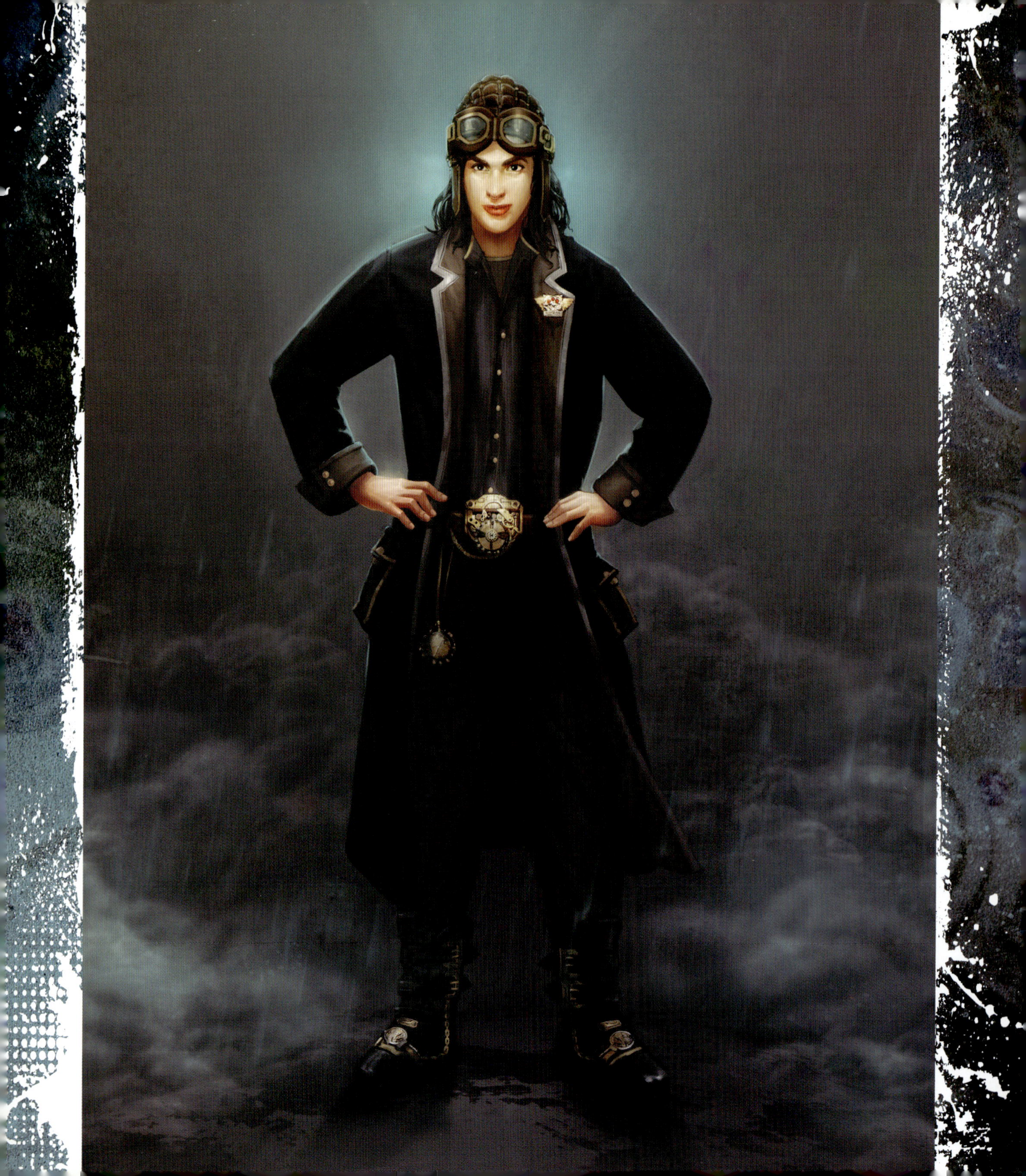

Fun and Games

Steampunk's unique setting lends itself well to video games and creates intriguing atmospheres. ***Final Fantasy VI*** (1994) and ***Final Fantasy VII*** (1997) took the franchises' traditional fantasy setting and coated it with a thick layer of steampunk, complete with spaceships and cowboys. The rather more laid-back ***Myst*** (1993) takes the player on a journey through a mysterious Jules Verne-inspired abandoned island, with only a few ancient instruments for company. ***Myst*** was a huge success thanks to its unique aesthetic and take-your-time puzzles, which meant the player could never die.

Stealing Ideas

The ***Thief*** franchise, begun in 1998, nails steampunk, creating a perpetually-haunted city in which master thief Garrett is drawn into on-going battles between the tech-loving Mechanists and the nature-worshipping Pagans. Similar to ***Thief*** is ***BioShock*** (2007), in which the player is thrust into an underwater utopia-gone-wrong, marvellously rendered in brass surfaces and opulent objects. ***Dishonored*** (2012), meanwhile, depicts a city fuelled by whale oil in which the hero, Corvo, is able to possess rats and blast enemies with wind. What is notable about all these games is that they use a gothic, steampunk environment to effectively create a heady, gloomy atmosphere.

'As a subculture, we are not the spawn of Satan. People smile when they see us. They want to take our picture.'

Evelyn Kriete

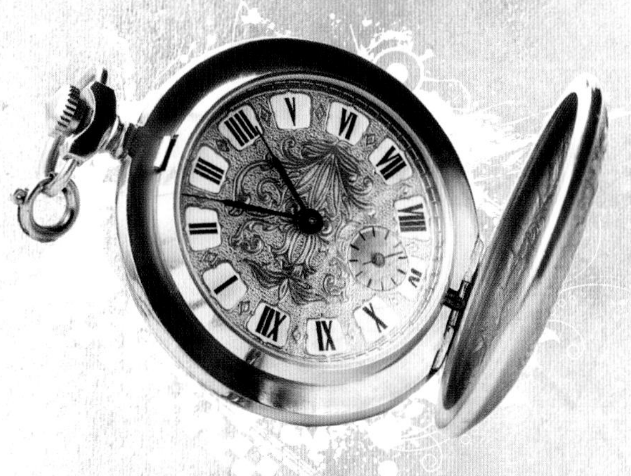

Steampunk Events

Every May, thousands of steampunk fans descend upon Morristown, New Jersey for the Steampunk World's Fair. Apparently the biggest convention of its sort, it includes panel discussions, speeches, role-playing games, performances of steampunk music and even prizes for the best facial hair. It's a great way for cosplayers and steampunk fans to show off their creations, but you can attend even if you don't fancy dressing up as a Victorian lord or lady, and you can pick up a costume and assorted steampunk goods while you're there. Even the fairly mundane meeting room at the Radisson Hotel which hosts the Steampunk World's Fair is renamed the 'Aether Trader'.

Meet the Steampunkers

Steamcon attracts steampunk fans on the other side of the States, in Seattle, Washington. Guests of honour have already included Tim Powers, James Blaylock and K.W. Jeter, and each convention is themed around ideas such as 'Weird Weird West' and 'Victorian Monsters'. In October, New Yorkers can experience steampunk performers at The Anachonism, a day-long event held in the city's trendy Lower East Side. Europeans can get a taste of steampunk at Weekend at the Asylum, held every September in the historical English city of Lincoln, where you can take part in a tea-drinking duel. While not strictly steampunk-focused, both goth festival Eccentrik in Raleigh, North Carolina, and comic convention Comic-Con in San Diego, California, have steampunk exhibitions and events.

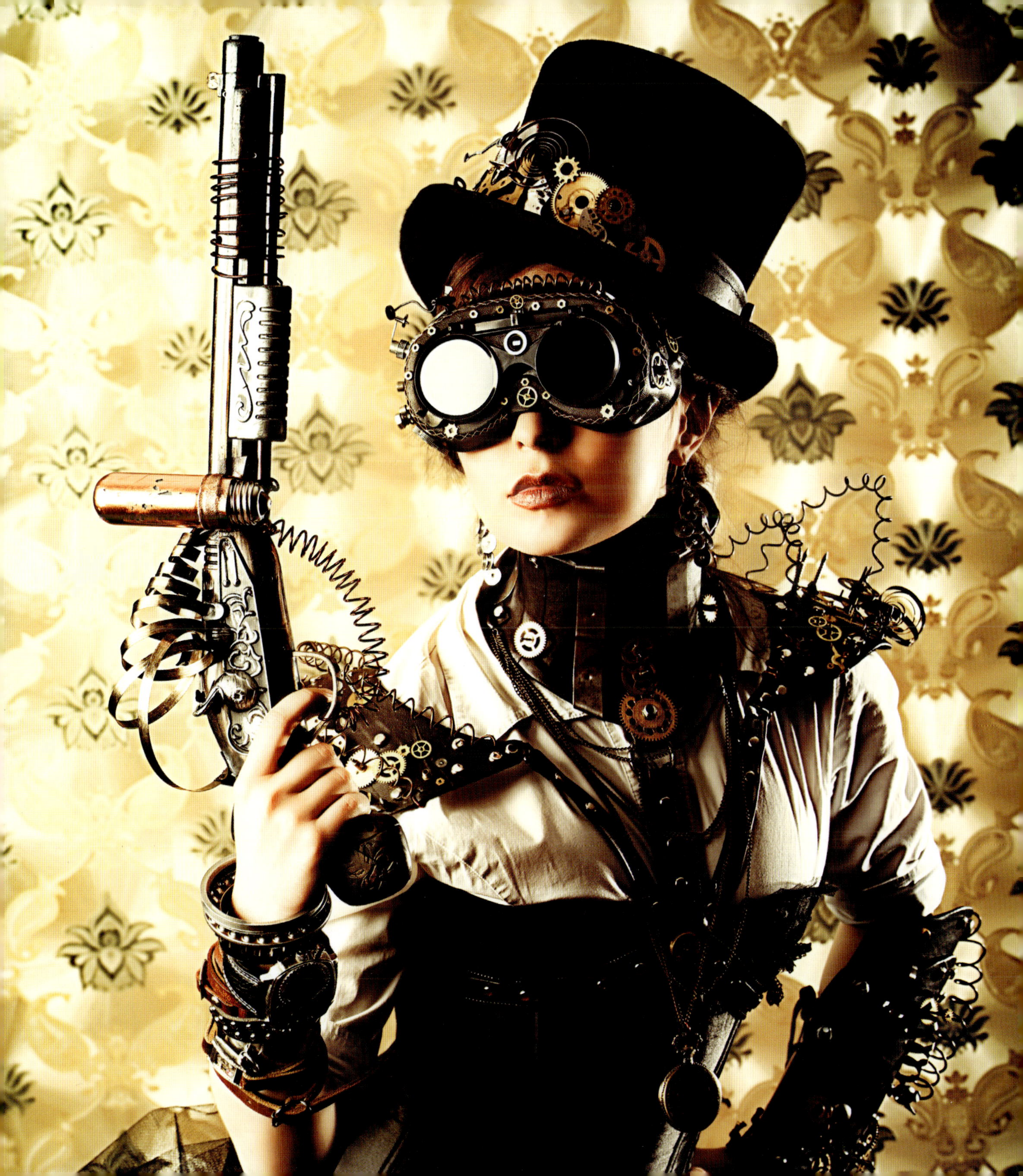

'With our antique clock parts we've taken all arts, fine art to fashion And now we're spreading worldwide to circle the globe with a furious passion'

Abney Park, 'Steampunk Revolution'

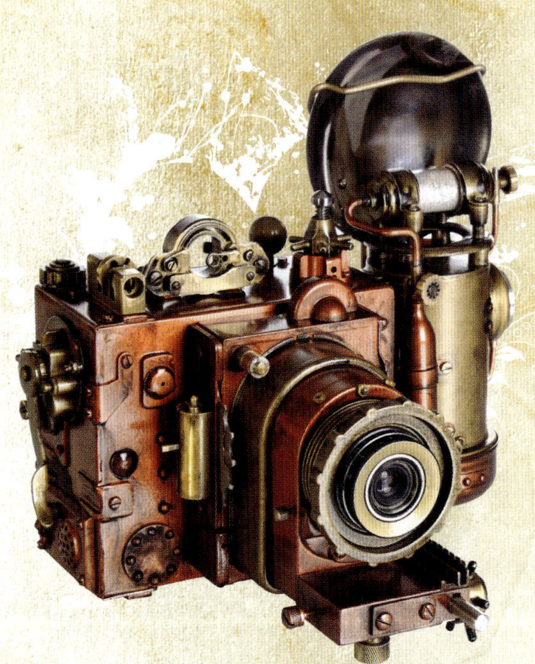

Marvellous Contraptions

A big part of the steampunk sub-culture is modding contemporary technology so it looks old-fashioned, and even a cog-laden iPhone case can show your love for all things Victorian. There are a number of online shops where you can pick up retro-future items: big sites such as Amazon and eBay will flog you brass USB drives and mechanical-looking MacBook Air skins, whereas more unique items can be purchased from www.cafepress.com. The latter supplies user-customized products, so you can create an amazing design for an iPad sleeve in Photoshop, upload it to the site and it'll be manufactured for you – and anyone else who wants it.

(Robotic) Handmade

Enormous internet craft store, etsy, is a great place to look for homemade steampunk items, and a number of shops on the store (Steampunknation, edmdesigns and Steampunk Vintage) have a complete range of products which make fabulous gifts for Verne-obsessed friends. The quaintly named UK-based Little Steampunk Shop (www.littlesteampunkshop.co.uk) includes exquisitely designed jewellery, cufflinks and homemade cards, and you can be sure you're picking up a unique item. RebelsMarket (www.rebelsmarket.com) is great for steampunkers on a budget, and you can pick up intricate watches or steampunk prints for a bargain.

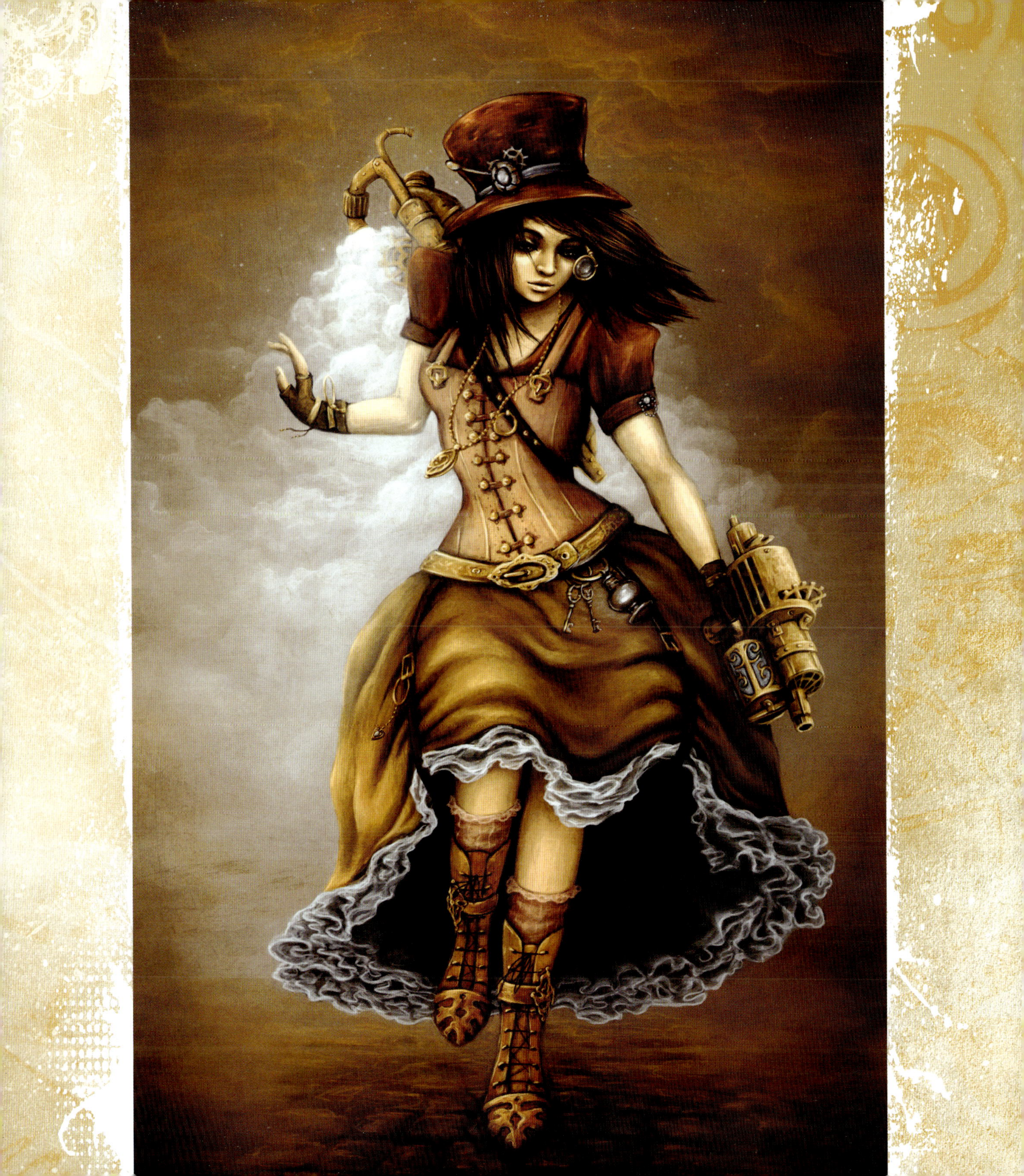

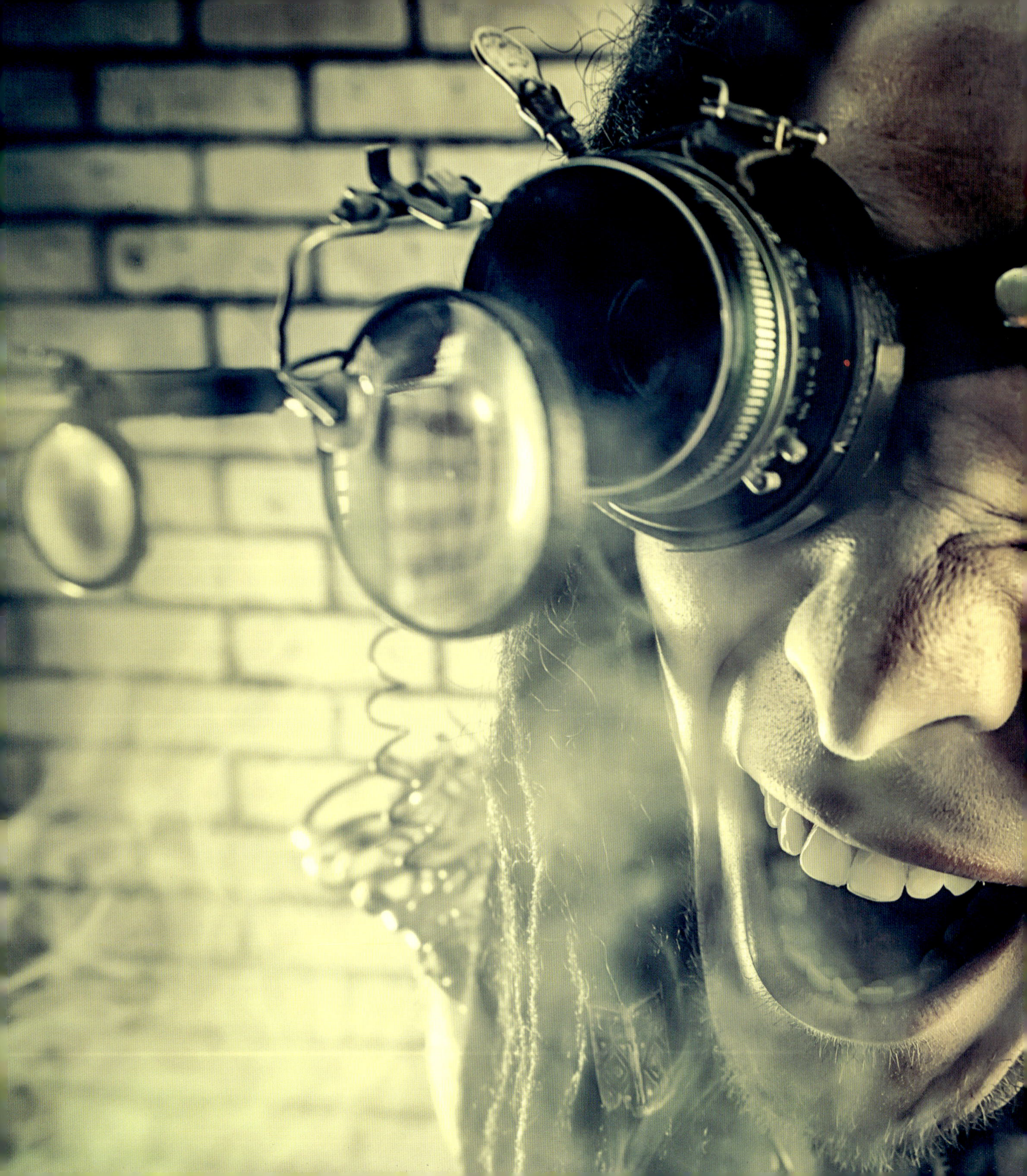

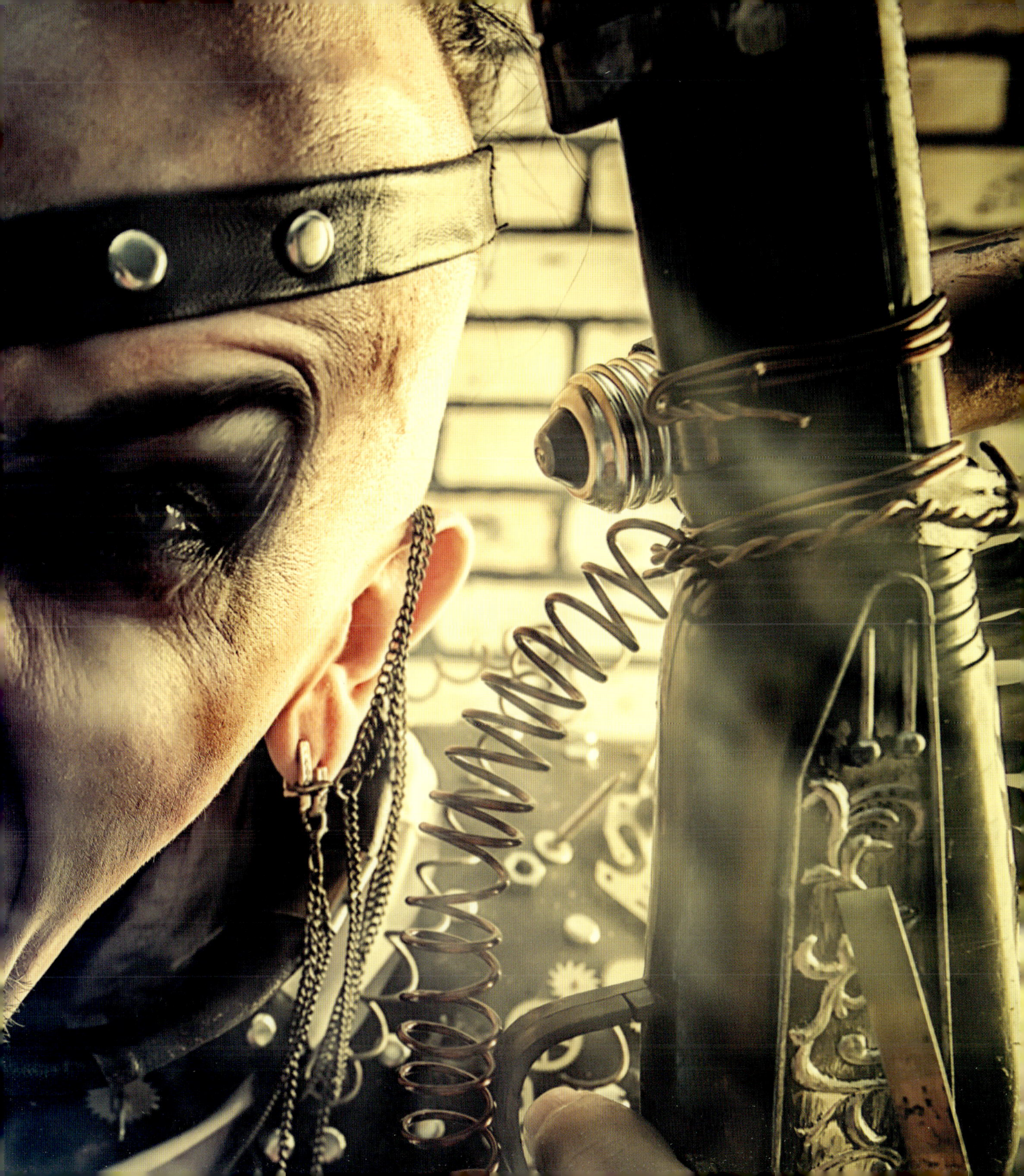

Find Out More

Full steam ahead – safely! Before visiting forums, or if you have any problems on fan sites, visit ***www.thinkuknow.co.uk*** for some online safety advice. It's also worth noting that all these websites were accessible at the time of going to press, but could be subject to change/removal/being sucked into another dimension.

The Big Three Authors

www.steamwords.wordpress.com / @kwjeter: K.W. Jeter, the man who coined the phrase, occasionally blogs but is far more active on Twitter.

www.jamespblaylock.com: the author of ***The Digging Leviathan***'s official site includes short stories and essays downloadable as PDFs so you can read them anywhere.

www.theworksoftimpowers.com: yarr! Point yer internet compass at this site to find out more about the ***On Stranger Tides*** scribe.

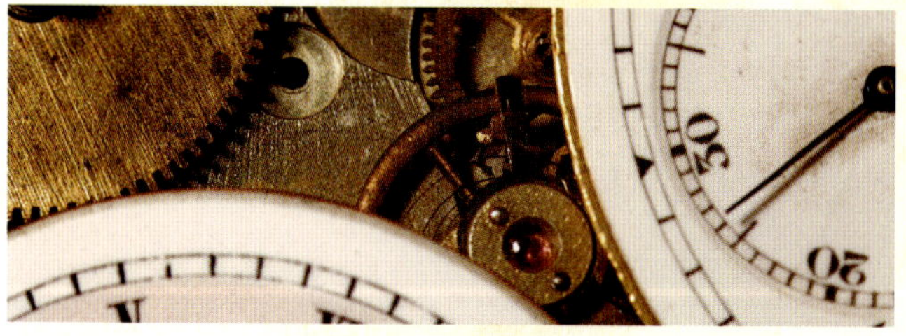

Other Great Steampunk Authors

www.philip-pullman.com: Phil's gone a bit serious since ***His Dark Materials***, but his official site includes lots of fascinating material, including his surprisingly good illustrations.

www.multiverse.org: Michael Moorcock's Miscellany's forum-like presentation is a little confusing, but hunt around and you'll find rare works, and you can even get in touch with the man himself.

www.nealstephenson.com / @nealstephenson: the author of ***The Diamond Age***'s official site and Twitter are insightful and thought-provoking.

www.stephen-baxter.com: ***The Time Ships***' author is now working with Terry Pratchett and you can keep up with his latest releases here.

www.chinamieville.net: China Mieville discusses influences on his mind-bending books.

www.philip-reeve.com: the popular author's site includes links to his blog, Twitter and upcoming novels.

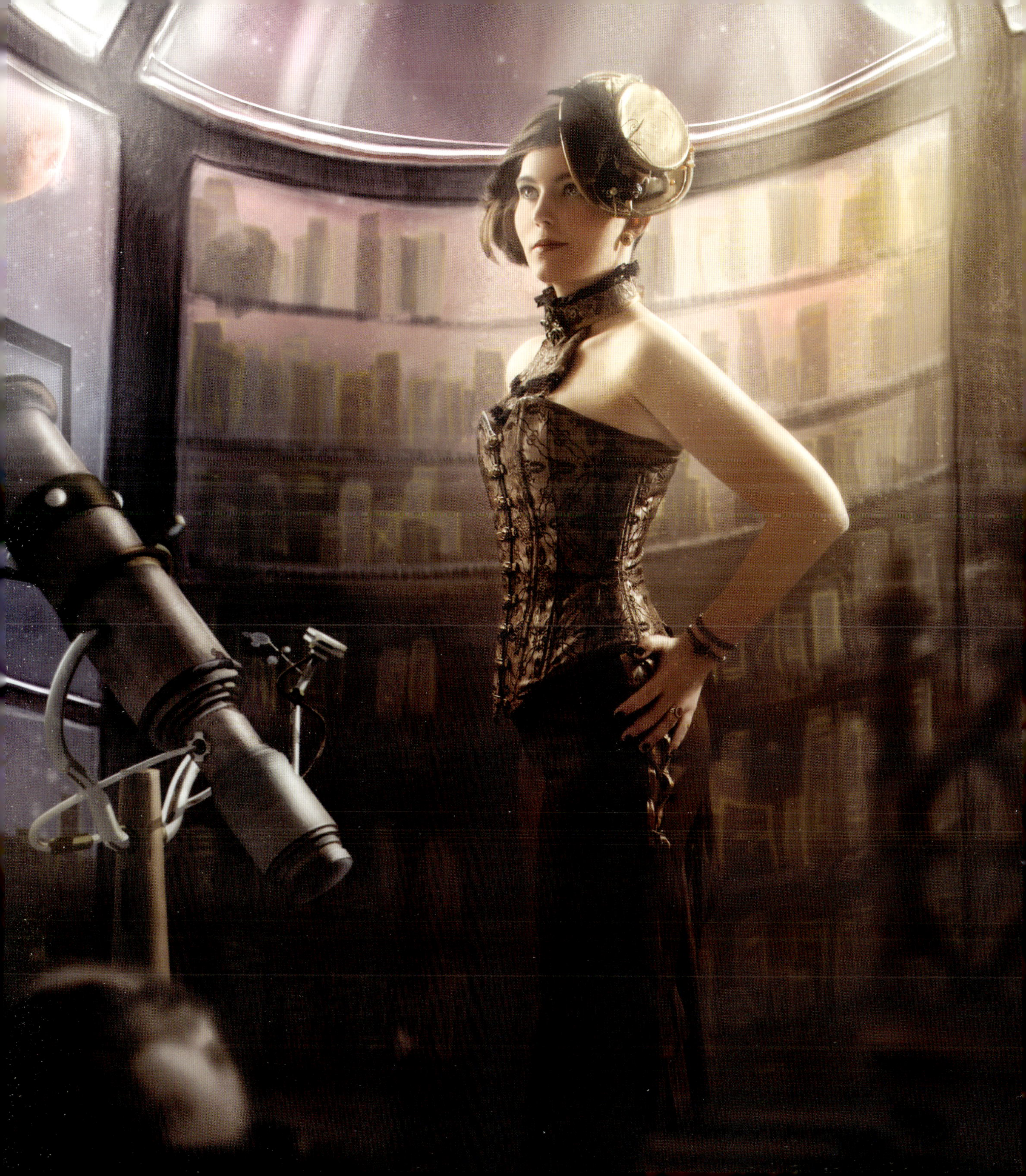

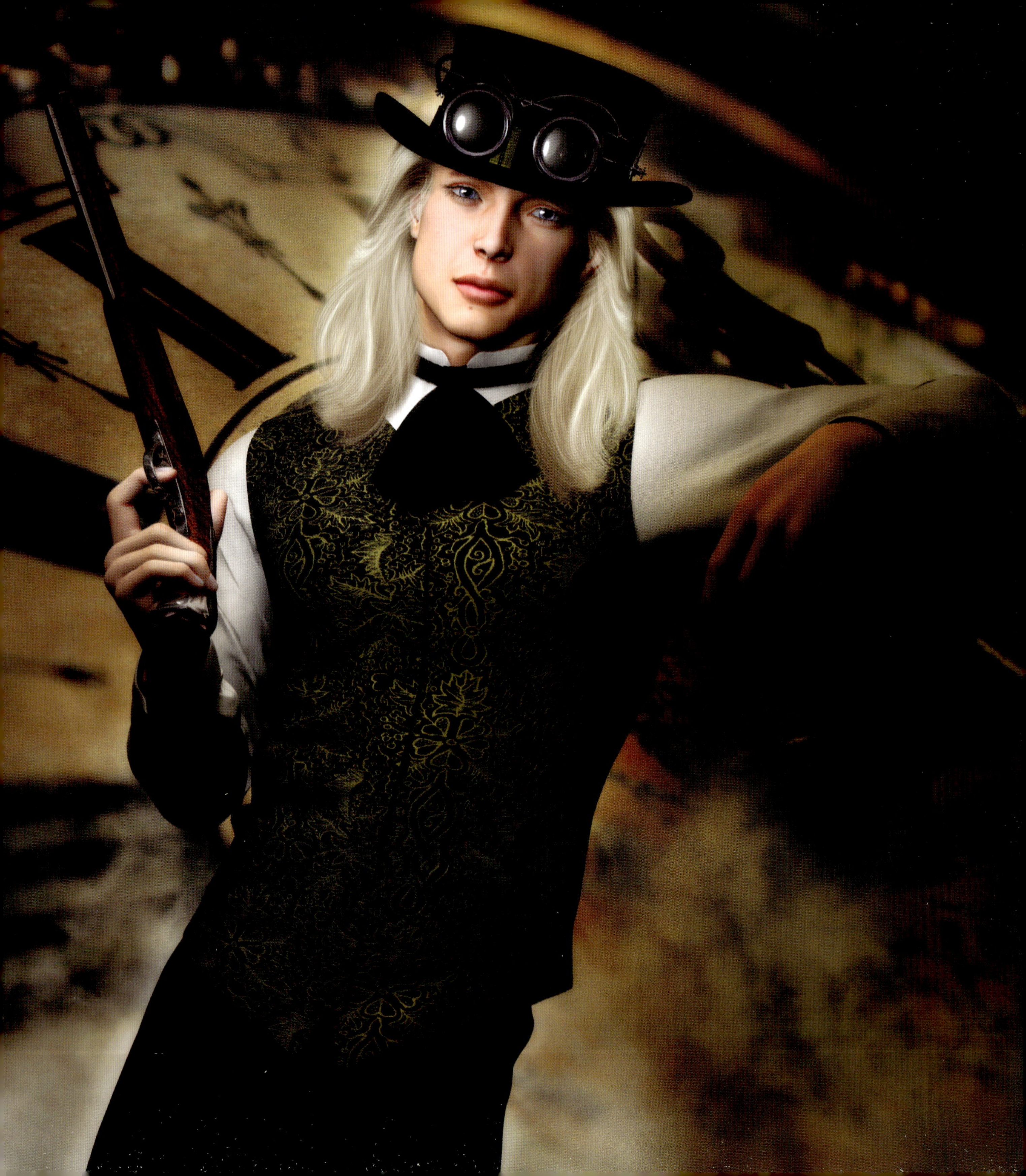

www.stephenhunt.net: run by the author with help from a fan, this site includes a frank rebuttal of rumours that he's actually J.K. Rowling.

www.ekaterinasedia.com: ***The Alchemy of Stone*** author is a frequent blogger who covers many aspects of popular culture.

www.gailcarriger.com: find out more about the ***Parasol Protectorate*** author on her official site.

www.scottwesterfeld.com: this globetrotting steampunk author's site is packed with updates on the adventures of plucky protagonist Deryn Sharp.

www.gdfalksen.com: Steampunk hero Falksen's site is a curated museum of artefacts from bygone times.

General Steampunk Resources

www.steampunk.wikia.com: a user-edited site packed with information on steampunk books, films and TV shows.

www.ministryofpeculiaroccurrences.com: the URL may be a mouthful, but this site is essential for the latest developments in the steampunk world.

Steampunk: An Illustrated History of Fantastical Fiction, Fanciful Film and Other Victorian Visions: Brian J. Robb's in-depth but accessible tome is packed with steampunk goodness.

www.steampunkscholar.blogspot.co.uk: analysis and essays on steampunk novels by Mike Perschon.

Steampunk Projects

www.steampunklab.com: loads of ideas and resources so you can put your fervent imagination to good use.

www.steampunkworkshop.com: more crazy steampunk projects, as well as general information on the sub-genre.

www.thesteampunkhome.blogspot.co.uk: ever wondered if you could make your home look like the interior of a zeppelin? This blog will show you how.

Steampunk Events

www.steamcon.org: visit here for everything you need to know about the annual steampunk convention in Seattle.

www.steampunk.synthasite.com: Weekend at the Asylum is a massive steampunk event in Europe.

www.steampunkworldsfair.com: a weekend long festival held in New Jersey.

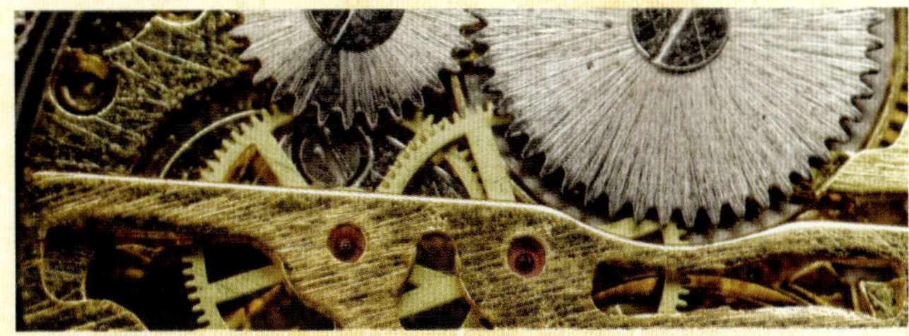

Acknowledgements

Biographies

Henry Winchester (Author)

Henry's love of science fiction, combined with an innate tendency to tinker with technological and old things, meant that a career as a steampunk inventor surely beckoned. But he stuck with the quill as there was a lower chance of blowing himself up, and since then he's made words for some of the grandest periodicals in the world, including *ImagineFX*, *PC Gamer* and *Stuff*. When he's not writing he likes nothing more than to jump on his safety bicycle and ride to one of the many fine Victorian drinking establishments which inhabit the glorious countryside around Bath.

G.D. Falksen (Foreword)

G.D. Falksen is an author, lecturer and public speaker. He is a consultant for Disney and blogs for Tor.com and ComicMix.com. Dubbed 'the unofficial face of Steampunk' by *Paper* magazine, he is one of the most recognizable figures in the steampunk literary genre and the related subculture. He is the author of The Hellfire Chronicles series and the Ouroboros Cycle series and his work has appeared in *Steampunk Tales*, *Steampunk Magazine*, *The Chap* and others. He has appeared as a guest at various Comic Cons, and been featured in *The New York Times*, on MTV and io9.com.

Links

Find out more about the fantastic artists, authors and sources of the steampunk quotes in this book:

www.flametree451.com

Picture Credits

The Artists

Special thanks to all the artists who have contributed artwork for this book:

Benjamin Carré/Pré aux Clercs 4; **Lindsey Look** 7; **Nicholas Kole** 8; **Katt Amaral** 11; **Jenny Lehmann** 12, 26; **Cris Ortega** 15, 50, 95; **Bernard Bittler** 16; **Pinkabsinthe** 18, 28, 90l; **Gina Roma** 22; **Reiner Eisenbeis** (Model/Styling/Makeup/Dress: **MADmoiselleMeli**) 24; **Patrick Hartz** (Model/Outfit/Makeup: **MADmoiselle Méli**) 29; **Lycilia-Art** (Model: **freexinshadows**) 30; **Jon Hodgson/© Cubicle 7 Entertainment Ltd** 33; **Timothy B. Tupaz** 34; **Nigel Quarless** 37; **Jason Juta** 38; **Doug Sirois** 43; **Cory Jespersen** 44; **Ram Singh** 46; **Benjamin Carré** 49, 103; **Alex Alsina** 52, 123; **Rita Fei** 86; **Jan Ditlev Christensen** 87; **Pavan Krushik Artworks** 90; **Brooke Gillette** 93; **Derek Cinalli** 96 & 97; **Kelley Hensing** 104; **John Barry Ballaran** 108; **Paul Alexandrescu** 114; **Matilde Søltoft** 119.

Other Picture sources

Courtesy of/© **Photoshot** (and the following): 84; **Loud and Clear Media/LFI** 61; **Columbia Pictures** 63; **Universal Pictures** 64; **Canal Plus** 65; **Warner Bros. Pictures** 66; **Walt Disney Pictures/Idols** 68; **2003 20th Century Fox/LFI** 71; **2003 20th Century Fox** 72; **Revolution Studios** 74; **Nippon Television Network** 75; **Photo by Universal Studios/Entertainment Pictures. © Copyright 2004 by Courtesy Universal Studios** 76; **Starstock** 79, 82; **New Line Cinema/LFI** 81; **PictureLux/LFI** 83; **Paramount Pictures** 88.

Courtesy of **Shutterstock** and the following: **Kiselev Andrey Valerevich** 19, 20, 25, 58, 117, 120; **YorkBerlin** 40; **Atelier Sommerland** 55, 107, 113; **Kachinadoll** 57, 100, 111, 124; and thanks to the following for recurring decorations: 3355m; AlexRoz; Chad McDermott; greglith; jayfish; Laborant; Mediagram; melis; Nneirda; Ociacia; Pergame; Rob Stark; Robyn Mackenzie; Sergej Razvodovskij; windu.

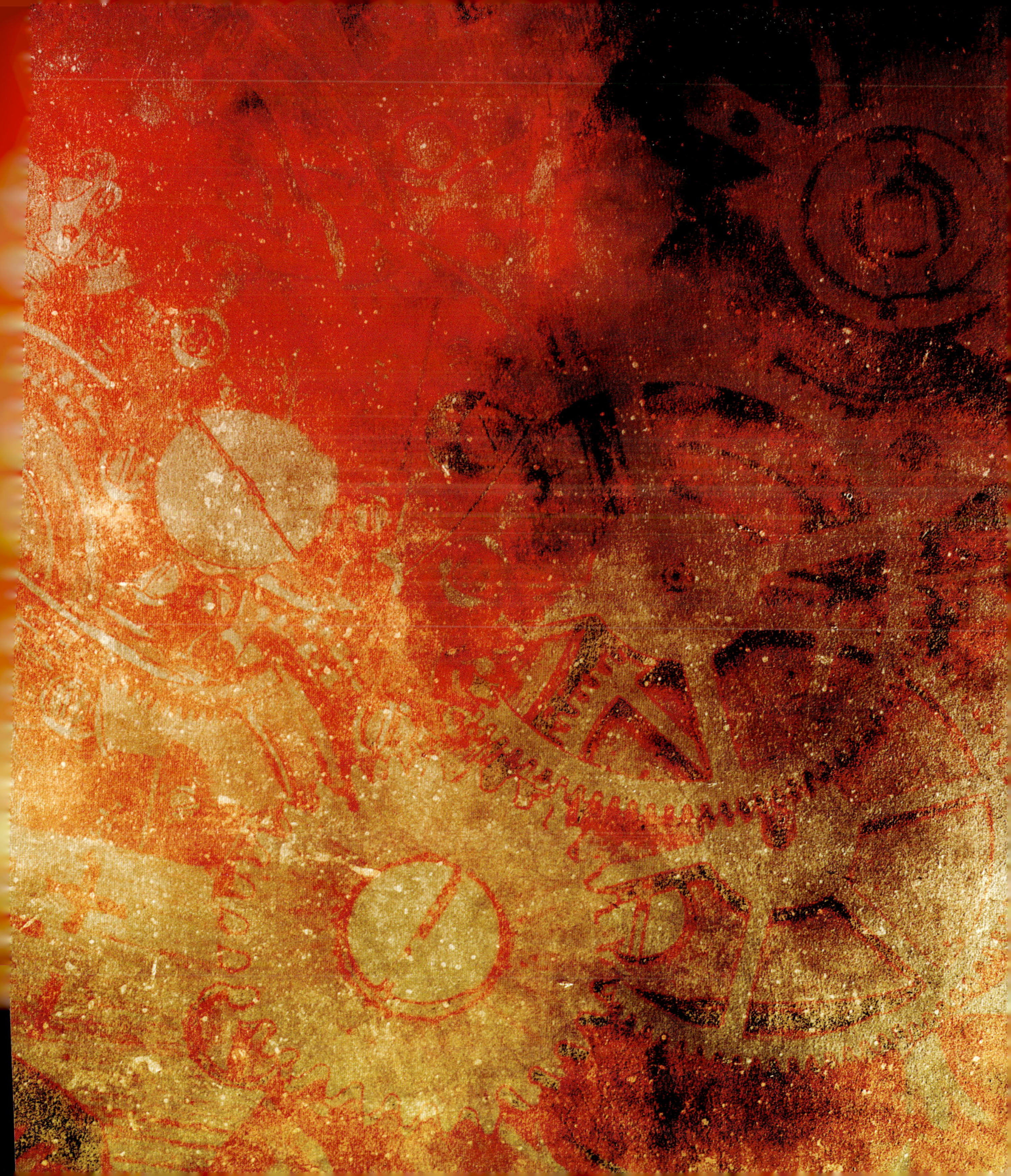

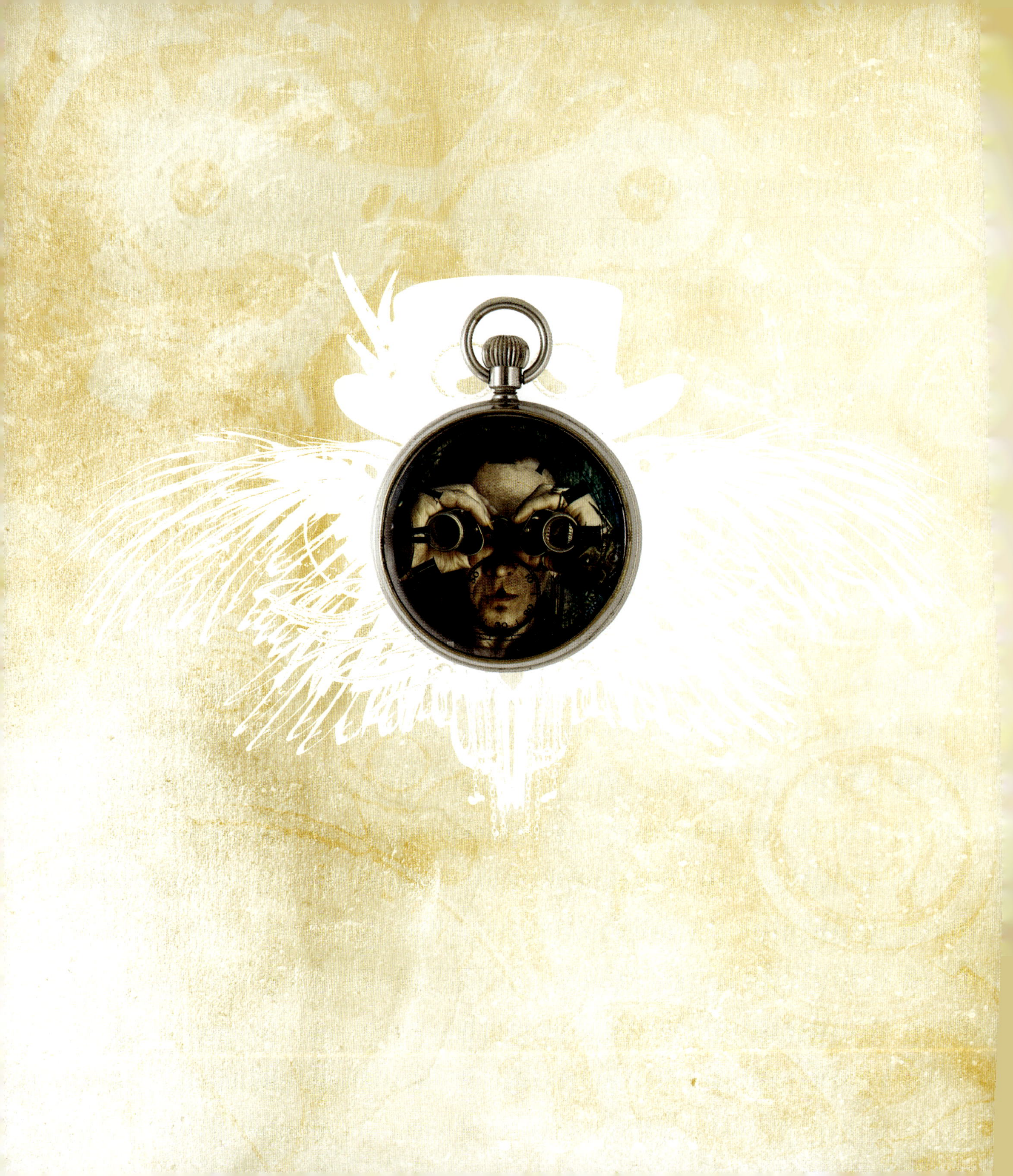